HABERMAS: AN INTELLE(

This book follows postwar Germany's leading philosopher and social thinker, Jürgen Habermas, through four decades of political and constitutional struggle over the shape of liberal democracy in Germany. Habermas's most influential theories – of the public sphere, communicative action, and modernity – were decisively shaped by major West German political events: the failure to denazify the judiciary, the rise of a powerful constitutional court, student rebellions in the late 1960s, the changing fortunes of the Social Democratic Party, NATO's decision to station nuclear weapons in Germany, and the unexpected collapse of East Germany. In turn, Habermas's writings on state, law, and constitution played a critical role in reorienting German political thought and culture toward a progressive liberal-democratic model. Matthew G. Specter uniquely illuminates the interrelationship between the thinker and his culture.

Matthew G. Specter is Assistant Professor of History at Central Connecticut State University. He has published in the journals *Modern Intellectual History* and *The European Legacy* and has presented his work at Harvard's Center for European Studies, the National Humanities Center, the German Historical Institute in Washington, DC, the Birmingham Civil Rights Institute, and the American Historical Association, as well as to audiences in Vienna, Frankfurt, Berlin, Cortona, and Haifa. Professor Specter received a Ph.D. from Duke University, and previously held the position of Postdoctoral Fellow at George Mason University.

"This is an original work of the first importance both for our understanding of Habermas – one of the most important European philosophers and political theorists of the twentieth century – and the political-intellectual history of the West German republic. In addition, it is an exemplary work of intellectual history; it shows convincingly how the disciplinary approach can reveal meanings and dimensions of a highly abstract body of thought that a purely conceptual interpretation inevitably misses."

– Gerald Izenberg, Washington University in St. Louis

"This is a remarkable piece of work. No other book has situated Habermas's thinking within its intellectual-historical context as deftly and with such sophistication. Specter digs widely and deeply into the German-language writings of Habermas's interlocutors (as well as his named and often unnamed adversaries) in each of postwar Germany's periods of crisis. His argument for a continuity (traceable through attention to the law) in Habermas's corpus is courageous and convincing." – John P. McCormick, University of Chicago

"I have found Matthew Specter's *Habermas: An Intellectual Biography* immensely rewarding. By showing how deeply Jürgen Habermas was implicated in debates over constitutional and legal theory in West Germany from the mid-1950s onward, Specter has given me a far clearer understanding than I was previously able to muster of a figure who has a strong claim to being the most important political thinker of the second half of the twentieth century – and of today as well. This is contextualizing intellectual history of the best kind. Specter never treats Habermas's interventions as mere 'discourse.' On the contrary, he enters into the substance of the theoretical issues that Habermas has addressed. Indeed, his own clear voice can occasionally be heard as he enters into a discreet and respectful dialogue with a man who did much for the transformation of German public culture in the years since 1945."

– Allan Megill, University of Virginia

"For lawyers, Jürgen Habermas is a political authority. His work symbolizes the change from 'state' to 'constitution,' from the ontological system of values to processuality, pluralism, and discourse. Matthew G. Specter pictures the 'political Habermas' and gives us a fascinating panorama of the intellectual scene in Western Germany on its way to 'normality.'"

– Michael Stolleis, Johann Wolfgang Goethe-University Frankfurt

"This book offers an eye-opening and richly historical account of the dominant intellectual figure of the Federal Republic. It enriches our understanding of Habermas, by placing him as part of the ongoing struggle to create a democratic Germany." – Adam Tooze, Yale University

Habermas: An Intellectual Biography

Matthew G. Specter

CAMBRIDGE
UNIVERSITY PRESS

CAMBRIDGE UNIVERSITY PRESS
Cambridge, New York, Melbourne, Madrid, Cape Town, Singapore, São Paulo, Delhi, Dubai, Tokyo, Mexico City

Cambridge University Press
32 Avenue of the Americas, New York, NY 10013-2473, USA

www.cambridge.org
Information on this title: www.cambridge.org/9780521738316

First published 2010
Reprinted 2010

A catalog record for this publication is available from the British Library.

Library of Congress Cataloging in Publication Data

Specter, Matthew G. (Matthew Goodrich), 1968–
Habermas : an intellectual biography / Matthew G. Specter.
p. cm.
Includes bibliographical references and index.
ISBN 978-0-521-48803-7 (hardback) – ISBN 978-0-521-73831-6 (pbk.)
1. Habermas, Jürgen. I. Title.
B3258.H324S66 2010
193–dc22
[B]
2010027358

ISBN 978-0-521-48803-7 Hardback
ISBN 978-0-521-73831-6 Paperback

For three great teachers – Tom de Zengotita, Frank Moretti, and Roman Zwarycz.

Contents

Acknowledgments

The intellectual, professional, and moral support of friends and colleagues on both sides of the Atlantic over nearly a decade has sustained and enlivened my work on this book. The book began as a dissertation at Duke University and it is to Malachi Hacohen, my mentor in the Duke History department, to whom I owe my deepest debts on this project. His intellectual and political passion, personal gentleness, and high integrity made him a superb mentor and professional model. I was also extremely fortunate to have the unstinting support over many years of the other members of my dissertation committee at Duke: Claudia Koonz, Anthony J. LaVopa, and William M. Reddy. Claudia's vigorous and detailed critiques of draft chapters of the dissertation were a great gift. Tony LaVopa's teaching, advice, and leadership role in the Triangle Intellectual History Seminar shaped my development as a historian. To him and the other coordinators of the Triangle Intellectual History Seminar, I owe a major part of my graduate education and professional development. Bill Reddy's courses oriented me to the major methodological and historiographical issues in the study of modern Europe, and offered an inspiring model for combining history and theory. Special thanks are also due to the two wonderful assistants to the Director of Graduate Studies I was fortunate to know during my time at Duke: Judy Martin and Revonda Huppert. For material support during the writing of the dissertation, I must thank numerous departments and agencies at Duke: the Department of History, for a multiyear departmental fellowship; the Center for European Studies; and the Graduate School for a summer international research grant. I would also like to thank the Friedrich Ebert Foundation of the German Social Democratic Party for a doctoral fellowship that supported research in Berlin, the International Center for Research in Cultural Studies (IFK) in Vienna for a residential fellowship, and the American Council on Germany for the

2004–05 Dr. Richard M. Hunt Fellowship for German History, Politics, Culture and Society which I held at the Max Planck Institute for European Legal History in Frankfurt.

For a wonderful 2003–04 year as a Junior Research Fellow at the IFK in Vienna, I want particularly to thank Lutz Musner, its associate director, and the IFK's amazing, wonderful staff – Viola Eichberger, Petra Radeczki, Eva Cesciutti, Brigitte Bargetz, Daniela Losenicky, and Romana Riedl – for creating such an inviting, lively, and warm environment in which to work. Conversations with senior and research Fellows Cornelia Vismann, Thomas Elsaesser, and Omer Bartov were particularly helpful. To all the "juniors" of 2003–04, a warm thank you for an unforgettable year of comradeship.

I am very grateful to Jürgen Habermas for his willingness to answer my questions on several occasions in person and in writing. Thanks are due also to members of Habermas's legal theory group who allowed me to interview them: Ingeborg Maus, Lutz Wingert, Klaus Günther, and Günter Frankenberg. Alfons Söllner was my first German sponsor and a source of great guidance. Ulrich Preuss, Ingeborg Maus, Detlev Horster, and Jürgen Seifert showed interest in my project in its earliest stages. Michael Stolleis, Cornelia Vismann, Ellen Kennedy, Alfons Söllner, Norman Birnbaum, Felicia Kornbluh, Nader Vossoughian, Doug Casson, Joel Revill, and Seth Rogoff all read and commented on early versions of dissertation chapters.

By far the best part of writing a book is the personal relationships that form in the process. For spirited conversations about Habermas, and German political thought generally, the most memorable and enjoyable were those I had with Hauke Brunkhorst and David Rasmussen at the Inter-University Consortium in Dubrovnik; with Cornelia Vismann in Vienna and Frankfurt; with Ulrich Preuss in Cortona; with Manfred Gangl, Alexander Kalyvas, and Christoph Moellers in Flensburg; with Detlev Horster and Jürgen Seifert in Hannover; with Anne Fritz Middelhoek in Berlin; and with Jeffrey Herf and Anson Rabinbach in Vienna. Thanks also to Joachim Perels, Micha Brumlik, and Thomas Henne for a discussion of militant democracy over dinner in Frankfurt; to Mattias Iser for sharing his paper on constitutional patriotism with me; to Bruno Schoch and Nicole Deitelhoff of the Institute for Peace Research in Frankfurt for an in-depth discussion of Habermas and the German peace movement in the 1980s; to Michael Stolleis for the warm welcome he extended me at the Max Planck Institute in 2004–05 and for several very helpful lunchtime conversations on my work; and to Thomas Henne of the Max Planck Institute for discussions of German constitutional law in the 1950s. Also warm thanks to Axel Honneth, Eva Illousz, Russell Miller, Regina Kreide, and Adam Tooze for their interest and suggestions. My editor at Cambridge University Press, Eric Crahan, made valuable suggestions for revisions and has guided the project expertly from the beginning. Celebrated German photographer Barbara Klemm generously donated the use of her photograph for the book's cover.

Revisions of the manuscript began during my 2005–08 tenure as a Postdoctoral Fellow in the history department at George Mason. For their support of my teaching and research at that time, I thank in particular T. Mills Kelly, Jack Censer, Mack Holt, Marion Deshmukh, Brian Platt, Randy Lytton, Chuck Lipp, Allan Tulchin, Chris Hamner, Steve Harris, Josh Arthurs, John Berndt Olsen, and Rebecca Scales. While in Washington, D.C., from 2005 to 2008, I especially enjoyed the intellectual camaraderie afforded by Claudia Verhoeven, Andrew Zimmerman, Johanna Bockman, and Andrew Rubin. Audiences at the Intellectual History Seminar at the National Humanities Center in the spring of 2006, as well the Mid-Atlantic German History Seminar at the German Historical Institute in the spring of 2007, provided useful input on Chapters 4 and 5 respectively. McKay Duncan and Hillary Ellison afforded me a summer research grant, which was much appreciated.

For their insight, encouragement, and friendship, I wish to thank, from my years in Durham, North Carolina, Dr. Roni Cohen, Dr. Susan Head, Jennifer Perlmutter, Fiona Barnett, Vince Brown, Jake Selwood, Ann Claycombe, Elisa Slattery, Munis Faruqui, Lisa Lee, Katja Altpeter, Doug Casson, Natania Meeker, Seth Rogoff, Joel Revill, and Rick Sawyer; from Vienna, Margarethe Szeless, Nadja Hahn, Roman Widholm, and Nicole Scheyerer; and from Frankfurt, Cornelia Vismann, Sebastian Martin, and Veronika Müller.

Since the fall of 2008, I have been a professor in the history department at Central Connecticut State University, and I'm delighted to acknowledge my colleagues there for the warm welcome and practical support I have received. In particular I wish to thank Dean Susan Pease for granting research reassigned time in the fall of 2008 and Louise Williams for serving as my faculty mentor since my arrival at CCSU.

This book is dedicated to the three extraordinary teachers who introduced me to Western philosophy and social thought at the Dalton School in New York City. For my introduction to the field of European intellectual history, I am pleased to acknowledge three wonderful and inspiring teachers from my undergraduate education at Harvard and Brown: John McCole, Chris Waters, and Mary Gluck. Friends Andrew Rubin, Michael Behrent, Liz Weinstock, and Nicole Barrett and my brother Evan Specter were always there for me, even when we were separated by oceans. I also acknowledge the love and support of my maternal grandparents, Matthew Brown and Edna Goodrich Brown. Above all, I am grateful to my extraordinary parents, Patricia and David, who first nurtured my passion for learning, always showed pride in me, and never doubted that the work I had chosen was valuable and important.

Finally, I wish to acknowledge the tremendous contributions and sacrifices made in the last year by my wife, Marjan Mashhadi, for the sake of my book. She read every version of the final drafts, made countless suggestions for improvements to the writing, and aided me with the thankless task of the index. I thank her for her love, friendship, and hard work, and I mark our first wedding anniversary with the completion of this book. As we enter the next chapter of our life, I embrace her.

HABERMAS: AN INTELLECTUAL BIOGRAPHY

Introduction

Jürgen Habermas, world-renowned as a social theorist, philosopher, and leading European public intellectual for more than five decades, is also one of the public figures most responsible for the liberalization of German political culture after World War II. This book departs from most studies of Habermas by focusing on his political and legal thought. While communication and the public sphere surely are leading leitmotifs of his life's work, they are not the concepts that best illuminate Habermas's historical significance. Rather, the dilemmas posed by the twentieth-century German experience with the rule of law and its absence provide the interpretive key that decodes the signature duality of his creative work, namely, as philosopher and social theorist, on the one hand, and as public, politically engaged intellectual, on the other. The focus of this study of the legal theme in Habermas's oeuvre furnishes a new interpretation of Habermas's intellectual career as a whole.

But Habermas's reconstruction of German political and legal thought illuminates more than just the meaning of his intellectual project. His reconstructive work on German tradition is also a window through which we observe the normative reorientation of West German political culture to a liberal-democratic model after 1945.

This book thus pursues a double task: Historical contextualization of Habermas adds much to our understanding of the impulses central to his theoretical project; at the same time, Habermas's theoretical and political writings provide a privileged vantage point from which to reconsider twentieth-century German history. Habermas's contributions to philosophy and social theory will endure, but from the mid-1950s to the mid-1990s, he was also a great reformer of German political culture. Habermas's work on German social, political, and legal theory and his grappling in particular with its concepts of state, constitution, and law helped to anchor West

Germany in the West. As such, his thought is part of the dramatic intellectual reconstruction and recovery work of the postwar period that enduringly liberalized and Westernized German politics and political thought.

Looking back in the mid-1980s, Habermas wrote: "The unreserved opening of the Federal Republic to the political culture of the West is the great intellectual achievement of the postwar period, of which my generation in particular can be proud."[1] Tracing the contours of this "opening" toward a Western model of liberal democracy is a central task of this book. Typically absent from Habermas's narration of his own history, however, is the fact that his own opening to the West was at first ambivalent and incomplete. Habermas was highly critical, for example, of the efforts of Chancellor Adenauer to anchor Germany in a West conceived as an anticommunist bulwark backed by the military power of the North Atlantic Treaty Organization (NATO), supporting instead a political party that argued for German neutrality in the emerging Cold War.[2] Habermas argued in the 1950s that *Westbindung* – being bound to or integrated in the West – was not worth the price of admission, as it were; Adenauer's anticommunism seemed to be purchased at the price of a failure to come to terms with the Nazi past.

Also foundational for the Frankfurt School tradition of "Critical Theory" from which Habermas emerged is sociologist Max Weber's view that the Occident's signature characteristic – instrumental rationality – had created an unshakeable "iron cage" of bureaucratized capitalist society. By contrast, Habermas sought to recover the "substantive" aspects of rationality – its quality as a faculty of practical reasoning and political deliberation. Due to the influence of Weber, he wrote, the tradition of Western Marxism had lost sight of the substantive dimension of Occidental rationalism.[3] Habermas sought to resolve his ambivalence by binding West Germany to an

---

[1] Jürgen Habermas, "Apologetische Tendenzen," in *Eine Art Schadensabwicklung* (Frankfurt/Main: Suhrkamp, 1986), 120–35.

[2] The party was the All-People's Party (*Gesamtdeutsche Volkspartei*) founded by CDU renegade Gustav Heineman. See Habermas, "Der verschleierte Schrecken," *Frankfurter Hefte* 13 (1958): 530–2; and Peter Dews, *Autonomy and Solidarity: Interviews with Jürgen Habermas* (London: Verso, 1987), 36, 39.

[3] Jürgen Habermas, *Theorie des kommunikativen Handelns*, Vol. I: *Handlungsrationalität und gesellschaftliche Rationalisierung*. Vol. II: *Zur Kritik der funktionalistischen Vernunft* (Frankfurt/Main: Suhrkamp, 1981).

ideal West that did not yet exist – a utopia based on an idealized portrait of Enlightenment Europe as the space of public deliberation and the rule of law.

Describing Habermas as a Westernizer – albeit an ambivalent one – begs the question of the identity of the West and Germany's relationship to it. But the most compelling recent work on the intellectual history of German democracy – its successful acculturation and institution building – has found it impossible to dispense with the categories of liberalization and Westernization.[4] Alfons Söllner's studies of the history of the establishment in West Germany of a "science of politics" highlights the role played by German emigrés to the United States, such as Ernst Fraenkel and Franz Neumann, and christens their contribution "normative Westernization."[5] Thus a scholarly consensus has emerged in the last decade that "normative Westernization" and "liberalization" are the best general terms we have for describing the multidimensional processes that recivilized West Germans after World War II.[6] Illuminating the concrete meaning of these general terms is one of the goals of this book.

Particularly fruitful for grounding these abstract concepts of Westernization and liberalization has been the study of what experiences were shared by the post–World War II generations. Until the late 1990s, a consensus obtained that there were two postwar

[4] Ibid., 6. Recent works in English that exemplify this research trend include Heinrich August Winkler, *Germany: The Long Road to the West* (Oxford, England: Oxford University Press, 2006); Konrad Jarausch, *After Hitler: Recivilizing Germans, 1945–1995* (Oxford, England: Oxford University Press, 2006); Thaddeus Jackson, *Civilizing the Enemy: German Reconstruction and the Invention of the West* (Ann Arbor: University of Michigan Press, 2006); and Jan-Werner Müller, *A Dangerous Mind: Carl Schmitt in Postwar Europe* (New Haven, CT: Yale University Press, 2003). See also Ulrich Herbert, "Liberalisierung als Lernprozess: Die Bundesrepublik in der deutschen Geschichte," in Ulrich Herbert ed., *Wandlungsprozesse in Westdeutschland: Belastung, Integration, Liberalisierung* (Göttingen: Wallstein, 2000), 7–49; A. Dirk Moses, *German Intellectuals and the Nazi Past* (Cambridge, England: Cambridge University Press, 2008); Jan Werner-Müller, ed., *German Ideologies Since 1945: Studies in the Political Thought and Culture of the Bonn Republic* (New York: Palgrave Macmillan, 2003).

[5] Alfons Söllner, "Normative Westernization? The Impact of the Remigres on the Foundation of Political Thought in Post-War Germany," in Werner-Müller, *German Ideologies*, 40–60.

[6] "Recivilizing" is Jarausch's term. The Westernization paradigm is associated with historians from Tübingen, for example, Anselm Döring-Manteuffel. Not all West German "Westernizers" or "Occidentalists" were liberal democrats, however.

generations in West Germany most responsible for the transformations of its political culture. The first, the so-called founder generation, was born before 1900 and therefore experienced World War I and the Weimar Republic. Among them were Konrad Adenauer (1876–1967) and Kurt Schumacher (1895–1952),[7] leaders of the postwar Christian Democratic Union (CDU) and Social Democratic Party (SPD), respectively. The other leading protagonist was supposedly the "'68ers," the generation born between 1938 and 1946. Figures such as Joschka Fischer, Rudi Dutschke, Rainer Werner Fassbinder, and others challenged the political establishment and their fathers, mothers, and teachers for their silence about their Nazi past.[8] Recent scholarship has shifted attention to the generation in between: Those born between 1922 and 1932 were too young for the army but old enough to be recruited to auxiliary combat duties in the Hitler Youth. Those born between 1938 and 1946 experienced the end of the war only as young children. Habermas was not among those who had the "gift" of late birth. Boys as young as twelve were enlisted to help with the antiaircraft artillery (*Fliegenabwehrkanone*). Born in 1929, Habermas was recruited to the Hitler Youth in 1944 and sent with his youth cohort to help man the antiaircraft artillery of the western wall defenses.[9] Scholars have defined Habermas's generation as the "*Flakhelfer* generation," in reference to their teenage experiences on the western front, but they disagree on the exact dates that define the cohort.[10]

This terminology is commonly understood, as the 2005 obituary of political scientist and activist Jürgen Seifert (b. 1928) shows:

> It was a stroke of luck for the development of the Federal Republic of Germany after the war that the leading minds of the anti-aircraft support generation (*Flakhelfer-Generation*) – such as Habermas, Dahrendorf, Luhmann, Grass and Enzensberger – were not only the ideational shapers (*Innenausstatter*) of this historic period, but were the ones to give democracy its spiritual anchor for decades.[11]

---

[7] Schumacher led the SPD from 1945 until his death in 1952.

[8] See Clemens Albrecht, *Die Intellektuelle Gründung der Bundesrepublik* (Frankfurt/Main: Campus Verlag, 1999), 500.

[9] Dews, *Autonomy and Solidarity: Interviews with Jurgen Habermas*, 78 (orig. March 23, 1979).

[10] Albrecht prefers 1926–37 for the *Flakhelfer* generation. See the discussion in Moses, *German Intellectuals and the Nazi Past*, 45–56.

[11] Alexander Cammann, "Uber die Zaune und Sperren hinweg. Zum Tod von Jürgen Seifert," *Vorgänge: Zeitschrift für Bürgerrechte und Gesellschaftspolitik* 170:44 (2005) 2, 128–9.

The list of academic and literary intellectuals from the *Flakhelfer* generation reads like an honor roll of West German academic accomplishment. To name only the most well-known: Kurt Sontheimer (1928–2005), Niklas Luhmann (1927–98), Ralf Dahrendorf (b. 1929), Hans-Magnus Enzenberger (b. 1929), Günter Grass (b. 1929), and Hans-Ulrich Wehler (b. 1931).[12] Another popular label for this group is the "skeptical generation," as they were categorized by sociologist Helmut Schelsky. Like Schelsky, the psychoanalytically-oriented social critics Alexander and Margarete Mitscherlich also argued that a generation that experienced the collapse of Nazi ideals developed a political disposition skeptical of all utopias, whether of the left or the right. Habermas's robust idealism does not fit well within the paradigm of the skeptical generation, however.

More promising is the notion of the "'45ers." Historian A. Dirk Moses proposes that the *Flakhelfer* generation, which he calls "the '45ers," is the one most responsible for the "discursive democratization" of the Federal Republic – the "... key generation ... uniquely placed to commence the process of republican value development."[13] He is not alone in this judgment.[14] Moses calls them the '45ers because the collapse of the Nazi regime and the beginning of liberal freedoms marked "...the turning point of their lives and the beginning of their own (and Germany's) intellectual and emotional (*geistige*) reorientation."[15] Two important studies of Habermas's intellectual biography[16] both emphasize the centrality of 1945 as a marker of Habermas's generational identity. Habermas fits this paradigm

[12] Other '58ers whose careers intersected with Habermas's include Hermann Lübbe (b. 1926), Karl Otto-Apel (b. 1922), Gustav Rohrmoser (b. 1927), Martin Kriele (b. 1927), and Robert Spaemann (b. 1927); historians Andreas Hillgruber (1925–89), Hans Mommsen (b. 1930), Helga Grebing (b. 1930), Ernst Nolte (b. 1923), and Gerhard Ritter (b. 1929); political scientists Iring Fetscher (b. 1922), Karl-Dietrich Bracher (b. 1922) Thomas Ellwein (b. 1927), Helge Pross (1927–86), Martin Greiffenhagen (b. 1928), Wilhelm Hennis (b. 1923), Horst Ehmke (b. 1927), and Peter von Oertzen (b. 1924); the jurists Peter Häberle (b. 1934), Ernst-Wolfgang Böckenförde (b. 1931); the sociologists Oskar Negt (b. 1934), M. Rainer Lepsius (b. 1928), and Ludwig von Friedeburg (b. 1923); the theologian Dorothée Sölle (1929–2003); and the journalist Christian Geissler (b. 1928).

[13] Moses, *Intellectuals*, 50.

[14] See the concurring judgment of historians Lutz Niethammer and Hans-Ulrich Wehler, September 1, 2008: *Frankfurter Allgemeine Lesesaal*, "Sind die 68er politisch gescheitert?"; available at www.faz.net.

[15] Moses, *Intellectuals*, 51.

[16] Martin Beck Matůstìk, *Jürgen Habermas:A Philosophical-Political Profile* (London: Rowman and Littlefield, 2001); Moses, *Intellectuals*, n. 4.

perfectly: "'What really determined my political life was 1945,' wrote Habermas. 'At that point the rhythm of my personal development intersected with the great historical events of the time.'"[17] In an interview in 1979, Habermas recalled that he had in 1945 wished for a great rupture – an "explosive act" that would "sweep away" everything that came before.[18] He describes himself as transfixed by the radio broadcasts of the Nuremberg trials in 1945–6, from which he first learned of the Holocaust and its atrocities.[19] Thus 1945 has been called Habermas's "existentially motivated philosophical birthday."[20] The *Flakhelfer*'s generational affinity for the liberal rule of law bolsters the argument for recognition of law's centrality for Habermas's project:

> A historicizing approach might recognize that the experience of compulsion and politicization in the Hitler Youth until 1945, and of civil society and the rule of law thereafter, afforded the '45ers a unique perspective on the virtues of the Federal Republic.... The new order was patently superior, humane, and liberal because it safeguarded the private sphere from state violation. This is the primal experience of liberalism. The forty-fivers did produce an answer to the Nazi past: the Federal Republic as a project of consolidation and reform.[21]

Philosopher Martin Beck Matŭstìk makes the same point about Habermas's attachment to constitutionalism: that Habermas "invested his lifework in German constitutionalism" and is best seen as a mediator between the "securing generation" and a "revolting generation." Matŭstìk's core thesis suggests that "... Habermas's work and his philosophical-political profile emerge integrally through debates and dialogues with his era's two generations."[22] The problem with this formulation is that it abstracts from the way the securing and revolting impulses were mixed in Habermas's generation from the start. This book agrees with Moses on the importance of this generation's historic role and proposes instead the label "the '58ers." This locution is the one Habermas prefers and has gained

[17] Dews, *Autonomy and Solidarity*, 73 (orig. May 29, 1978).
[18] Ibid., 75; (orig. March 23, 1979).
[19] Ibid., 43; (orig. December 16, 1977).
[20] Matŭstìk, *Jürgen Habermas*, 5. Matŭstìk follows Albrecht's definition of the *Flakhelfer* generation: 1926–37.
[21] Ibid., 64.
[22] Ibid., 69.

traction in the self-description of other representatives of his generation, such as Jürgen Seifert and Oskar Negt. "I am, if anything, a '58er and cannot speak for the '68er generation," Habermas has stated on more than one occasion.[23]

While the question of whether to name Habermas a '45er or a '58er is primarily semantic, this study emphasizes 1958 for several reasons beyond Habermas's endorsement of the latter. First, the locution '58er obliquely articulates the rivalry between the older, less-heralded generation and the younger, more famous '68er one; it is tinged with irony. Second, the '58er label directs our attention away from Habermas's teenage years, about which we have very little evidence. Third, it directs our attention toward the years in which Habermas emerged as a public intellectual with meaningful contributions to the German debate on the state and constitution. The year 1958 is a good placeholder for the approximate year when members of Habermas's generation, then in their thirties, began to take important positions in universities and the media. A fourth reason to prefer '58er to '45er is that between 1945 and 1958, a dramatic turn occurred in Habermas's work. The inchoate nature of Habermas's thought before the late 1950s thus bolsters the argument for the '58er label. The making of Habermas into a '58er – his search for a method in the contexts that shaped him – is the subject of Chapter 1.

The '68ers' self-description as cultural and political revolutionaries heightened the '58ers' sense of generational difference. Although they too had challenged the cultural and political continuities of restoration, the '58ers distanced themselves from the politics of the '68ers, whom Habermas at times demeaned as playing at revolution; the '68ers, in turn, denounced the '58ers for being too conservative. Habermas has portrayed himself as "injured" in 1969 by the claim of the protesting generation that they were the first to truly challenge the postwar continuities with the fascist past.[24] Habermas's support

[23] In Peter Winterling. "Das Gewissen der Demokratie. Der Philosoph Jürgen Habermas wird 80," June 18, 2009; Jürgen Seifert, "Vom '58er' zum '68er.' Ein biographischer Rückblick," *Vorgänge* 124 (Jg. 32, Heft 4), 1–6.; Oskar Negt: *Achtundsechzig. Politische Intellektuelle und die Macht* (Göttingen: Steidl Verlag, 2008). Yet another name for the generation, the "'48ers," proposed by Harold Marcuse (2001) seems not to have caught on.

[24] Conversation between Inge Marcuse and Habermas at the Korcula (Yugoslavia) Summer School in 1969, as recalled by Habermas in a 1988 interview. Cited in Matuštik, *Jürgen Habermas*, 91.

for the ideals of the 1968 generation – for greater "democratization" of the university and social relationships generally and against the silence and repression of the past – was matched by strong reservations about the means the younger generation was employing. He represented himself as the more mature conscience of a reformism that was as radical as it was realistic. Before 1967, the relationship between the liberal and moderately conservative wing and the leftist wings of the '58er generation held.[25] After 1968, the '58ers split into camps, divided by the question of whether the cultural and political rebellions of 1967–9 did more to consolidate or threaten the achievements of *Rechtsstaatlichkeit* (constitutionalism) and democracy.[26]

That intragenerational debate – the "civil war" of the '58ers – dominated Habermas's political outlook from the 1970s though 1989. In an essay from 1978, Habermas strongly identified with the ideals of the left-wing publishing house *Suhrkamp*, whose cultural authority, he believed, was "militantly called into question" in the 1970s. Habermas claimed:

> If there was ever anything (in Germany, that is) to the expression, "the spirit stands on the left," then it was during those years, when despite the massive social restoration, the memory of Nazism and the tradition which it had broken was kept alive … by an intellectual left that could place its stamp on the cultural milieu with a certain conviction that it had been entrusted with the task. All this, however, is now over.[27]

The "*Tendenzwende*," an ideological shift to the right that began around 1972, culminated in CDU leader Helmut Kohl's victory over the Social-Liberal coalition that had governed West Germany from 1969 to 1982. Habermas reads the *Tendenzwende* as the updating of arguments and themes from the interwar German conservatives Carl Schmitt (1888–1985) and Arnold Gehlen (1904–76): the "liberals who … drifted into the neoconservative camp" and merely

---

[25] Moses, *Intellectuals*, 49.

[26] While figures such as Lübbe, Luhmann, Scheuch, Rohrmoser, Sontheimer, Hennis, and Maier viewed the late 1960s generation's demand for greater "democratization" of the university and other social spheres as regressive, dangerous left-wing idealism, Habermas belonged to the other group, which included Seifert, Ehmke, Häberle, Enzenberger, Grass, and Walser.

[27] Habermas, "Introduction," in Habermas, ed., *Observations on "The Spiritual Situation of the Age": Contemporary German Perspectives*, trans. by Andrew Buchwalter (Cambridge, MA: MIT Press, 1985), 2.

"… reactivated an existing source of argumentation by removing it from politically discredited contexts."[28] However, one historian has argued that Habermas "… time and again … mischaracterized the positions of the German neo-conservatives."[29] While Habermas's use of the label "neoconservative" is generally more enlightening than obscurantist, its historical significance lies in the fact that it attests to a decades-long intragenerational struggle for cultural hegemony in West Germany.

On dozens of occasions over the last several decades, interviewers have asked Habermas to describe his intellectual and political development. Without fail, the cornerstone of these autobiographical narratives is his depiction of the 1950s as a decade of conservative "restoration." We intellectuals on the left, Habermas wrote in 1978, "… move along a beaten path first cleared by the liberal intelligentsia during the Adenauer phase of restoration."[30] By "restoration," Habermas means the failure to make a clean break with both Nazi ideology and the species of radical conservatism that predates 1933.[31] His conventional description of the 1950s has been superseded by more balanced scholarly portrayals that emphasize the rapid modernization that occurred in these years, albeit under conservative trusteeship.[32] "You cannot imagine how closed a world it was," he has said of this period.[33] Habermas's depiction of the 1950s as an entirely "closed world" dovetails neatly with the pride he expresses in his generation's contribution to the "opening" of Germany to the West. The central deficiency of the postwar restoration period for Habermas was the contradiction between the new

---

[28] Ibid., 12.

[29] See Jerry Muller, "German Neoconservatism, ca. 1968–1985: Hermann Lübbe and Others," in Werner-Müller, *German Ideologies*, 161–84.

[30] See, for example, Habermas's introduction to *On the Spiritual Situation of the Age*, 14; Dews, *Autonomy and Solidarity*, 35 (orig. December 16, 1977).

[31] The notion of the 1950s as a restoration era originates from the left-wing Catholic publicists Eugene Kogon (1903–87) and Walter Dirks (1901–91), who promoted a view of a "missed revolutionary" moment and the return of the old politicians as a restoration. See Kogon, *Die Restaurative Republik. Zur Geschichte der Bundesrepublik Deutschland. Gesammelte Schriften* (Berlin: Quadriga, 1996), 3; and Moses, *Intellectuals*, 41–5.

[32] The modernization paradigm is associated with the historians Hans-Peter Schwarz, Axel Schildt, and Arnold Sywotteck, eds., *Modernisierung im Wiederaufbau. die Westdeutsche Gesellschaft der 50er Jahre* (Bonn: Dietz, 1993).

[33] Dews, *Autonomy and Solidarity*, 192 (orig. December 6, 1984).

beginning announced by the Allied occupation forces and the reality of continuities with the Third Reich. That the two spheres – the university and the state – that were intended in theory to play key roles in democratizing Germany were fatally flawed from the outset is the contradiction that provoked Habermas's political awakening and shaped his initial trajectory.

During his university studies at Bonn and Göttingen from 1949 to 1954, Habermas had two major experiences of disillusionment. The first was a crushing realization concerning Martin Heidegger (1889–1976). It was a great shock for him to discover that the philosopher he so admired had written in 1935 of the "… inner truth and greatness of the Nazi movement." The discovery came when Heidegger republished his 1935 lectures on metaphysics in 1953 – without retraction of the astonishing passage. Instead, he appended an explanatory note that the "greatness" denoted "… the encounter between global technology and modern man."[34] This provoked an intense response from Habermas in an essay on the subject that first brought him to the attention of readers of the feuilleton pages.[35] As he recalled much later, "Then I saw that Heidegger, in whose philosophy I had been living, had given this lecture in 1935 and published it without a word of explanation – that's what really disturbed me."[36] His second great shock was the discovery of the Nazi past of both of his dissertation supervisors in philosophy at the University of Bonn, Erich Rothacker (1888–1965) and Oskar Becker (1889–1964).[37] Stumbling on books written during the 1930s and 1940s by his *Doktorvater*, Habermas discovered that the teachers most important to him had been convinced Nazis. Habermas's disappointment with Heidegger, Rothacker, and Becker highlighted the failure of the new German state to take the task of denazification of the universities seriously. Habermas's disappointment eventually

[34] Discussed in Matůstìk, *Jürgen Habermas*, 14.

[35] Habermas, "Mit Heidegger gegen Heidegger denken. Zur Veröffentlichung von Vorlesungen aus dem Jahre 1935," *Frankfurter Allgemeine Zeitung* (July 25, 1953). Reprinted in *Philosophisch-Politisch Profilen* (Frankfurt/Main: Suhrkamp, 1971), 67–75.

[36] Dews, *Autonomy and Solidarity*, 77 (orig. March 23, 1979).

[37] Rothacker, a party member from 1933, worked for the Ministry of Propaganda on popular education (*Volksbildung*) and was a "… contact person for the students who organized the burning of books." Becker was an anti-Semite and remained an active Nazi Party member until the end. From Matůstìk, *Jürgen Habermas*, 18.

developed into a broader critique of what the historian Fritz Ringer famously identified as the antimodern "mandarin" mentality of pre-1933 German university professors. "Ringer reconstructs the portrait of a world which in fact did not disappear, as he believes, in 1933," Habermas wrote in 1971.[38] In Habermas's political writings, the "mandarin mentality" is a term that symbolically condenses all the authoritarian, irrationalist, or antidemocratic attitudes against which Habermas defines himself. The threat of reactionary, "young conservative," "antimodern," or "counter-enlightenment" thought regaining traction in German political culture is never far from Habermas's mind. Whether the threat is always as real as Habermas seems to think is debatable. One critic has written that Habermas's political writings are particularly marked by this preoccupation: "They are without exception – related to a deep anxiety concerning the continuing influence of the mandarin mentality on the political culture of the Federal Republic."[39] But this critique errs in resorting to metaphors drawn from psychology to analyze Habermas's preoccupations: "Habermas's 'Four Horsemen' – Heidegger, Schmitt, Jünger and Gehlen – appear again and again in his political writings with such frequency and regularity that one is tempted to speak in terms of a response to a trauma."[40] Trauma and anxiety are concepts unnecessary for decoding the cultural-political logic of responding to the German mandarins.

Nonetheless, passions do run high concerning Schmitt's legacy in particular. Of the conservative mandarins, it is Carl Schmitt whose legacy still seems most dangerous to Habermas. At a conference on Schmitt's thought in Germany in the 1990s, Habermas confronted one of the participants with intense anger: "Tell me one thing that Carl Schmitt wrote that my generation failed to address in our critiques! Name one thing!"[41] Habermas noted in the early 1990s that a major source of Schmitt's appeal in the 1950s was that many postwar

[38] Habermas, "Die Deutsche Mandarine," *Minerva* (London) 9:3, 422–8. Fritz Ringer, *The Decline of the German Mandarins: The German Academic Community, 1890–1933* (Cambridge, MA.: Harvard University Press, 1969).

[39] Max Pensky, "Jürgen Habermas and the Antinomies of the Intellectual," Peter Dews, ed., in *Habermas: A Critical Reader* (Oxford, England: Blackwell, 1999), 221.

[40] Ibid.

[41] Author's conversation with a legal scholar at the Max Planck Institute for Legal History, Frankfurt am Main, January 2005.

Germans were alienated by the different tone struck by such influential "preachers of atonement" as the philosopher Karl Jaspers.[42] Banned from teaching on account of his Nazi Party membership and writings, Schmitt refused to participate in the official denazification procedures, was exiled to Plettenberg, and was never permitted to return to the university. This exclusion heightened Schmitt's appeal because, in Habermas's words "... there came into being an aura of something conspiratorial and initiatory around him."[43] Schmitt's student, Ernst Forsthoff (1902–74), established a regular summer course at Ebrach in which Schmitt's contemporaries, Hans Barion, Arnold Gehlen, Werner Conze, and Franz Wieacker, participated, as did interested students.[44] Meanwhile, categorized by the Allies as mere "*Mitläufer*" (fellow travelers), Schmitt's Weimar-era students received only slaps on the wrist and managed to become leading figures in West German legal scholarship. Intellectually active until his death in 1985, Schmitt was able to keep his arguments actively circulating in the West German intellectual field.

In 1949, Walter Dirks, a publicist behind the notion of the restorative character of the Bonn Republic, wrote that the attainment of the Basic Law was no cause for celebration.[45] By contrast, Habermas remembers the Allied occupation as a time in which "... [W]e learned that the *Rechtsstaat* in its French or American or English form is a historic achievement. This is an important biographical difference between those who experienced what a half-hearted bourgeois republic like the Weimar Republic can lead to, and those whose political consciousness was formed at a later date."[46] It was well known that Konrad Adenauer had invited ex-Nazis to enter his cabinet, as evidenced by his appointment of Nuremberg laws commentator Hans Globke (1898–1973) as his personal secretary and Hans-Christoph Seebohm (1903–67), a member of the small postwar nationalist German Conservative Party, as Minister of Transportation. Habermas has recounted the story of how he was disgusted to hear "Deutschland, Deutschland, über alles" sung

---

[42] Habermas, "Carl Schmitt in the Political-Intellectual History of the Federal Republic," in *A Berlin Republic: Writings on Germany*, trans. by Steven Rendall, intro. by Peter Uwe Hohendahl, 108; orig. *Die Zeit* (December 3, 1993).

[43] Ibid., 110.

[44] See Dirk van Laak, *Gespräche in der Sicherheit des Schweigens – Carl Schmitt in der Geistesgeschichte der frühen Bundesrepublik* (Berlin: Akademie, 1993).

[45] Moses, *Intellectuals*, 46.

[46] Dews, *Autonomy and Solidarity*, 75 (orig. March 23, 1979).

at one of their campaign meetings in 1949.[47] Had Habermas not believed to some extent in the new beginning signified by the Bonn Republic, the anger he recalls feeling at the Seebohm appointment would not make sense. Redeeming the promise of the *Rechtsstaat* – its validity-claim, to use a Habermasian locution – is an agenda rooted in Habermas's experience in the 1950s.

Habermas's primary contribution to the liberalization and Westernization of German political culture was the sustained manner in which he recast German political and legal thought. A number of recent intellectual histories of twentieth-century Germany have lent concreteness to the liberalization and Westernization paradigms, but the role played by constitutional law in the cultural reorientation has fallen between two stools – that of the historians and that of the legal scholars. This book aims to bridge that gap. Habermas dissolved long-standing antinomies in concepts of law and state that had contributed to the polarization of German politics from the German Empire (1871–1918) to the reunification of Germany in 1990. Three vexed conceptual relationships preoccupied Habermas throughout his career: of state and civil society, of legality and legitimacy, and of constitutionalism (*Rechtsstaatlichkeit*) or the rule of law (*Rechtsstaat*) and democracy. All three problems stem from the peculiarities of German statism.

ANTINOMY I: STATE AND CIVIL SOCIETY

German statism is a view of governance rooted in the late eighteenth-century history of Prussia and the history of the German Empire, but with consequences still visible at present. The concept of "*Staat*" is synonymous with neither "state" nor "government" or "nation" but rather connotes a community that aspires to "a higher grade of moral quality than *Gesellschaft* (society)."[48] Its key features were a view of the state centered on the executive branch, a treatment of the executive and administration as a politically neutral mediator entirely above the fray of competing interests in civil society, a metaphysical view of the state as a source of social integration and ethical guidance, and a dissociation of the rule of law from

[47] Ibid.

[48] Erhard Denninger, "Judicial Review Revisited: The German Experience," *Tulane Law Review* 59 (1984–5), 1013.

democracy.[49] Statists viewed the executive branch, including the civil service, as above the fray of competing interests in civil society and therefore potentially an impartial judge (*pouvoir neutre*). Two centuries of German statism made the question of the boundary between state and society an important problem in German politics. In the Prussian General Code of 1794, the state was counterposed to civil society as the privileged agent that could stand above partisan politics and identify a common good. Civil servants, including university professors, needed to be expert, moral, and loyal to the state.[50] Hegel's *Philosophy of Right* (1821) inscribed the contrast between a "universalistic" state and a "particularistic" society. Hegel's notion of an impartial class of bureaucrats (*Beamten*) stems from this vision.[51] For one important analyst writing in 1960, the dichotomy between the state conceived of as a realm that is "political" and society conceived of as private, "prepolitical," and nonpolitical found its fullest theoretical expression in the German constitutional law of the nineteenth century.[52] For an American-imposed democracy to become a real, living democracy, Habermas ultimately reasoned, civil society had to emancipate itself from the state.[53] The problem, according to Habermas's early analysis, was that state and civil society appeared "fused" and "interlocked." Disentangling the idea of civil society from the idea of the state required an extensive coming to terms with the German idea of the state and the related notion of a boundary between the "political" and "social" spheres.

ANTINOMY II: LEGALITY AND LEGITIMACY

"With the conceptual pair, legality and legitimacy, much mischief was done; that explains the reactionary posture of many jurists."[54]

49 Werner-Müller, *A Dangerous Mind*, 5, 248.

50 See Gregg Kvistad, *The Rise and Demise of German Statism: Loyalty and Political Membership* (Providence, RI: Berghahn, 1999), 23.

51 G. W. F. Hegel, *Grundlinien der Philosophie des Rechts* (Hamburg: F. Meiner, 1967).

52 Horst Ehmke, *Wirtschaft und Verfassung* (Karlsruhe: C. F. Müller, 1961), 5.

53 Author's conversation with Günther Frankenberg, professor of public law, legal philosophy and comparative law at the J. W. Goethe University, June 25, 2005, Frankfurt am Main.

54 Habermas, "Ziviler Ungehorsam – Testfall für den demokratischen Rechtsstaat. Wider den autoritären Legalismus in der Bundesrepublik," in *Die Neue Unübersichtlichkeit* (Frankfurt/Main: Suhrkamp, 1985), 38.

So wrote Habermas in 1983. The mischief of which he wrote has a distinguished German intellectual pedigree. It links its greatest social theorists, Karl Marx (1818–83) and Max Weber (1856–1920), to its most infamous jurist and political theorist, Carl Schmitt (1888–1985), apologist for the Third Reich. In Marx, legality and legitimacy were radically divorced from one another. Liberal constitutional order did nothing to resolve the social contradictions of capitalism. The legitimacy of the social order depended on the transformation of the economy and the sublation of the alienated political sphere into a new egalitarian form of society and economy. Ingeborg Maus, a colleague from Habermas's University of Frankfurt legal theory group, has written of Habermas's "emphatic critique of a tradition in legal theory that goes back to Marx": "... Marx's fundamental critique of bourgeois formal law, which insisted that the latter was exclusively repressive in character, failed to recognize the elements of formal law which forged the basis for individual liberty and which were discarded by the systems of Eastern bloc socialism to devastating effect."[55] While Habermas's political writing of the late 1950s contained an orthodox Marxist critique of the liberal *Rechtsstaat*, a reappraisal of liberal legality was already under way by the publication of *The Structural Transformation of the Public Sphere* in 1962.[56] Habermas's recasting of German political thought involved a sustained engagement with and ultimate rejection of the Marxist critique of legality as merely formal and bourgeois.

In the *Theory of Communicative Action* (1981), Habermas characterized Max Weber as a legal positivist who had failed to grasp the normative dimension of law. Weber's contributions to the debate on legality and legitimacy are found in his posthumously published *Economy and Society*.[57] Like Marx, Weber viewed the rule of law as

[55] Ingeborg Maus, "Liberties and Popular Sovereignty: On Jürgen Habermas's Reconstruction of the System of Rights," in "Habermas on Law and Democracy: Critical Exchanges," *Cardozo Law Review* 17 (4–5), 829. Karl Marx, "On the Jewish Question," (1843) is the *locus classicus* of the argument.

[56] Habermas, "Reflexionen über den Begriff der Politischen Beteiligung," in Ludwig von Friedeburg, Christoph Oehler, and Friedrich Weltz, eds., *Student und Politik: eine soziologische Untersuchung zum politischen Bewusstein Frankfurter Studenten*, (Neuwied: Luchterhand, 1961), 11–55; "On the Concept of Political Participation" hereafter.

[57] Max Weber, *Economy and Society: An Outline of Interpretive Sociology* [1920], Günther Roth and Claus Wittich, eds., trans. by Ephraim Fischoff et al. (Berkeley: University of California Press, 1978).

a functional mechanism for the preservation of capitalism. Law was neither a true expression of the popular will nor a reflection of moral values beyond the law, but rather the most rational way of ordering a "disenchanted" world, that is, a world in which traditional worldviews have given way to a polytheistic clash of ultimate values.[58] The legitimacy of legality depends only on two conditions: As Weber puts it, legitimacy rests on "... belief in the legality of enacted rules and the right of those elevated to authority under such rules to issue commands."[59] Weber can be categorized as a legal positivist because he did not distinguish between de facto and *de jure* legal order. Habermas engaged in a close critical reading of Weber's writings on the legality-legitimacy problem, arguing that Weber had ensnared himself in a vicious circle.[60] Habermas argued that Weber's positivist conception of law resulted in a decisionistic concept of legitimacy.

Weber was a decisionist because he followed Nietzsche in arguing that value decisions were strictly irrational; the choice of what to consider a god and what a demon ultimately was arbitrary and ungrounded. In his last political writings from 1918, Weber prescribed a strong role for the president as the solution to the problem of a weak German parliament incapacitated by parties and bureaucracy. The directly elected president would have "superior democratic legitimacy" compared with the mere rule of law produced by an enfeebled parliament.[61] A parliament dominated by bureaucratic and party-political forces was enclosed within an "iron cage" of instrumental reason. Only a Caesarist politician, a charismatic leader, could provide this machine with direction. But the choice of this direction was unmoored in any theory of the collective good. Thus would "charismatic legitimacy" make up for the steering deficit of "rational-legal" legitimacy. Both Weber's positivist conception of law and his decisionistic concept of legitimacy were symptomatic of the

---

[58] See David Dyzenhaus, "Legitimacy of Legality," *University of Toronto Law Journal* 46:1 (Winter 1996), 129–80.

[59] Weber, *Economy and Society*, 215.

[60] Habermas, *Theory of Communicative Action*, Vol. 1: *Reason and the Rationalization of Society*, trans. by Thomas McCarthy (Boston: Beacon Press, 1984), 265. Compare Habermas, *Legitimation Crisis*, trans. by Thomas McCarthy (Boston: Beacon Press, 1975), 97.

[61] Carl Schmitt, *Legality and Legitimacy*, trans. and ed. by Jeffrey Seitzer with an intro. by John P. McCormick, (Durham, NC: Duke University Press, 2004), xv.

undemocratic cast of German liberalism on the eve of the Weimar Republic. Clearly, Habermas found it necessary to work through Weber to work through the problems of a statist view of democracy.[62] Weber's thought belonged to the tradition of German statism because of his orientation to the executive branch and his tendency to dissociate the rule of law from democratic sources of legitimation.

Habermas's concern about Weber has remained acute throughout his career.[63] At a conference held in Heidelberg in 1964 to commemorate the centenary of Max Weber's birth, Habermas dissented from the portrayal of Weber as a liberal, emphasizing instead the dangerous decisionist element in his thought: "If we are to judge Weber here and now, we cannot overlook the fact that Carl Schmitt was a 'legitimate pupil' of Weber's."[64] The main link between Schmitt and Weber is that Schmitt "... exploited Weber's reduction of legal legitimacy to 'belief' in the law's validity."[65] Schmitt's influence over the Federal Republic's political thought and culture was one of the main factors that led Habermas to the law.

For any thinker concerned with the distorting legacies of German statism for democratic practice, Schmitt's thought was unavoidable.[66] German statism declined in the postwar years, and new conceptions of the relationship of legality and legitimacy emerged that were not entangled in Weberian or Schmittian aporia. Habermas's recasting of German political thought contributed to the decline of German statism in philosophy and practice.

ANTINOMY III: LIBERAL CONSTITUTIONALISM AND DEMOCRACY

The existence of an irreconcilable tension between constitutionalism and democracy has been deemed "one of the core myths" of modern political thought.[67] It is easy to see why this myth could

---

[62] Compare Ulrich Preuss, "Communicative Power and the Concept of Law," in "Habermas on Law and Democracy: Critical Exchanges," Part I, *Cardozo Law Review* 17:4–5 (March 1996), 1179–92.

[63] For discussion of the Weber-Habermas connection, see Chapters 3, 4, and 5.

[64] Otto Stammer, ed., *Max Weber and Sociology* [1965] (Oxford, England: Blackwell, 1971), 66.

[65] John McCormick, "Introduction," *Legality and Legitimacy*, xl.

[66] Müller, *A Dangerous Mind*, 5.

[67] Stephen Holmes, "Precommitment and the Paradox of Democracy," in John Elster and Rune Slugstad, eds., *Constitutionalism and Democracy* (Cambridge, England: Cambridge University Press, 1988), 197.

take hold in Germany. When the *Rechtsstaat* first developed in Germany, civil and political rights were grants of the state. Liberal constitutionalism in Germany initially accompanied a monarchy, not a republic. For Marx, Weber, and Schmitt, liberal constitutionalism and democracy pointed in different directions. Habermas's mature project in political theory was to show the conceptual and practical connections between the rule of law and democracy. To an American audience, this may seem a touch banal. In the German context, however, making the case for the connection between the two involved a staggering feat of overcoming German tradition. In Schmitt's hands, a tension between liberalism and democracy is inflated into an irreconcilable contradiction: In his *Constitutional Theory* (1928), Schmitt asserted that "… the entire effort of constitutionalism was aimed at repressing the political."[68] In his *Concept of the Political* (1927), an abstruse, vitalist concept of "the political" is proffered, by which Schmitt insisted that the state must retain the critical power to decide how to meet existential threats. In *Crisis of Parliamentary Democracy* (1923), Schmitt argued that liberalism and democracy were fundamentally alien to one another: the former having to do with an antiquated faith in public, rational debate and the latter essentially linked to finding mechanisms for identifying ruler and ruled.

The lesson the drafters of the Basic Law drew from the failure of the Weimar Republic was that the constitution should elevate certain basic rights beyond the reach of the legislature's power to amend. Article 1 announces that "The dignity of man is inviolable." Article 20 declares the constitution "a democratic, federal and social state (*Sozialstaat*)." Article 79, paragraph 3 bars any amendment that would impinge on "… the basic principles laid down in Articles 1 and 20." Article 79 for this reason is sometimes called the "perpetuity clause." The "free democratic basic order" announced in Article 21 and repeated numerous other times in the Basic Law is usually invoked to limit rights. The Basic Law departed from legal positivism by asserting the "… universal and extralegal character of these rights which exist prior to and irrespective of their official recognition by the state."[69] The Basic Law restored the *Rechtsstaat* but

[68] Carl Schmitt, *Verfassungslehre* (Berlin: Duncker & Humblot, 1928), 41.
[69] Rainer Grote, "Rule of Law, *Rechtsstaat*, and État de Droit," in Christian Starck, ed., *Constitutionalism, Universalism and Democracy – Comparative Analysis* (Baden-Baden, Germany: Nomos Verlagsgesellschaft 1999), 286.

also revolutionized its meaning: By curtailing the power of the state and suppressing political movements hostile to the "free democratic basic order," the Basic Law was restorative; by positing a higher law beyond positive law, it announced a departure from Weimar legal positivism. The Basic Law "... recreated the formal *Rechtsstaat* – a state based on the rule of positive law (*Gesetz*) – but now that law is "subject to the suprapositive notion of justice or *Recht*.... In short, the *Rechtsstaat* far from being an end in itself, now serves the constitutional state (*Verfassungsstaat*)."[70] The idea of law in the Basic Law was intended to be a normative one, not simply a statement of fact.

The growth of a Federal Constitutional Court with powers of judicial review is a landmark in the establishment of the separation of powers and therefore in the liberalization of German politics. Judicial review powers did not exist in Weimar.[71] The astonishing rise of the Federal Constitutional Court has helped to build one of the strongest human rights cultures in the world. Despite this record of achievement, though, Habermas consistently viewed the high court and the constitutional lawyers as a poor substitute for the robust democratic debate of basic values and policy choices. While he never went as far as Schmitt in contrasting liberalism and democracy, he clearly saw a tension between the two. At times, Habermas was sceptical of German democracy's "precommitment" to basic rights because this commitment appeared to freeze the democratic process. He did not always value the "democracy enabling" elements of constitutional precommitment.[72] This was so for Habermas when the concept of the free democratic basic order was instrumentalized in the Cold War and again in the context of German reunification. Habermas's political philosophy is universalist but not foundationalist: The rhetoric of human dignity that forms the heart of the constitution does not possess a sacred, foundational quality for him.

Habermas's antifoundationalist position makes political sense, however, because even a foundationalist, dignitarian constitution

---

Cited in Brian Z. Tamanaha, *On the Rule of Law: History, Politics, Theory* (Cambridge, England: Cambridge University Press, 2004), 109.

70 Donald Kommers, "German Constitutionalism: A Prolegomenon," *Emory Law Journal* 40 (1991), 846.

71 The Weimar constitution created a high state court, *Staatsgerichtshof*, to hear constitutional disputes between branches and levels of government, but this was a specialized tribunal outside the regular judiciary.

72 "Precommitment is justified because it does not enslave but rather enfranchises future generations." Holmes, "Precommitment," 216.

can be highly repressive. A jurisprudence interpreting the Bonn Republic as a "militant democracy" (*streitbare Demokratie*) developed in the 1950s. On this basis, a neo-Nazi party (Sozialistische Reichspartei Deutschlands – SRP) and the Communist Party (Kommunistische Partei Deutschlands – KPD) were declared to be enemies of the basic order and banned in 1952 and 1956, respectively. This jurisprudence also was revived during the state's confrontation in the 1970s with left-wing domestic terrorism.[73] Habermas's writings contain a critique of postwar West Germany: The shadow side of Germany's success in dethroning German statism in favor of a robust liberal constitutionalism is that too much power has been concentrated within the Federal Constitutional Court. By highlighting Habermas's engagement with decisions of the Federal Constitutional Court over four decades, we can see the extent to which Habermas has always been a democrat first and a liberal second.[74]

The Bonn Republic sometimes has been mischievously called the "Karlsruhe Republic." If a party failed to achieve its objective by parliamentary majority, the party's next step inevitably was to make the "trip to Karlsruhe" – the seat of the Federal Constitutional Court – to challenge the law's constitutionality.[75] Since the 1970s, a marked "judicialization of politics" has been noted by observers of German politics from across the political spectrum, with democracy "… circumscribed by and in favor of judicial power."[76] At different times and for different reasons, both left and right complained that the political process was truncated by the hegemony of the constitution.[77]

For leftists, both the 1956 ban on the Communist Party and the rejection of plebiscites opposing atomic armament in the late 1950s rankled. For rightists, a number of free speech cases in the 1960s

[73] See Jeremy Varon, *Bringing the War Home: The Weather Underground, the Red Army Faction, and Revolutionary Violence in the Sixties and Seventies* (Berkeley: University of California Press, 2004), 254–89.

[74] See, for example, Charles Larmore, *The Morals of Modernity* (New York: Cambridge University Press, 1999).

[75] Philip Blair, "Law and Politics in Germany," *Political Studies* 26:3 (1978), 348–62.

[76] See Grote (1999), cited in Tamanaha, *Rule of Law*, 110; Erhard Denninger, "Judicial Review Revisited: The German Experience," *Tulane Law Review* 59 (1984–5), 1013–31.

[77] Kommers, "German Constitutionalism," 849; Denninger, "Judicial Review," 1023–6.

were seen as oppressive. During the thirteen years of coalition rule by the Social Democrats (SPD) and Free Democrats (FDP) from 1969 to 1982, the Federal Constitutional Court frequently acted as a brake on the liberal-SPD Parliament.[78] A pronounced legalism of German politics resulted that recapitulated some of the original problems of statism: "The search for authoritative, definitive and hence legally binding resolution of conflict are [*sic*] still vital features of German political life."[79] One German law professor worried in the mid-1980s that while the judicial review functions of the Court are generally positive, the risk remained that

> ... an autocratic admistration of justice might dangerously narrow the concept of pluralism to a monistic view of civic values. Such a constricted perception of values, if practiced by the Constitutional Court and other high courts, might suffocate the still delicate flowering of democracy, of freedom of speech, and of active citizenship which in Germany needs more intense care than in the robust grassroots democracy of the United States.[80]

On the other hand, the Basic Law has had a democratizing effect in another way: It empowers any German citizen to file a constitutional complaint. Over 50 percent of the cases heard by the Court since 1949 were brought by individual plaintiffs.[81] Moreover, the judges selected to sit on the Court are elected by a committee of Parliament and serve only a single, nonrenewable term of twelve years.[82] Despite these democratic mechanisms of accountability, Habermas has long believed that German judges have now, and for generations have had, too much power. "Judges should obey, not reason!" is how one law professor and colleague of Habermas's from the University of Frankfurt recalls the general thrust of Habermas's position.[83]

---

78 Denninger, "Judicial Review," 1023.

79 Blair, "Law and Politics," 361.

80 Denninger, "Judicial Review," 1031.

81 Kommers, "German Constitutionalism," 840. A total of 78,000 individuals filed complaints with the Federal Constitutional Court from its founding until 1990. Judges in lower courts cannot rule something unconstitutional but must refer it to the Federal Constitutional Court.

82 Article 94, Section 1. Party membership on the Bundestag's Judicial Selection Committee is proportionate to the strength of each party in the Bundestag as a whole.

83 Author's conversation with Klaus Günther, professor of legal theory, criminal law, and criminal procedure, University of Frankfurt, June 7, 2005, Frankfurt am Main.

Thus do we arrive at the central paradox of Habermas and the institutional culture of German law. The Federal Constitutional Court was designed as a kind of "social superego"[84] for a German polity the founders did not entirely trust with democracy. This elicited a backlash from Habermas, who rejected its paternalism. In the context of civil disobedience actions that he supported in the 1980s, Habermas warned: "Historical experience speaks for the systematic prejudice of representatives of the state and – God knows! – of scholarly jurisprudence. Again and again these generations retreat from certain historical challenges which [require] corrections or jurisprudential innovations."[85] The persistence of German statism is particularly manifest in Schmitt's legacy. The recurrent temptations of Schmitt's political theory for both the German left and the German right cause Habermas tremendous consternation. Habermas's *Between Facts and Norms* was designed in part to respond to the German left's temptation to develop Schmitt's antithesis from a left-wing perspective.[86] *Between Facts and Norms* represents a solution to the problem of the alleged contradiction between liberalism and democracy by describing them as "internally related" to one another and mutually supportive.

Meanwhile, as a '58er, Habermas was keenly aware of the value of the rule of law, the absence of which is a defining experience of his generation. He saw the *Rechtsstaat* as a historic feat.[87] He recently stated that in the 1950s he came to regret not having studied law.[88] He also described his political identity in the early 1960s (and ever since) as a member of the "... constitutionally-loyal Left to the left of the Godesburg SPD."[89] In the words of long-time colleague and friend Ulrich Preuss, "With Habermas, the law was always an obsession."[90] Another colleague from the University of Frankfurt notes that Habermas was always a "legalistic" thinker in some

---

[84] Ingeborg Maus, "Justiz als Über-Ich. Zur Funktion von Rechtsprechung in der 'vaterlosen Gesellschaft'," in Werner Faulstich and Gunter E. Grimm, eds., *Sturz der Götter? Vaterbilder im 20 Jahrhundert* (Frankfurt/Main: Suhrkamp, 1989), 121.

[85] Habermas, "Recht und Gewalt," in *Die Neue Unübersichtlichkeit: Kleine Politische Schriften V* (Frankfurt/Main: Suhrkamp, 1985), 112.

[86] Werner-Müller, *A Dangerous Mind*, 195.

[87] Ibid., n. 48.

[88] Author's private correspondence with Habermas, June 7, 2005.

[89] Ibid.

[90] Author's conversation with Ulrich Preuss, July 2001, Cortona.

regards.[91] And Habermas has jokingly referred to himself during the years he was writing his magnum opus of legal and political theory as "a lay jurist."[92] This phrase captures something quintessential about Habermas's presence both within and outside the professional community of German jurists.

Constitutional law was a magnet for Habermas because of the burdens carried by the law in West Germany after 1945. Assuming these burdens was Habermas's major strategy for changing the political culture. Clearly, he was fascinated by the law. Perhaps this was due to its ambivalent, mercurial character that presented obstacles to the generations that sought to make of West Germany a more democratic and liberal political culture but also furnished resources for the struggle. Why Habermas found it necessary and appealing to become a kind of "lay jurist," and how Habermas worked through the institutional, political, and intellectual dimensions of liberal constitutional order in Germany are the central questions addressed by this book.

Chapters 1 and 2 excavate the political and intellectual contexts of Habermas's earliest political theory, written between 1956 and 1963. These chapters describe how debates in German constitutional theory and a series of revolutionary decisions by the Federal Constitutional Court shaped the findings of Habermas's first book-length study, *The Structural Transformation of the Public Sphere* (1962). Habermas's theory of the public sphere evolved from a question of praxis. The practical problem was how to respond to the multifaceted crisis of the Social Democratic Party after its electoral defeat in 1957. The theoretical dimension concerned the normative deficit in Critical Theory. In these chapters, we observe Habermas navigating the major schools of constitutional theory in the 1950s and the legacies they carried from the Third Reich. Three major legal debates in the 1950s are shown to be relevant to Habermas's intellectual development: The first concerned the extent to which a welfare state was constitutionally mandated, the second concerned whether constitutional principles could be seen as expressions of a

[91] Author's conversation with Klaus Günther, June 10, 2005, Frankfurt am Main.

[92] Habermas, "Der Philosoph als wahrer Rechtslehrer," in Habermas, *Die Nachholende Revolution: Kleine Politische Schriften VII* (Frankfurt/Main: Suhrkamp, 1990), 52.

higher "natural law," and the third concerned the interpretation of the basic rights section of the constitution.

Chapter 3 examines the evolution of Habermas's thought between 1961 and 1981, with a focus on the critical years 1964–9. It argues that the groundwork for one of his masterworks, *The Theory of Communicative Action* (1981), was laid before 1968, a fact with significant implications for how his career is understood as a whole. The positions Habermas took between 1964 and 1969 responded to a pervasive discourse on "technocracy," or rule by experts, in which all political tendencies in West German society from the far left to the conservative right participated. Contextualizing Habermas as a participant in this debate helps to explain why Habermas accepted the radical left-wing students' critique of the university but rejected their broader hostility toward modern science and technology. Faced with visions of technological utopia on both the left (e.g., Herbert Marcuse) and the right (e.g., Schelsky), Habermas inquired into the relationship of scientific expertise to political practice thematized by Max Weber. His turn to Weber helped Habermas to recognize what was wrong with both the German university structures and the student opposition: Both missed the connection between legality and legitimacy. While student protestors undervalued legality, the technocratic conservatives declared democratic legitimation of policy choices obsolete. The political crises of the late 1960s were the theater in which Habermas began to work out his mature solution to the question of how to combine legality with legitimacy.

The argument of Chapter 4 is that Habermas's three major theoretical positions in the 1980s – the theory of modernity, the concept of constitutional patriotism, and his advocacy of civil disobedience in the face of West German nuclear armament – have a remarkable coherence that has been overlooked. Each position represents an interlocking piece of an answer to a pressing political question: What was the nature of West Germany's link to the West? Was it based on strategic interests or moral values? The political crisis engendered by the public debate on the stationing of intermediate-range nuclear missiles in 1980–3 caused a major realignment of the governing coalition and presented strategic challenges to Habermas as a political thinker. The chapter traces Habermas's rejection of the positions of both the neoconservatives around Helmut Kohl and the neutralist (anti-NATO) left around Oskar Lafontaine and his creative reconceptualization of Germany's political relationship to the West. It also shows the interplay between his philosophical account of modernity (including the critique of poststructuralism) and his political interventions in *Historikerstreit* and in the Euromissile controversy.

Chapter 5 is the first sustained attempt to contextualize Habermas's imposing statement of his mature political theory, *Between Facts and Norms: Contributions to a Discourse Theory of Democracy* (1992). It shows how the work subtly reflects the hopes raised by German reunification and the disillusionment experienced in its wake. It describes Habermas's intellectual agenda in 1984–9 when he began work on the book. It recounts how Habermas aligned himself with the jurists who in 1989–90 argued that a reunified Germany required an entirely new constitution. The chapter explores how Habermas's republican commitment to self-determination vied for primacy with his anxieties as a liberal. Habermas feared that absorption of the former East Germany would jeopardize his life's work: the liberalization and Westernization of German political culture. *Between Facts and Norms* is not only a kind of epitaph for the Bonn Republic but also a surprisingly revealing testament – the closest thing we have to Habermas's intellectual autobiography.[93]

No other scholar has argued for the centrality of the legal theme in Habermas's oeuvre as a whole; most prefer to characterize his *Between Facts and Norms* as a decisive marker of a "legal turn" or a "liberal turn" in his thought, the two being used interchangeably. This study argues that there is no such turn. 1968 has been framed as the turning point at which Habermas "devolved" from progressive leftist to "reform-minded legal scholar."[94] But this notion of a "turn" obscures dramatic continuities in Habermas's thought: His political analysis since publication of *The Structural Transformation of the Public Sphere* has been framed in the language of German legal theory. This pervasive leitmotif attests not only to Habermas's personal fascination with the law but also to the consistency of his committment to the goal of a "radical reform" of German politics and political culture. This book vigorously rejects the claim that the arc of Habermas's career as a political theorist can be characterized

93 Author's conversation with Ulrich Preuss, July 2001, Cortona.
94 Matůstìk, *Jürgen Habermas*, 93.

as one that moves from "radicalism to resignation."[95] Habermas is aware that some readers on the left believe that *Between Facts and Norms* betrays the traditions of the Frankfurt School: "Even if readers do not always see the 'end of critical theory' in [my] project, they frequently think it defuses the critique of capitalism and just gives in to political liberalism."[96] This study defends Habermas from these charges, arguing that Habermas's renovated liberal ideal is not only a radical solution to the problem of German statism but also an important contribution to progressive political theorizing generally.

Habermas's repeated interventions in West German public constitutional and political debates over four decades illustrate the struggle of German civil society with the state. The German Empire, the Weimar Republic, and the Third Reich bequeathed both authoritarian and democratic ideas about law and constitutions to the postwar Federal Republic. Habermas's career as a theorist is a dramatic effort to work through, preserve, and transform those legal legacies into a usable past. In the intellectual work of Jürgen Habermas, one can trace the itinerary of the West German transition to a liberal-democratic republic.

---

95 William Scheuerman, "From Radicalism to Resignation: Democratic Theory in Habermas's *Between Facts and Norms*," in Peter Dews, ed., *Habermas: A Critical Reader* (Oxford: Blackwell, 1999), 153–77.

96 Habermas, "Response to His Critics," *Cardozo Law Review* 17:4–5 (1996), pt. II, 1545.

1 The Making of a '58er: Habermas's Search for a Method

Habermas's critical reconstruction of the meaning of the eighteenth-century Enlightenment for twentieth-century (and twenty-first-century) moderns is one of his enduring contributions. Habermas's first major work, *The Structural Transformation of the Public Sphere* (*Transformation* hereafter), is rightly seen as marking a break with the negative view of the European Enlightenment represented by Theodor Adorno and Max Horkheimer's 1947 *cri de coeur*, *The Dialectic of Enlightenment*. *Transformation* is Habermas's celebrated account of the transformation of the active, critical debating publics that existed in the era of the European Enlightenment into the passive, managed citizenry of the postwar welfare state. While the first half of *Transformation* traces the historical rise of a "bourgeois public sphere" of rational deliberation in the salons, masonic lodges, and coffeehouses of Europe, the second half of the work describes the decline of this sphere to the point of near extinction. West Germany's public sphere was in eclipse, Habermas concluded. His diagnosis was that it had been occluded by the interpenetration of state and society. The task of Critical Theory as articulated in *Transformation* was to reinvent the public sphere that once had tamed the Leviathan of the absolutist state. Although Habermas's *Transformation* shared Adorno and Horkheimer's cultural pessimism about the stultifying effects of mass communication, it also demonstrated a countervailing interest in the immanent critique of liberal ideals. Thus Habermas's book can be read as a *cri de coeur* too, but on behalf of the norms of liberal society.

From where did the impetus come for this consequential paradigm shift in the Frankfurt School tradition of Critical Theory? Habermas provided us with a clue in 1989: "I conceived it within a theoretical framework that had been outlined in Hegel's philosophy of right ... elaborated by the young Marx, and ... received its specific shape in the

German constitutional law tradition since Lorenz von Stein."[1] This chapter's argument takes Habermas's hint as a point of departure. It contends that the most decisive intellectual stimuli to his reformulation of Frankfurt School cultural pessimism came from his encounter with a distinct intellectual field: the West German constitutional law and political science of the 1950s. The yield of reading *Transformation* alongside three minor works from the same period – "On the Concept of Political Participation" (1961, written in 1958), "On the Classical Doctrine of Politics and Its Relation to Social Philosophy" (1963), and "Natural Law and Revolution" (1963) – clearly supports this interpretive strategy. Constitutional lawyers in the 1950s divided into three distinct groupings or informal "schools." Each of the three recapitulated positions first claimed during the Weimar Republic. Two prominent students of Carl Schmitt – Werner Weber (1904–76) and Ernst Forsthoff – adapted and modernized arguments first made by their teacher in the 1920s and 1930s. The judges on the Federal Constitutional Court in the 1950s were influenced by the Weimar-era writings of Rudolf Smend (1882–1975), a key interlocutor of Schmitt's in Weimar and one of the most influential teachers of law in postwar West Germany. The theoretical positions held by Wolfgang Abendroth (1900–85) restated and updated those of an important Weimar-era Social Democratic jurist, Hermann Heller (1891–1933). Each of these schools – that of Schmitt, Smend, and Abendroth – considered one branch of the new government in Bonn its preferred "guardian of the constitution": These were the executive, the judicial, and the legislative branches, respectively. Because they do not fit neatly within any one of these three schools of political/legal theory, Habermas's early political writings constitute a challenging *bricolage* and have been subjected to intense scrutiny.[2] One controversy turned on Habermas's reception of Schmitt's political thought, which seemed to some critics to indicate a fundamental illiberalism in Habermas's early works, a puzzling anomaly in the oeuvre of Germany's most prominent left-liberal thinker. But characterizing Habermas as a "left-Schmittian" critic of liberal democracy did not do him justice;

[1] Habermas, "Further Reflections on the Public Sphere," in *Habermas and the Public Sphere*, ed. Craig Calhoun (Cambridge, MA: MIT Press, 1992), 431–61.

[2] See Ellen Kennedy, "Carl Schmitt and the Frankfurt School," *Telos* 71 (Spring 1987), 37–66, with responses from Martin Jay, Alfons Söllner, and Ulrich Preuss, 36–117.

greater contextualization is necessary to reshape our understanding of his earliest works.[3]

The priority Habermas attached to the legislative branch enables us to disentangle the three main strands of his synthesis: his attraction to Abendroth's work, the utility for him of the Schmitt school, and his ambivalent response to the Smend school. Picking up the thread of these debates, Habermas found arguments that oriented and invigorated him; his engagement in them had two lasting effects. The first was to reanimate a significant branch of Frankfurt School tradition – the political and legal theory of the Weimar-era theoreticians Franz Neumann (1900–54) and Otto Kirchheimer (1905–65) – a tradition significant for the rapprochement it signified between Marxist political economy and the liberal constitutionalist ideal of the *Rechtsstaat*, or rule of law-based state. Second, by interrogating German legal theory in the 1950s, Habermas joined the minority within the constitutional law profession who were struggling toward mastery of the Nazi past of their field, a process of coming to terms with the past (*Vergangenheitsbewältigung*) critical to reconstructing German political culture.

THE POLITICAL THEORY DEFICIT IN WEST GERMANY IN THE 1950S

When Habermas arrived at the Institute for Social Research in Frankfurt in 1956, he had no special interest in legal theory, nor were Horkheimer or Adorno equipped to provide him with orientation to it. Rather, he was working on a grant-funded study of the concept of ideology.[4] Habermas first came to Adorno's attention with his critique of Heidegger in 1953, of which Adorno approved. Having discovered Marx only in 1953–4, Habermas was beginning a lasting reorientation of his intellectual habitus from the *Geisteswissenschaften* (humanities) to the *Sozialwissenschaften* (social sciences). Habermas earned a Ph.D. in philosophy in 1954 in Bonn with a thesis on Schelling. His discovery of Heidegger's Nazi commitments later that year caused a break and a search for new sources of orientation. Habermas encountered Marcuse's pre-1933 writings in 1956; it is plausible that these helped him to make the transition away

---

[3] Ibid.
[4] Dews, *AS* (November 1984) 150.

from Heidegger.[5] The pre-Frankfurt Habermas was quite invested in theological themes as well.[6] Open to new impulses, Habermas did not encounter a coherent tradition of Critical Theory when he arrived at the Institute. As Habermas recalled in 1981, "For me there was no Critical Theory, no coherent teaching. Adorno wrote culture-critical essays and taught seminars on Hegel. He brought to us a certain Marxist background – that was all."[7] The Critical Theory of the interwar period was largely invisible to him at the time, in retrospect, little more than a "sunken continent."[8]

Habermas had never formally studied sociology or political science; both were young and weak disciplines in West Germany, only recently reconstituted after their evisceration by the Third Reich.[9] Habermas thus found himself learning the two disciplines "on the job."[10] In addition, Habermas was forced to become an autodidact in these fields owing to the fact that the theory of the state (*Staatswissenschaft*) had never been central to the Frankfurt School's concerns. The absence of state theory in Horkheimer's 1931 design of the Institute illustrated the Frankfurt School's initial preference for social over political categories of analysis.[11] As one historian has observed of the classic phase of Critical Theory, "The commitment to society as the fundamental category [of social analysis] implied the dissolution of political science themes into sociological and social-psychological questions."[12] Historians recently have

---

5 See Matŭstìk, *Profile*, 19.

6 For Habermas's youthful Heideggerianism, see Matŭstìk, *Profile*, 11–17; for the intellectual formation of a "redemptive republican," see Moses, *German Intellectuals*, Chap. 5.

7 Axel Honneth, Eberhardt Knödler-Bunte, Arno Widmann, "Dialektik der Rationalisierung,"[October 1981], in *Die Neue Unübersichtlichkeit* (Frankfurt/Main: Suhrkamp, 1985), 171.

8 Ibid., 169.

9 See Wilhelm Bleek and Hans J. Lietzmann, *Schulen in der deutschen Politikwissenschaften* (Opladen: Leske & Budrich, 1999); Alfons Söllner, Rainer Elsfeld, Michael Th. Greven, and Hans Karl Rupp, *Political Science and Regime Change in 20th Century Germany* (New York: Nova Science Publishers, 1996).

10 Author's private correspondence with Habermas, June 7, 2005.

11 Helmut Dubiel, *Kritische Theorie der Gesellschaft. Eine einführende Rekonstruktion von den Anfängen bis Habermas* (München: Weinheim, 1985).

12 Hubertus Buchstein, "Franz Neumann im Schatten der Kritischen Theorie. Eine Bemerkung zum Verhältnis von Kritischer Theorie und Politikwissenschaft mit drei bisher unbekannten Texten Neumanns,"

recovered the neglected and misunderstood tradition represented by Neumann and Kirchheimer.[13] But in 1956, the Institute's interwar publication, *Zeitschrift fur Sozialforschung*, in which Neumann and Kirchheimer had written many of their most important works, was kept in the Institute basement. "Horkheimer was terribly afraid of us opening the chest in the basement that contained a complete series of the journal," Habermas recalled.[14] Horkheimer was concerned about the radicalism of the *Zeitschrift* and sought to contain its influence on the postwar reputation of the Institute.

As important as this tradition is to a full historical picture of the Frankfurt School, neither Neumann nor Kirchheimer was the most important influence on Habermas's emerging political theory. This was due, in part, to the fact that when Habermas composed *Transformation*, there was no "stimulus from the history of ideas" that might have encouraged Habermas to focus on the political sociology of democracy:

> Not merely Kirchheimer's trenchant studies from the late 1920s and early 1930s but also all the discussion by social democratic and trade union–oriented legal and constitutional experts, both among themselves and with their authoritarian counterparts, formed part of a tradition of social democratic thought that had been either destroyed or protractedly interrupted by Nazism and remained suppressed until late in the 1960s. In ... [West Germany], this tradition was only maintained by Wolfgang Abendroth. Habermas – and even more so others of his generation – knew only more recent work by Kirchheimer, Neumann and Fraenkel.[15]

In the summer of 1957, Habermas's assignment to an empirical research project led him into the field of legal theory and its Weimar roots for the first time. *Student und Politik* (*Students and Politics*), a

Internationale wissenschaftliche Korrespondenz zur Geschichte der deutschen Arbeiterbewegung 25 (Berlin, 1989), 1–30.

[13] See William Scheuerman, *Between the Norm and Exception: The Frankfurt School and the Rule of Law* (Cambridge, MA: MIT Press, 1994); idem, "Neumann vs. Habermas: The Frankfurt School and the Rule of Law," *Praxis International* 13 (1993): 50–67; idem, ed. *The Rule of Law under Siege: Selected Essays of Neumann and Kirchheimer* (Berkeley: University of California Press, 1996).

[14] Cited in Wiggershaus, *The Frankfurt School*, 544; Honneth et al.,"Dialektik," 169.

[15] Wiggershaus, *The Frankfurt School*, 559.

"sociological inquiry into the political awareness of Frankfurt students," was part of an Institute series on the relationship of university and society. The idea behind the project was to assess the political attitudes of university-educated elites. Habermas was tasked with writing the theoretical introduction.[16] Simitis, a fellow *Mitarbeiter* at the Institute, introduced Habermas to the field of constitutional law.[17] Also a young researcher at the Institute, Simitis recently had completed his dissertation in law under Abendroth at Marburg.[18] Habermas's introduction to *Students and Politics* was entitled, "The Concept of Political Participation." While the book did not appear in print until 1961, Habermas's essay was complete in 1958. Although Adorno considered the essay a "tour de force" – the best analysis of the current political situation he had read – Horkheimer was alarmed by what he considered its radical Marxist politics.[19] Horkheimer had become deeply conservative, even a defender of the Christian Democratic Union, since returning from exile in the United States in 1950. But the tensions between Horkheimer and Habermas were personal as well as political.

Horkheimer was an "authoritarian" who "bullied" all the young assistants, according to Habermas.[20] In the late summer of 1958, Horkheimer wrote to Adorno that Habermas's introduction "presents theses similar to those in the article in the *Philosophische Rundschau*" – a 1957 article on "Marx and Marxism" by Habermas – that Horkheimer had seen as grounds for dismissal from the Institute.[21] Horkheimer wrote to Adorno that

> The word "revolution," probably under your influence, has been replaced by "the development of formal democracy into material

---

[16] For further discussion of the methods and findings of *Student und Politik*, see Wiggershaus, *The Frankfurt School*; and Alex Demirovic, *Der Nonkonformistische Intellektuelle: Die entwicklung der Kritischen Theorie zur Frankfurter Schule* (Frankfurt/Main: Suhrkamp, 1999), 223–63.

[17] Author's private correspondence with Habermas, June 7, 2005.

[18] Spiro Simitis, "Die Faktischen Vertragsverhältnisse," Ph.D. dissertation, University of Marburg, 1956; idem, *Der Sozialstaatsgrundsatz in seinen Auswirkungen auf das Recht von Familie und Unternehmen* (Habilitationsschrift, University of Frankfurt, 1963).

[19] Adorno to Horkheimer (March 15, 1960). Cited in Wiggershaus, *The Frankfurt School*, 554.

[20] Author's private correspondence with Habermas, June 7, 2005.

[21] Horkheimer to Adorno (September 27, 1958). In Max Horkheimer, *Gesammelte Schriften Bd. 18: Briefwechsel 1949–73*, eds. Günzelin Schmid-Noerr, Alfred Schmidt.(Frankfurt/Main: Fischer, 1996), 437–52.

democracy, of liberal democracy into social democracy." ... How is a people which is "being held in the shackles of bourgeois society by a liberal constitution" to change into the so-called political society, for which, according to Habermas, it is "more than ripe," other than by violence?[22]

Horkheimer's displeasure with Habermas's radicalism had two concrete consequences: First, *Students and Politics* was not published in the series for which it was originally intended, and second, Horkheimer rejected Habermas's *Habilitation* proposal on the public sphere.[23] The *Habilitation* is the second doctoral thesis required of German professors. Habermas's time as *Assistent* at the Institute (1956–9) thus came to a close when Habermas left to work with Abendroth in Marburg. Financed by a government grant, Habermas was able to work with Abendroth on expanding the theses of his essay on political participation: The result was *Transformation*, completed in August 1961 and published the following year.

Why Abendroth? Abendroth maintained close ties with left–Social Democratic political scientists at the Berlin *Hochschule für Politik* and elsewhere.[24] Relations between Marburg and the Institute for Social Research in Frankfurt were strained, however. The Institute consciously abstained from projects on the history of the workers' movement or the Marxist theory of revolution.[25] According to Abendroth, "Adorno and Horkheimer didn't wish to have much contact with "... an outcast – so was I viewed by the majority of university colleagues and the bourgeois press."[26] For a student of

[22] Ibid. Translated in Wiggershaus, *The Frankfurt School*, 554.

[23] Wiggershaus explains that Horkheimer would have allowed him to habilitate with a thesis on a different subject; Adorno's enthusiasm for the project was insufficient to protect him.

[24] Among them Martin Drath, Osip Flechtheim, Eugen Kogon, Ernst Wilhelm Meyer, and Ernst Fraenkel. For an account, see the following: Hubertus Buchstein "Wissenschaft der Politik, Auslandswissenschaft, Political Science, Politologie. Die Berliner Tradition der Politikwissenschaft von der Weimarer Republik bis zur Bundesrepublik," in Bleek and Lietzmann, *Schulen*, 183–212; Alfons Söllner, *Deutsche Politikwissenschaftler in der Emigration. Ihre Akkulturation und Wirkungsgeschichte, samt einer Bibliographie* (Opladen: Westdeutscher Verlag, 1996).

[25] Demirovic, *Der Nonkonformistische Intellektuelle*, 239. Abendroth was invited only once to Frankfurt to discuss the 1957 court proceedings against the editor of a socialist journal.

[26] Barbara Dietrich, Joachim Perels, eds., *Wolfgang Abendroth, Ein Leben in die Arbeiterbewegung* (Frankfurt/Main: Suhrkamp, 1977), 240.

Adorno's, Habermas's choice of mentor was unusual – in retrospect, a legible trace of his discontent with the prevailing dominance of social and cultural theoretical paradigms over political and legal ones at the Institute in the 1950s and sign of his relative radicalism on the question of workers' rights.

Various facets of the West German political context from 1956–62 were crucial for Habermas's turn to political and legal theory and for shaping the largely pessimistic conclusions he reached in *Students and Politics* and *Transformation.* There were five key issues for Habermas in these years: the 1956 decision of the Federal Constitutional Court to ban the Communist Party, Christian Democratic Union (CDU) political strength and Social Democratic Party (SPD) weakness in the national elections of 1957, the SPD's ideological transformation at Bad Godesburg from a Marxist party to a "people's party" in 1959, the North Atlantic Treaty Organization (NATO) decision to arm West Germany with nuclear weapons in 1957, and the ruling against an antinuclear plebiscite by the Federal Constitutional Court in 1958. All five dimensions of the political context reveal Habermas as an activist in the public sphere at the same time that he was becoming a theorist of it.[27]

THE POLITICAL CONTEXTS OF A '58ER

For the drafters of the Basic Law, nothing was more important than that Bonn should not be Weimar. The architects of the 1949 West German constitution considered the fundamental lesson of the Weimar Republic to be that liberalism could no longer afford to be agnostic about its own ultimate value. German judges reasoned that the Basic Law was more substantive than procedural, more value-oriented than value-neutral on the fundamental question of the goals, or identity, of the state. Unlimited tolerance, they argued, expressed an unhealthy relativism about basic values that in Weimar had been politically suicidal. Political parties openly committed to the destruction of the republican state form had exploited constitutional guarantees of freedom of association, using them as a Trojan horse to subvert democracy from within. The founders of the Basic Law thus reasoned that boundaries needed to be drawn, gates

[27] U. W. Kitzinger, *German Electoral Politics: A Study of the 1957 Campaign* (Oxford, England: Clarendon Press, 1960).

erected. Where the Weimar constitution was seen as a "document without a decision" in Schmitt's terms, the Basic Law embodied a decision – in favor of democracy. Militancy meant setting limits, deciding what was inside and outside. Inside the gates was the "free democratic basic order" (*freiheitliche demokratische Grundordnung* – *fdgo* hereafter) – a phrase that appears numerous times in articles of the constitution but is nowhere defined.

In accordance with this philosophy, Article 21, Section 2 of the constitution reads: "Parties which by reason of their aims or the behavior of their adherents, seek to impair or abolish the free democratic basic order or endanger the existence of the Federal Republic of Germany shall be unconstitutional."[28] In 1951, Chancellor Adenauer initiated actions under Article 21 against both the neo-Nazi Socialist Reich Party (SRP) and the Communist Party (KPD). The Court deemed unconstitutional the SRP in 1952 and the KPD in 1956. In both cases, the party's property was confiscated, and the party and all its surrogate organizations – current and future – were dissolved. The judges of the Federal Constitutional Court expressed an admirable concern that the law might be abused by the government to eliminate "troublesome" opposition parties. Thus they reasoned that the Court "... is justified in eliminating them from the political scene, if, but only if, they seek to topple supreme fundamental values of the *fdgo* embodied in the Basic Law."[29]

In April 1957, Adenauer's government publicly declared its willingness to station tactical nuclear weapons on German soil. In response, eighteen prominent German scientists signed the Göttingen Manifesto warning about the dangers inherent in nuclear war. In September, Adenauer's government rebuffed the plan of Polish Foreign Minister Rapacki for a nuclear-free central Europe[30] and went on to defeat the Social Democrats later that month for the second time in a decade. The CDU expanded its proportion of the vote from 45.2 percent in 1953 to 50.2 percent and gained an absolute majority in the Parliament for the first time.[31] Despite his advanced age, Konrad Adenauer came to seem unbeatable. The

[28] Donald Kommers, *The Constitutional Jurisprudence of the Federal Republic of Germany* (Durham, NC: Duke University Press, 1989), App. A, 509.

[29] Cited in Kommers, *Jurisprudence*, 221. The phrase "*streitbare Demokratie*" first appears in this case, BVerfGE 5, 85.

[30] Nick Thomas, *Dissent and Democracy: Protest Movements in West Germany* (London: Berg, 2003), 34.

[31] The seats were apportioned 270 for the CDU and 169 for the SPD.

Adenauer-Erhard government presented itself as the only guarantee of security – military or social – and developed modern advertising slogans that articulated this – "No experiments," "You have what you have," and "Prosperity for all."[32]

The December 1957 decision of NATO to equip European member states with nuclear weapons spurred nationwide protests from a diverse range of West German citizens. In January 1958, the "Struggle Against Atomic Death" (*Kampf den Atomtod*) campaigns began; Habermas participated in its Frankfurt branch. On March 25, 1958, the Parliament voted to ratify the NATO decision, even though 52 percent of adults polled in West Germany and West Berlin were opposed. On April 17, 150,000 people marched in Hamburg. On May 20, 20,000 people demonstrated in Frankfurt; 40,000 people turned out in Hannover in June. That same month, Habermas wrote an article in the Frankfurt student magazine *Diskus* arguing for a plebiscite.[33]

At the end of April, leading SPD politician Erich Ollenhauer introduced a bill in Parliament calling for a plebiscite; the government rejected this as a maneuver incompatible with representative democracy. Supported by the unions, several Social Democratic–controlled cities and states then tried to carry out plebiscites at the level of the *Länder* (federal states) – notably Hamburg, Bremen, and Hesse. These efforts failed because the Federal Constitutional Court decided on July 30, 1958 that the plebiscites were not compatible with parliamentary government.[34] The SPD let the movement die slowly over the next few months rather than risk further confrontation with the popular chancellor.[35] The weapons were stationed in late 1959.[36]

In November 1959, a historic conference of the SPD was held in Bad Godesburg. After a decade of intraparty debate, and the SPD's consecutive defeats at the polls in 1953 and 1957, the SPD adopted a

---

32 Habermas, *Strukturwandel*, 323–4; *Transformation*, 219–20.

33 Habermas, "Unruhe, erste Bürgerpflicht: Römerbergrede gegen die Atombewaffnung des Bundeswehr," *Diskus* 8:5 (1958). See Wiggershaus, *The Frankfurt School*, 551.

34 8 BVerfGE 104; see Kommers, *Jurisprudence*, 86–91.

35 The movement reconstituted itself as the Easter March of the Opponents of Nuclear Weapons in Hamburg in 1960, which drew 1,000 in 1960 before peaking in the wake of the Cuban Missile Crisis at 100,000. See Thomas, *Dissent*, 37–8.

36 Thomas, *Dissent*, 34.

new platform in 1959. The conclusion of the conference was that if the party were to again win elections, it must transform itself from a working-class party into a "people's party" (*Volkspartei*). Although it had espoused an evolutionary, parliamentary path to socialism since the 1890s, with the Godesburg platform the party took a further step away from its Orthodox Marxism. The choice for socialism became an ethical choice as opposed to a decision to align oneself with an immanent historical process. Lobbying by representatives of the reform wing at hundreds of party meetings between the spring of 1958 and the fall of 1959 prepared this success. Herbert Wehner, a former Communist, threw his weight behind the program, which added to its credibility with the rank and file. The platform was heralded as a step in the right direction by the more than 320 of the 340 delegates who approved it.[37]

In February 1960, the SPD party executive demanded that the league of German socialist students, the *Sozialistischer Deutscher Studentenbund* (SDS), accept the Godesburg platform. Three months later, an organization of students dissatisfied with the platform formed. On October 8, 1961, shortly after completing *Transformation*, Habermas joined Abendroth and political scientist Osip Flechtheim in attending the long-planned founding of a group of "sponsors" of the German Socialist Students League (SDS) opposed to the Godesburg reforms.[38] This founding meeting took place in the *Studentenhaus* of the University of Frankfurt; 260 academics, writers, unionists, and active SDS functionaries were present. In November 1961, the party executive expelled the members of both the SDS and the Association of Socialist Sponsors from the SPD, which now included Habermas. The SDS's unwillingness to compromise on the issue of atomic weapons, as well as Abendroth's critique of the Godesburg platform published in the SDS paper *Standpunkt*, were two of the factors behind the decision to expel the groups.[39]

---

[37] The Bad Godesburg party platform of November 13–15, 1959 was the first complete redraft of the party program since 1925, and it remained in force through 1989. See Anthony Nicholls, *Freedom and Responsibility: The Social Market Economy in Germany, 1918–1963* (Oxford, England: Oxford UP, 1994), 386.

[38] Wiggershaus, *The Frankfurt School*, 561.

[39] Ibid., 561–2. Wiggershaus follows the account of Tilman Fichter and Siegward Lonnendonker, *Kleine Geschichte des SDS: Der Sozialistische Deutsche Studentenbund von 1946 bis Auflösung* (Berlin: Rotbuch Verlag, 1977), 46.

In the years 1959–61, therefore, Habermas's relationship with Abendroth deepened. While Habermas worked on his *Habilitation*, he also joined Abendroth in the Socialist Sponsors group. To understand the significance of Abendroth's legal theory for Habermas and why Habermas followed Abendroth out of the SPD, we need to understand what was being debated at Godesburg. Sketching briefly Abendroth's position in the debate on the social-market economy (*soziale Marktwirtschaft*) illustrates how far to the left both Abendroth's and Habermas's positions were on the political-economic spectrum of debate. Generally, Abendroth argued that the idea of the social-market economy and "acclamation for the economic miracle" were the two most characteristic "ideologies of the Restoration period."[40]

Godesburg, the culmination of a half decade of rethinking the party's core positions, reconceived socialism as an ethical position. The "ethical socialist" ideas of the 1920s Kantian Leonhard Nelson (1882–1927) were revived. Overtures were made to the churches, a gesture unthinkable before Kurt Schumacher's death in 1952. A leading historian of the SPD explains that the Godesburg platform replaced the theory of class struggle "... with a conviction in 'basic values' and 'basic demands' which could be grounded in different ways."[41] The platform announced that the tradition of "democratic socialism ... in Europe" declared its roots in "Christian ethics, in humanism and in classical philosophy."[42] Instead of class conflict and the socialization of means of production, there would be demand for a more just distribution of wealth. From now on, the state "... is responsible for a forward-looking policy to control the business cycle, and should restrict itself mainly to indirect methods of influencing the economy."[43] To Abendroth, however, the Godesburg platform exchanged the rigor of historical materialism for a bundle of "inert values."[44] Writing in 1976, Abendroth recalled the signficance of the Godesburg platform as "only a variant of the dominant opinion, instead of a real alternative" and in many ways to the right of the CDU's Christian Socialist-influenced Ahlen Program of

[40] Dietrich, *Leben*, 209, 246.
[41] Suzanne Miller and Heinrich Potthof, *Kleine Geschichte der SPD. Darstellung und Dokumentation, 1848–1980* (Bonn: Verlag Neue Gesellschaft,1983).
[42] Nicholls, *Social Market Economy*, 367.
[43] Ibid.
[44] In Dietrich, *Leben*, 209, 246.

1947.[45] The social-market economy and "social partnership ideal," expressed in the law on worker "codetermination" of workplace conditions (the *Betriebsverfassungsgesetz*), were "illusions" that masked the contradiction of class interests.[46]

After 1957, however, there were only a few Marxists who still held influence in the SPD. A reform of the party's economic doctrines had begun around 1951, when its leading economist, Karl Schiller (1911–94), promoted a Keynesian program combining competitive markets with increased purchasing power.[47] Schiller called this idea the "market economy of the left"; only a minimum of state planning would be incorporated.[48] "The freedom-loving socialist solution … tries to find the 'solution of the third way,'" he wrote.[49] The rightward trend in the SPD was a response to the actions of Adenauer's finance minister, Ludwig Erhard, whose brain trust was the Freiburg "neoliberal" school of economists.[50]

Had the neoliberals not shifted the terms of debate, Schiller's reformist program would not have been taken as seriously as it was within the SPD.[51] Schiller coined the phrase, "As much competition as possible, as much planning as necessary"; from 1953 to 1959, this was the SPD's consistent message.[52] Schiller wanted a fundamentally liberal economic system modified by steering mechanisms and full-employment strategies of a Keynesian type.[53] Nevertheless, Schiller was far from being accepted by the whole of the SPD.[54] Viktor Agartz (1897–1964), Erik Nölting, and Hermann Veit represented the side of the party that still believed in the socialization of major industry. Schiller's ideas disturbed the middle ranks of the party and the German trade union federation founded in 1949, the *Deutscher Gewerkschaftsbund* (DGB).[55] At the DGB conference in

[45] Ibid., 246
[46] Ibid.
[47] Nicholls, *Social Market Economy*, 253, 365.
[48] Ibid., 372, 374.
[49] Ibid., 307. Schiller would later serve as Economics Minister from 1966–71 and Finance Minister from 1971–2.
[50] Walter Eucken (1891–1950), Franz Böhm (1895–1977), Wilhelm Röpke (1899–1966), and Alfred Müller-Armack (1901–78) were the most important. For background, see F. X. Kaufmann, *Sozialpolitische Denken: Die Deutsche Tradition* (Frankfurt/Main: Suhrkamp, 2003).
[51] Nicholls, *Social Market Economy*, 308.
[52] Ibid., 319.
[53] Ibid.
[54] Ibid., 308.
[55] Ibid., 308–9.

October 1954, DGB leader Agartz denounced market economics as incompatible with socialism.[56] Abendroth described Agartz in retrospect as a like-minded comrade whose 1954 book was "... one of the most important political documents of the time."[57] Habermas's proximity to the Abendroth-Agartz wing of the SPD shows that he rejected the reinvention of the party along Keynesian lines.

In 1949, the concept of a "*sozialer Rechtsstaat*" had been elastic enough to unite the left and right wings of the party. When parliamentarian Carlo Schmid introduced the concept in the deliberations of the Parliamentary Council in 1948, he cited Weimar jurist Hermann Heller (1891–1933) as his main inspiration.[58] Abendroth and Schmid then were united in their endorsement of Heller's theory. By 1959, though, the idea of a *sozialer Rechtsstaat* had attained two meanings: one reformist and the other transformist.[59] Habermas and Abendroth interpreted the Godesburg platform as a weak reformist version of the *Sozialstaat* goal. By contrast, Habermas adhered to Abendroth's transformist account of the social *Rechtsstaat*. The roots of the divergence at Godesburg have a specific legal geneaology in addition to the economic one. They can be traced to a heated 1954 debate between the leading constitutional lawyers in West Germany over the correct interpretation of the Basic Law: Did it contain a "decision" for a social welfare state, and if so, with what implications for the idea of a "liberal" state based on law? Could social justice be reconciled with strict equal treatment under the law?

DEBATING THE CONSTITUTIONALITY OF SOCIAL RIGHTS: ABENDROTH VERSUS FORSTHOFF

In 1954, a heated debate was underway in the Association of Professors of Constitutional Law (*Vereinigung der Deutschen Staatsrechtslehrern*) between the Abendroth camp and the Schmitt camp over whether the Basic Law contained a "decision" for a social welfare state with a

[56] Ibid., 374–5.

[57] Dietrich, *Leben*, 224.

[58] See Hans Gerber, "Die Sozialstaatsklausel des Grundgesetzes" [1956], in *Verfassung: Beiträge zur Verfassungstheorie*, ed. Manfred Friedrich (Darmstadt: Wissenschafliche Buchgesellschaft, 1978), 340–410.

[59] With thanks to Professor Günther Frankenberg for discussion of this point.

capitalist basis or a socialist democracy. Drafted by the Parliamentary Council in 1948, the Basic Law's Article 20, Section 1 refers to a "democratic and social federal state" (*demokratischer und sozialer Bundesstaat*). Article 28, Section 1 of the Basic Law begins: "The constitutional order in the states (*Länder*) must correspond to the principles of republican, democratic and social government based on the rule of law (*sozialer Rechtsstaat*) within the meaning of the Basic Law."[60] Article 79 dictated that no future change to the constitution could overturn Article 20. Because of their formidable claims to legitimacy, the *Sozialstaat* clauses generated great controversy.

Wilhelm Grewe, a prominent legal advisor to Adenauer, spoke for the majority of conservatives when he mocked the idea of a "social state" as a "substance-less blanket-concept."[61] Schmitt pupil Ernst-Rudolf Huber wrote that the constitutional provisions contained only the vaguest notion that economic freedom be subjected to the principle of social justice, that is, the guaranteeing of an existence worthy of human life; there were no implications for a particular form of social or economic organization.[62] Forsthoff shared this view, adding that "no word has a more ambiguously plural meaning or is easier to misuse.... The danger of a boundless expansion of 'the social' according to political wishes is already apparent."[63] Schmitt similarly complained that political parties in postwar Western Europe had merely "decorated" their names with the adjective "social." Schmitt's hostility to social democracy was captured in his assertion that "... the word *Sozial* remains a foreign word in German."[64] He claimed that the word "social" had always had the polemical connotation of an insurgent society besieging the state. For a statist, this was problematic. In 1953, Schmitt wrote of

[60] Das Bonner Grundgesetz [1949]. Translations taken from Kommers, *Constitutional Jurisprudence*, App. A: "Provisions of the Basic Law," 508–9.

[61] Cited in Hans Zacher,"Das Sozialstaatsziel," in *Handbuch des Staatsrechts der Bundesrepublik Deutschland*, eds. Josef Isensee and Paul Kirchhof, Bd. I (Heidelberg: 1987), 1087.

[62] E. R. Huber, *Wirtschaftsverwaltungsrecht*, 2 Aufl., Bd. I (Tübingen: Mohr, 1953), 25.

[63] Ernst Forsthoff, "Verfassungsprobleme des Sozialstaats," [1954], in idem, *Rechtsstaatlichkeit und Sozialstaatlichkeit: Aufsätze und Essays* (Darmstadt: Wissenschaftliche Buchgesellschaft, 1968), 163.

[64] Schmitt, "Nehmen, Teilen, Weiden: ein Versuch der Grundfrage jeder Sozial- und Wirtschaftsordnung vom Nomos her richtig zu stellen," [1953], in *Rechtsstaatlichkeit und Sozialstaatlichkeit: Aufsätze und Essays*, ed. Ernst Forsthoff (Darmstadt: Wissenschaftliche Buchgesellschaft, 1968), 104.

the emerging German welfare state: "Before such a state divides or redistributes, it must take, be it through taxes or duties, [or] distribution of work places.... But only a God, who created the world out of nothing, can give without taking, and even he, only in the realm of the world created by him out of nothing."[65] Thus Schmitt saw the welfare state as a kind of sacrilege.

Forsthoff elaborated Schmitt's critique. The urge to reinterpret the *Rechtsstaat* in social terms was comprehensible, he conceded, but the emerging body of social security, labor, rent, and housing law "... detonates the *rechtsstaatlichen* structure of the constitution."[66] Social policy should be a matter for administrative law, not constitutional law.[67] Forsthoff protested against the "adjectival diminution" of the *Rechtsstaat* ideal: "Liberal, bourgeois, national, social and chiefly, national socialist *Rechtsstaat*. They all indicated stations of decline."[68] In dramatic contrast, Abendroth used the concept of a democratic and social *Rechtsstaat* as the unifying interpretive principle for his reading of the Basic Law as a whole.[69] Through this hermeneutic lens, one could reshape "the inherited thought of the liberal *Rechtsstaat*."[70] The two principles, *Rechtsstaatlichkeit* and *Sozialstaatlichkeit*, were not antithetical.

Articles 20 and 28, Abendroth argued, were a reminder by the framers that the basic rights enumerated in the Basic Law should not be construed too narrowly as a "... restorative or conservative endorsement of the existing social and economic order"; rather, they "... [held] open the possibility of ... enlarged social rights and another system of social order."[71] Abendroth sought to reconceive the rights he viewed as negative and exclusionary rights against the state as "participatory" or "social" rights, stating: "The constitution

---

[65] Schmitt, "Nehmen, Teilen, Weiden," 112, 113.

[66] Forsthoff, "Begriff und Wesen des Sozialen Rechtsstaates," [1954], in idem, *Rechtsstaatlichkeit und Sozialstaatlichkeit*, 187.

[67] Ibid., 167.

[68] Ibid., 8–12.

[69] The concept of the social *Rechtsstaat* was a "fundamental principle" (*Rechtsgrundsatz*) legitimating the entire system of the Basic Law and not a mere statute (*Rechtssatz*).

[70] Ibid., 87.

[71] "Begriff und Wesen des sozialen Rechtsstaates. Ausspräche zu den Berichten in den Verhandlungen der Tagung der deutschen Staatsrechtslehrer zu Bonn am 15. und 16. Oktober 1953. Die auswärtige Gewalt der Bundesrepublik," eds. Wilhelm G. Grewe, Eberhard Menzel, *Veröffentlichungen des Vereins der deutschen Staatsrechtslehrer*, 12 [1954], 91.

is aimed at extending the idea of a substantively democratic constitutional state (which means especially the principle of equality ... and the idea of self-determination) to the entire economic and social order." Only this would give "... real content to the ideal of a state committed to social rights."[72] In Articles 20 and 28, he explained, both concepts – *Sozialstaatlichkeit* and *Rechtsstaatlichkeit* – are "directly bound up with the moment of democracy." In the "... binding of these three moments – *Rechtsstaat*, *Sozialstaat* and democracy – we catch a glimpse of the legal heart of our system."[73] Abendroth's assertion that *Sozialstaatlichkeit* could not be understood outside "the unity" of these other "contributing moments" brings the radicalism of the program into view. He was not merely saying that the state should extend social rights in T. H. Marshall's sense or that of the British Labour Party. What he was arguing for is that rights *qua* rights could not be conceived of apart from the democratic principle of self-determination. Abendroth's program therefore oscillated unstably between a reformist commitment to social rights and a transformist one in which rights were sublated in the Hegelian-Marxist sense into a broader concept of participatory democracy and collective economy.

In West German legal scholarship, the positions of Forsthoff and Abendroth are presented as the classic antipodes of the social-welfare debate in the 1950s. But set in the broader frame of the debate on the social-market economy discussed in the context of Bad Godesburg earlier, the two have more in common than appears at first sight. By the time Habermas read and appropriated Abendroth's and Forsthoff's writings at the end of the 1950s, the positions each had championed had been defeated or marginalized. The SPD and CDU had converged in the political center with rival versions of the "social-market economy." For the leaders and majorities of delegates to the two major political parties, neither a fully planned economy nor a minimal "night-watchman state" were any longer considered realistic. But Habermas did not recognize that the Abendroth-Forsthoff debate on the future of liberal constitutionalism had been eclipsed by events. To him, they still remained the most important guideposts for thinking through the relationship of liberalism, democracy, and socialism.

[72] Ibid., 87.
[73] Ibid., 84.

THE MEMORY OF THE THIRD REICH IN WEST GERMAN CONSTITUTIONAL THEORY

To understand why Habermas found Abendroth's legal theory appealing requires some understanding of the rival positions in the field – those of the Schmitt, Smend, and Abendroth schools. Part of Habermas's attraction to Abendroth's theoretical positions was that Abendroth was a true outsider in the West German academy – an uncompromising and uncompromised symbol of antifascist resistance to all conservative restoration tendencies in society.[74] Abendroth belonged to a small group of Social Democratic professors within the Association of Professors of Constitutional Law who sought explicitly to renew the legal theory of Hermann Heller.[75] Martin Drath (1902–76),[76] Helmut Ridder (1919–2007), and Hermann L. Brill (1895–1959)[77] also belonged to this left grouping.[78] A professor of public law in the juristic faculty of the Free University, Berlin, Drath was the only student of Hermann Heller to obtain a chair in Germany. In 1951, he was elected to the Federal Constitutional Court as a representative of the SPD, a position he held for two six-year terms. Abendroth remembered him as "one of the few real democrats" in Germany in the 1950s.[79] Drath invited Abendroth to Berlin, but Abendroth believed that he had more intellectual freedom in Marburg. Drath was a product of the Frankfurt *Akademie der Arbeit* milieu around labor lawyer Hugo Sinzheimer (1875–1945) and became *Dozent* in the *Hochschule für Politik* during the last years of the Weimar Republic, eventually rising to a position on the bench of the Federal Constitutional Court. Habermas became interested in Heller after reading Abendroth's

[74] See, most recently, Richard Heigl, *Oppositionspolitik. Wolfgang Abendroth und die Entstehung der Neuen Linken, 1950–1968* (Hamburg: Argumentations-Verlag, 2008).

[75] Author's private correspondence with Habermas, June 7, 2005. See Ingeborg Maus, "Hermann Heller und die Staatsrechtslehre der Bundesrepublik," in *Der soziale Rechtsstaat. Gedächtnisschrift für Hermann Heller 1891–1933*, eds. Ilse Staff and Christoph Müller. (Baden-Baden: Nomos, 1984), 126.

[76] See Michael Henkel and Oliver Lembcke, "Der Staat als Lebensaufgabe: Martin Drath (1902–76)," *Kritische Justiz* 36 (2003), 445–61.

[77] Brill was honorary professor in Frankfurt after 1947 and from 1953 in Speyer.

[78] Günther, *Denken*, 94.

[79] Dietrich, *Leben*, 207.

debate with Forsthoff over the Basic Law. As Habermas explained in an interview, "I read Heller's *Staatslehre* but was not particularly impressed. Heller's influence came through Abendroth whose *Auseinandersetzung* with Forsthoff at the teachers' conference on constitutional law I found to be of extreme interest."[80] Abendroth sought to build on the legacy of Heller's effort to combine material theories of justice with legal positivism. Like Heller, Abendroth eliminated suprapositive legal principles in favor of basic legal principles (*Rechtsgrundsätze*) in positive constitutional law.

Ridder and Abendroth saw the *Sozialstaat* principle as the key to holding open the West German constitution for socialist democracy.[81] Abendroth interpreted Article 1, Section 1, "The dignity of man is inalienable," as an injunction to "... prevent the human being from turning into a mere function of the social-political system." In recognition of this, the sovereign democratic lawgiver must realize the social state.[82] Abendroth trusted simple majorities of the legislature to interpret the constitutional state goals (*Staatsziele*) correctly. The basic rights catalogue was misunderstood, Abendroth believed, if treated as a "... fixed guarantee of the dominant social and economic order." For this reason, he resisted the tendency of the Federal Constitutional Court to ascribe to basic rights a "suprapositive" status, that is, a source of validity beyond the "positive" constitutional text, usually legitimated by arguments from natural law, be they Christian or rationalist. "Suprapositive" values should find no place in constitutional interpretation, Abendroth argued. In 1956 he wrote, in reaction to the Court's ban on the Communist Party, that by reaching for "pregiven legal ideas of community" and a suprapositive "value order" in a class-divided society, the Court privileged an illusory homogeneity of class interests. The concretization of values in a real democracy must come "... from the people and not the jurists."[83] Abendroth's sensitivity to how the Court

80 Author's private correspondence with Habermas, June 7, 2005.

81 See Helmut Ridder, "Enteignung und Sozialisierung," in *VVDStRL* 10 (1952): 124–49.

82 Wolfgang Abendroth, "Zum Begriff des demokratischen und sozialen Rechtsstaates im Grundgesetz der Bundesrepublik Deutschland,"[1954], in *Rechtsstaatlichkeit und Sozialstaatlichkeit: Aufsätze und Essays*, ed. Ernst Forsthoff (Darmstadt: Wissenschaftliche Buchgesellschaft, 1968), 114–43.

83 Wolfgang Abendroth, "Das KPD-Verbotsurteil des Bundesverfassungsgerichts. Ein Beitrag zum Problem der richterlichen Interpretation von Rechtsgrundsätzen der Verfassung im demokratischen Staat," in idem,

instrumentalized arguments from natural law to defend the "free democratic basic order" against threats from the left and the right made him the precursor to a generation of leftist critics of postwar German jurisprudence.[84] Habermas also absorbed Abendroth's critique of the doctrine of "militant democracy" by which the Federal Constitutional Court established the limits of permissible political speech and action.[85]

It was never Abendroth's intent to describe an ideal socialist constitution. The constitution contained "no ultimate decision" between socialism and capitalism, he believed. Rather, he saw Article 20 as the critical "transformer" that would "hold open" the constitutional realm for social change.[86] This is the sense in which his vision of the *sozialer Rechtsstaat* was transformist rather than reformist. The achievements of democracy were to be guarded and preserved, but as long as capitalism existed, democracy would remain in danger. Because workers spent so much of their lives in the workplace, Abendroth believed, democracy could not be restricted to the "formal political" level; it had to extend to the inside of economic organizations. He viewed the unions as the "natural guardian of democracy" and believed that their strength would determine whether the constitutional provisions describing the Federal Republic as a "democratic and social *Rechtsstaat*" (Articles 20 and 28) would become meaningful.[87] The SPD should remain a working class party, emphasizing the centrality of its union members.[88] Thus, in the intraparty debates over reform in the 1950s, Abendroth represented the positions furthest to the left on codetermination in

Antagonistische Gesellschaft und Politische Demokratie (Neuwied: Luchterhand, 1967), 139.

84 See in particular Ulrich K. Preuss, *Legalität und Pluralismus: Beiträge zum Verfassungsrecht der Bundesrepublik Deutschland* (Frankfurt/Main: Suhrkamp, 1973).

85 This theme is developed further in Chapters 2 and 4.

86 Jürgen Seifert, "Demokratische Republik und Arbeiterbewegung in der Verfassungstheorie von Wolfgang Abendroth," *Kritische Justiz* 1 (1985), 14–27.

87 Compare Helmut Ridder, *Zur verfassungsrechtlichen Stellung der Gewerkschaften im Sozialstaat nachdem Grundgesetz fur die Bundesrepublik Deutschland* (Stuttgart: Fischer, 1960).

88 See Wolfgang Abendroth, "Zur Funktion der Gewerkschaften in der westdeutschen Demokratie," 59–68, and "Staatsverfassung und Betriebsverfassung," 103–10, in *Bürokratischer Verwaltungsstaat und soziale Demokratie*, eds. Herbert Sultan and Wolfgang Abendroth (Hannover: Norddeutsche Verlagsanstalt Goedel, 1955).

the workplace and the socialization of industry. Abendroth had been imprisoned by the Nazis throughout the Third Reich and had been elected to the governing body of the newly established Association for the Professors of Constitutional Law as a symbolic gesture of reparation (*Wiedergutmachung*).[89]

Of the hundred professors who had been members of the law professors' professional association during the Third Reich, only four were excluded from rejoining at its refounding in 1949.[90] The "coordination" (*Gleichschaltung*) of the jurists had begun on April 1, 1933, when the state ministries of justice suspended all Jewish judges, prosecutors, and district attorneys. Karl Linz, the chairman of the German Federation of Judges, trusted Hitler's assurances that the independence of the judiciary would be maintained. In the same year, the Nazis purged the law schools of about a third of their professors, making room for a new generation of professors who would retain their posts well into the 1960s. Nearly half the university professors who found positions after the war owed their careers to the Nazis. Only 17 percent of the full professors who were dismissed by the Nazis returned to their posts. Hans-Carl Nipperdey, Ulrich Scheuner, Hans-Peter Ipsen, and all the others who had participated in shaping the National Socialist legal system returned to their chairs and continued to dominate German legal thinking in the 1950s, just as they had in the 1930s and 1940s. Their commentaries on laws continued to appear, as if nothing had happened, in new editions prepared by the old authors.[91]

Other works from the Nazi period were confined in separate sections of libraries, known as "poison lockers," and kept out of sight.[92] The legal field was a complete failure at mastering its own past. This permitted the Schmittians to retain their prominent place in the academic and public discussion of matters pertaining

---

[89] Manfred Walther, "Die Positivismus-These als Selbstanklage? Hat der juristische Positivismus die deutschen Juristen wehrlos gemacht?" *Kritische Justiz* 21 (1988), 323–54.

[90] In addition to Schmitt, Reinhard Höhn (1904–2000), Ernst-Rudolf Huber (1903–90), and Otto Koellreutter (1883–1972) were barred. See Michael Stolleis, *Geschichte des öffentlichen Rechts in Deutschland*. Vol. 3: *Staats- und-Verwaltungsrechtswissenschaft in Republik und Diktatur, 1914–1945* (München: C.H. Beck, 1999).

[91] Ingo Müller, *Hitler's Justice: The Courts of the Third Reich* (Cambridge, MA: Harvard University Press, 1991; orig. 1987), 237.

[92] Bernhard Schlink, "Why Carl Schmitt?" in *Constellations* 2–3 (1996), 435.

to politics and the constitution. Schmitt's permanent loss of his academic chair made him a significant exception to the rule.[93] Through a network of informal seminars held over several decades in Ebrach, Schmitt continued to exercise a wide influence within the profession and on a host of other academic disciplines after 1945.[94] Two of his doctoral students – Werner Weber and Ernst Forsthoff – were Nazi Party members who retained their positions during the Third Reich. After the war, both escaped their denazification proceedings unscathed and continued their careers uninterrupted.[95] Forsthoff took the Berlin chair evacuated when Hermann Heller was driven out in 1933. The most important postwar center of the Schmitt school was in Heidelberg: Ernst-Wolfgang Böckenforde, Helmut Quaritsch, Günther Krauss, Joseph H. Kaiser, Herbert Krüger, Rolf Stödter, and Roman Schnur all were based there. The Schmittians created a mouthpiece for their views in a journal founded in 1962, *Der Staat*.[96]

In a decade in which a great number of political parties in Europe included the word "social" in their names, Forsthoff and Werner Weber brought an anachronistic, pathos-drenched concern for the fate of "the political." They resumed the Schmittian discourse in Weimar that treated the President of the Reich as the real "guardian of the constitution." Forsthoff and Weber clung to the Schmittian view of the executive and civil service as a neutral force "above" society that represented the general will.[97] In 1954, Forsthoff wrote that in Weimar the state was "neutral" and above all social interests; since then, the civil service had been "decimated" by the Americans and the presidency weakened by the Parliamentary Council. In 1992, Habermas summarized his critique of this Schmittian tradition: "The idea that the state as *pouvoir neutre* rises above the pluralism of civil society was always ideological."[98] For Habermas, the Schmittians are the statists par excellence.

---

[93] Ingeborg Maus, "Gesetzesbindung der Justiz und die Struktur der nationalsozialistischen Rechtsnormen," in *Recht und Justiz im 'Dritten Reich*, eds. Ralf Dreier and Wolfgang Sellert (Frankfurt/Main: Suhrkamp, 1989), 82.

[94] Dirk von Laak, *Gespräche in der Sicherheit des Schweigens – Carl Schmitt in der Geistesgeschichte der frühen Bundesrepublik* (Berlin: Akademie, 1993).

[95] Steven Remy, *The Heidelberg Myth* (Cambridge, MA: Harvard University Press, 2002), Chap. 3.

[96] See Günther, *Denken*, 126.

[97] Forsthoff, "Verfassungsprobleme," 150.

[98] Habermas, *Between Facts and Norms*, 175.

Viewed in his Weimar intellectual context, Schmitt was, like Smend (1882–1975), Heller (1891–1933), and Hans Kelsen (1881–1973), part of a generational revolt against the legal positivism of the Empire. Schmitt and his peers rebelled against what they saw as rationalism, formalism, and relativism in jurisprudence and sought new substantive foundations for law.[99] He saw in the Nazi Party a bearer of plebiscitary legitimacy that would give "substance" to democratic structures that otherwise could provide merely "formal" legality. Arguing for the legality of Chancellor Franz von Papen's coup against Prussia in 1932, (Prussia's Social Democratic-led coalition government was defended by Hermann Heller), Schmitt became the Nazi Party's ablest legal theoretician. *The Concept of the Political* (1927) outlined a critique of pluralist democracy. In it, Carl Schmitt argued that "… one seldom finds a clear definition of the political." Often it is used negatively, he argued, to distinguish it from economics, morality or law; only positive definitions associate it with the state. "Where definitions of the political utilize the concept of power as the decisive factor, this power appears mostly as state power, for example, in Max Weber's 'Politics as a Vocation.'"[100] But Schmitt believed that "the political" had an "… inherently objective [and] autonomous nature." To him, the focus on state power begged the question of a criterion: "The state thus appears as something political, the political as something pertaining to the state – obviously an unsatisfactory circle."[101] Schmitt blamed the hegemonic political and economic liberalism of the nineteenth century for obscuring the true nature of politics. Only where there is a "real possibility of physical killing" – of existential negation of the enemy – can "politics" be said to exist. By failing to recognize its economic and intellectual enemies, liberalism misunderstood them as mere competitors or debating adversaries, Schmitt believed.[102] "With great passion, political viewpoints were deprived of every validity and subjugated to the norms and orders of morality, law and economics."[103] Liberalism thereby engaged in a series

[99] Schlink, "Why Carl Schmitt?" 435.

[100] Carl Schmitt, *The Concept of the Political* [1932], trans. George Schwab, with a Foreword by Tracy Strong (Chicago: The University of Chicago Press, 1996), 20.

[101] Ibid.

[102] Ibid., 28.

[103] Ibid., 72.

of category mistakes. The *Rechtsstaat* prioritizes the freedom of the individual, Schmitt explained, but, in doing so, represses its need to defend itself with the blood of its own citizens: "In case of need, the political entity must demand the sacrifice of life. Such a demand is in no way justifiable by the individualism of liberal thought."[104] Liberalism "negates" the state and the political. As a consequence, it offers no "positive" theory of the state. Rather, it has only "... attempted to tie the political to the ethical and to subjugate it to economics. It has produced a doctrine of the separation and balance of powers [but] this cannot be characterized as a theory of state or a basic political principle."[105] Schmitt convicted liberalism of lacking the strength of its own convictions.

Werner Weber (1904–76) followed his teacher Schmitt in asserting that the West German democracy established in 1949 lacked legitimacy in part because it denied or misrecognized its political nature. Weber was representative of those who became prominent professors of law in the first decades of the Bonn republic. A student of Carl Schmitt's in Bonn during the Weimar period, he served in the Prussian Ministry of Science and Education and held chairs in law from 1935 until the end of the Third Reich. In the 1950s, he gained a relatively wide readership for a series of books and pamphlets in which he applied Schmitt's analysis of the Weimar constitution to the West German Basic Law (*Grundgesetz*). An effort to reconstitute Schmitt's interwar critique of liberal democracy on the postwar terrain, the publication of *Tensions and Forces in the West German Constitutional System* in 1951 caused a sensation among the West German intelligentsia. Distilling the essential questions of institutional design in the 1950s, the text is a classic of 1950s radical conservative political thought.

Each of Weber's critiques of the constitution was made in the name of the sovereignty of the people. The division of powers, an enduring feature of the *Rechtsstaat*, was described as a fateful "division of sovereignty"; political parties mediated and thereby diluted the sovereign popular will. Federal and regional constitutional courts exerted a countermajoritarian power of judicial review. The dilution of popular sovereignty accompanied the rise of a decadent legalism. In sum, the cunning force of "the political" was, in Weber's words,

[104] Ibid., 60.
[105] Ibid., 61.

"outwitted" by constitutional design. But beneath these rhetorical invocations of democratic sovereignty lay Werner Weber's true anxieties – preeminently, the fear that the judicial branch would be strengthened at the expense of the executive branch.

Adenauer's chancellor democracy needed all its power to wage the Cold War, Weber asserted. The emergency powers afforded by Article 48 of the Weimar constitution were a necessary tool for a state – the right to declare a "state of exception," in Schmitt's famous phrase. Without emergency powers, the state would not be able to defend its existence from internal or external threats. In the late 1960s, the question of emergency powers would become a major cleavage point in the public debate. The Basic Law, Weber wrote, shapes the political order "according to a system of abstractions," namely, the idea of divided branches of government. As Weber argued plaintively, though, "How can one make it clear to the people that its lord is three powers?"[106]

Werner Weber's text is also a quasi-Nietzschean lament for a lost world of risk: "The Basic Law ... gives us a picture of a constitutional life without risk, of calming security and a practically bucolic peace."[107] Because he conceived law and power as insoluble antinomics, Weber could write statements such as the following: "The elastic power, which the Weimar constitution still had, is replaced in the Basic Law by a thin-walled system of glass brittleness" or "... certainly, the unbridled vital power of the political, which one does not evade in Weimar, appears outwitted in the Basic Law."[108] His metaphorical contrast of the elasticity of the old order to the brittleness of the new expresses the conviction that the ability to assert power is the defining aspect of the political: The "... system of written constitutions, that is ossified in traditional formulae and constructions ... leaves us helpless against the actual political power game of our time."[109]

An émigré to the United States, Frankfurt school jurist Otto Kirchheimer labeled Weber's work "a curious spectacle" and a "brilliant, if dangerously lopsided indictment" of the Basic Law.[110]

106 Weber, *Spannungen*, 42.
107 Ibid.
108 Ibid., 38.
109 Ibid., 40.
110 Otto Kirchheimer, "Review of Werner Weber," *American Political Science Review* 46:3 (September, 1952), 885.

Similarly, Abendroth described it as a "... clever and useful attempt to represent political and public law problems" but nonetheless an example of the tradition and ideology of the authoritarian state (*Obrigkeitsstaat*).[111] Kirchheimer noted that Weber described Hitler's seizure of power in 1933 as the "... volcanic eruptions of the state's eternal tendency towards self-preservation."[112] Kirchheimer's judgment on this obscurantism needs no updating:

> [It is] somewhat astonishing to meet again – without prior attempt at some sort of inventory – the old clichés: "the all-embracing power of the state," with an acknowledged authority of its own ... "the strong executive," which neutralizes party-politics and preserves the permanence of the state ... [the idea of the civil service as an elite] and the people construed as an elementary organized force distinct from and opposed to the pluralism of oligarchic power groups....[113]

The popularity of Werner Weber's book illustrates that the cultivated pathos of German statism had public appeal beyond the academy. However, the Association of Professors of Constitutional Law was careful to police scandalous statements by the members of the Schmitt school,[114] much of whose writings were considered taboo by the Federal Constitutional Court. The result was that of the three major paradigms in West German jurisprudence of the 1950s, it was Smend's that rose to dominate. Smend became the single most cited and influential legal philosopher of the many-faceted West German social project of integration.[115] Broken by tyranny and war, postwar West German society was fractured among ex-Nazi Party members and ex-Communists, burdened with an enormous number of war-injured people and widows, and home to a refugee population of 13 million Germans expelled from the Eastern territories of the Third Reich. What could hold these groups together? The Federal Constitutional Court considered itself responsible for integrating a society riven by potentially dangerous cleavages. In Smend's *Theory of Integration* (1928), the Court found a suitable means of legitimating both its powers of judicial review (which had failed to take root

---

111 Wolfgang Abendroth, "Foreword," in *Bürokratischer Verwaltungsstaat und soziale Demokratie: Beiträge zu Staatslehre und Staatsrecht der Bundesrepublik*, eds. Herbert Sultan and Wolfgang Abendroth (Hannover: O. Goedel, 1955), 3.

112 Kirchheimer, "Review of Weber," 886.

113 Ibid., 887.

114 See Günther, *Denken von Staat her.*

115 Ibid.

during the Weimar Republic) and its ambition to integrate West German society.

Smend's theory also played a dramatic role in preventing Germans from coming to terms with the Nazi past, though. Smend's influence on jurisprudence in the 1950s illustrates the broader thesis that under Adenauer, West Germany chose integration and forgetting of the past over timely justice.[116] By embracing Smend's theory of democratic integration, the vast majority of judges and professors who had implemented and promoted Nazi law acquired an ingenious alibi for their former actions. These jurists claimed that the traditional legal methods they had inherited from the Empire had tied their hands, forcing them to execute laws without regard to any so-called extralegal (i.e., moral or political) considerations.[117] According to this version of legal positivism, law was a closed system; the judge lacked agency and simply "applied" the statute to the case at hand in a mechanical fashion. The jurists who had embraced Nazi ideology and applied the state's racist laws argued that they had only been following orders: "The law is the law." Moral considerations were not part of their legal habitus. As judges, they argued, they had no choice but to implement it. This was the genesis of the myth of judicial positivism.

The rise of this myth also was facilitated by the positive reception afforded by the officials of the Allied Occupation to another important Weimar theorist, Gustav Radbruch (1878–1949). After 1946, Radbruch, a former Minister of Justice in the Weimar Republic, encouraged judges to evaluate law from the perspective of suprapositive values, for example, justice, which he conceived as an expression of natural law. The legality of the laws was not sufficient to legitimate them. "Positivistic legal thought … a tradition nearly unbroken for many decades, dominated the jurists. Legal wrong [*gesetzliches Unrecht*] was as much of a contradiction in itself as unwritten law."[118] Lacking any cynical motive, Radbruch

---

116 See Jeffrey Herf, *Divided Memory: The Nazi Past in the Two Germanys* (Cambridge, MA: Harvard University Press, 1997); Norbert Frei, *Adenauer's Germany and the Nazi Past: The Politics of Amnesty and Integration*, trans. Joel Golb (New York: Columbia University Press, 2002).

117 For legal theory in the Empire, see Peter Caldwell, *Popular Sovereignty and the Crisis of German Constitutional Law: The Theory and Practice of Weimar Constitutionalism* (Durham, NC: Duke University Press, 1997).

118 See Gustav Radbruch, "Gesetzliche Unrecht und Übergesetzliches Recht" [orig. *Süddeutsche Zeitung* 1 (1946), 105–8]; reprinted in *Rechtsphilosophie*, 6th ed., Erik Wolf (Stuttgart: Köhler, 1963), 347.

unwittingly aided in the construction of the alibi of judicial positivism. Jurists in the 1950s then hid behind the moral authority Radbruch deservedly enjoyed. "Positivism, with its conviction 'law is law' [*Gesetz ist gesetz*], did in fact make the German class of jurists [*Juristenstand*] defenseless against laws of an arbitrary and criminal content. For this reason, positivism is not at all in the position to ground the validity of laws on its own."[119] Radbruch's assertion was seized as an opportunity by such influential figures as the first president of the Federal Constitutional Court, Hermann Weinkauff, who helped promote the renaissance of arguments from natural law that had dominated the first half of the decade.[120] In an influential essay published September 12, 1945, entitled, "Reappraisal of Legal Philosophy," Radbruch renounced legal positivism for its weakness in the face of Nazism:

> Such an attitude towards the law and its validity [i.e., positivism] rendered both lawyers and people impotent in the fact of even the most capricious, criminal or cruel laws. Ultimately this view that only where there is power is there law [*Recht*] is nothing but the affirmation that might makes right.[121]

By mid-decade, the jurists had embraced a self-serving myth, blaming their moral failures in the Nazi era on legal positivism. As one scholar explains,

> Hubert Schorn, a retired County Court judge, saw the "positivistic miseducation" of jurists as responsible, while Hermann Weinkauff, retired judge of the *Reichsgericht* and first president of the Federal Supreme Court, numbered arbitrary decisions by judges and legal murder by the courts among the "disastrous consequences of legal positivism."[122]

Schorn went on to author the most influential example of the myth: His *Judges in the Third Reich* was published in 1959.[123] The

---

119 Ibid.

120 For example, Weinkauff, "Der Naturrechtsgedanke in der Rechtsprechung des Bundesgerichthofes," in *Naturrecht oder Rechtspositivismus?* ed. Werner Maihofer (Bad Homburg vor der Höhe: Hermann Gentner Verlag, 1962), 554–76.

121 Stanley Paulson, "Lon Fuller, Gustav Radbruch and the 'Positivist' Theses," *Law and Philosophy* 13:3 (1994), 313.

122 Müller, *Hitler's Justice*, 221.

123 Hubert Schorn, *Der Richter im Dritten Reich* (Frankfurt: Klostermann, 1959).

contradictions in the myth of judicial positivism went unchallenged until the late 1960s, when a new generation of historians unveiled its falsity. The thesis that legal positivism tied the hands of Nazi judges was ultimately discredited by a generation of scholarship, and the exonerating function of the "Radbruch thesis" was thrown into relief.[124] As Manfred Walther concluded:

> The call to suprapositive law was no alternative to the legal thought of the Third Reich. The "new beginning" indicates much more continuity with the central elements of the legal thought in the fascist time, than has commonly been accepted. The Radbruch thesis has thus in terms of its historical reception had the function of concealing this continuity.[125]

In all the discussion of the alleged value-neutrality of Nazi judges and jurisprudence, the fact that "material justice" and "material illegality" had been the watchwords in Nazi criminal law was repressed because it did not fit with the claim that judges had been the victims of a "formalistic" training. In fact, the Nazi state had issued laws that left to judges the responsibility for filling in the content of blanket clauses such as "... with regard to the racial feelings of the people [*Volk*]." Nazi judges often went beyond what was officially required by the law to anticipate the underlying will of the *Führer*.[126] Nazi legal doctrines were in fact the exact opposite of legal positivism.[127]

Schmitt's explicit antipositivism went unmentioned. Directly contradicting the traditional formula of *Nulla poena sine lege* – no penalty can be retroactive and what constitutes a punishable offense must be clearly expressed in a statute – Schmitt had written in 1934 that "... no crime without punishment was more important than no punishment without law."[128] From his 1912 dissertation to his 1934 work, Schmitt was a critic of positivism. In 1932–33, both Schmitt

---

[124] Ibid., 314. See also Björn Schumacher, "Rezeption und Kritik der Radbruschen Formel," Ph.D. dissertation, University of Göttingen, 1985, 31–103; and Stanley Paulson, "On the Background and Significance of Gustav Radbruch's Post-War Papers," *Oxford Journal of Legal Studies* 26:1 (2006), 17–40.

[125] Walther, "Die Positivismus-These," 353.

[126] Müller, *Hitler's Justice*, 73.

[127] Ibid., 220.

[128] Ibid., 75. Schmitt, "Der Weg des deutschen Juristen," *Deutsche Juristen-Zeitung* 39 (1934), 698.

and Forsthoff had declared the era of legal positivism over.[129] Schmitt proposed "concrete order-thinking" (*konkretes Ordnungsdenken*) as the antidote to the abstract-rational law of the modern West.[130]

Concomitant to the critique of judicial positivism was the renaissance of natural law arguments. Numerous court decisions in the first postwar decade demonstrate that judges were making recourse to concepts of natural law, especially to negotiate cases stemming from the Nazi period. In a decision of February 8, 1952, the Federal Court (*Bundesgerichtshof*) addressed the question as to "... whether laws and ordinances can be considered 'law' in the true sense of the term, if their content offends against the claims of natural law or against the generally valid rules of conduct in the Christian-Western tradition."[131] An explicit rejection of legal positivism was articulated by the Federal Constitutional Court on October 23, 1951, arguing that even the framers of constitutions can create laws that "... will overstep the absolute bounds of justice."[132] As the *per curiam* opinion put it, "... the memory of 'legalized wrong' [*gesetzliches Unrecht*] is still fresh."[133] Other decisions of the Federal Constitutional Court in the early 1950s made reference to "moral law" or the "dictates of morality." In 1952, for example, an opinion read, "Commands issued by the sovereign which do not even aim at bringing about justice ... but which flagrantly ignore the rights and the dignity of human personality as they have been observed by all civilized peoples, do not create law."[134] Another 1952 decision of the Federal Constitutional Court similarly spoke of the "existence of suprapositive law."

Despite the fact that it was based on a false reading of the history of the Third Reich, Radbruch's account of what went wrong sealed the fate of legal positivism in the 1950s. With Kelsen in exile and Schmitt banned from teaching, Smend's theory was ideally placed to benefit from the weakness of the other paradigms. Moreover, his theory dovetailed neatly with the desires of business and labor, church and state, to secure social peace.[135] The concept of

---

129 Müller, *Hitler's Justice*, 71.
130 Walther, "Die Positivismus-These," 349.
131 Ernst von Hippel, "The Role of Natural Law in the Legal Decisions of the Federal Republic," *Natural Law Forum* 4:1 (1959), 112.
132 Ibid.
133 Ibid., 113.
134 Ibid., 115.
135 Schlink, "Why Carl Schmitt?," 434.

integration thus was ideally matched to the demands of the public and the profession.[136] It was not until the 1970s that the number of lawyers who had taught and administered law during the Third Reich dwindled sufficiently to permit unbiased study of the positivism question.[137] Smend's intellectual hegemony on the Court in the 1950s resulted in decisions that alienated Habermas from the Court until 1958, when the famous *Lüth* judgment began to change everything.

---

136 Michael Stolleis,"Die Staatsrechtslehre der fünfziger Jahre," in *Das Lüth-Urteil aus (rechts)historischer Sicht: die Konflikte um Veit Harlan und die Grundrechtsjudikatur des Bundesverfassungsgerichts*, ed. Thomas Henne (Berlin: BWV, 2005), 297.

137 See Schlink, "Why Carl Schmitt?" 435.

2 Habermas as Synthesizer of German Constitutional Theory, 1958–1963

Four major themes in Habermas's writings from 1958 to 1963 reveal the influence of the debates and contexts discussed in Chapter 1. The first concerns the plebiscitary deformation of democracy; the other three concern the status of liberal constitutionalism. Habermas's investigation of the first issue seems to have led him in search of a normative theory of the political, something he did not find in American political science. On this point, German constitutional theory seized Habermas's interest, despite it being dominated by the statist approach – a fact that does not attest to a fundamental illiberalism in Habermas's early writings.[1] The repression of the Nazi past by the Smend school had the not-incidental effect of repressing the Social Democratic–republican tradition in legal theory. Indeed, the ideas of Sinzheimer, Kirchheimer, and Fraenkel did not resurface in West Germany until 1965,[2] and Heller's work resurfaced only in 1968, when a "… new generation sought a socially liberal, social-scientifically oriented and politically unreproachable author to reference."[3] In context, therefore, we can interpret Habermas's appropriation of conservative constitutional theory as a result of a historical lacuna. As Habermas wrote in response to a question about the influence of some of the leading contemporary German political scientists (for example, Hennis, Sontheimer, Sternberger) on his work:

> It is true that I was very much influenced in the late '50s by the Weimar *Staatsrechtslehrerdiskussion* and its aftermath (C. Schmitt, Forsthoff, Weber vs. Abendroth), but less so by Kirchheimer,

[1] Schlink, "Why Carl Schmitt?" 435.

[2] Walther, *Radbruch-These*, 353.

[3] Michael Stolleis,"Der Methodenstreit der Weimarer Staatsrechtslehrer – ein abgeschlossene Kapitel der Wissenschaftsgeschichte?" Sitzungsberichte der Wissenschaftlichen Gesellschaft an der J.W.-Goethe Universität, Frankfurt/Main, 39:1 (Stuttgart: Steiner, 2001), 19.

> Fraenkel and Neumann.... I hadn't read much of [the] contemporary stuff in the field of political science and theory (except the American literature on mass communication and political sociology – Kornhauser, Lipset, C.W. Mills, etc.). Until I discovered Rawls in the late '70s I was nourished in political theory almost only by the German *Staatsrechtslehre*.[4]

Viewed contextually, Habermas's early writings are a daring – even jarring – hybrid of existing discourses. Habermas's interdisciplinary reach seems to have been driven by the peculiarities of the West German intellectual field, which was structured by an empirical and positivist political science on the one hand, and a conservative statist constitutional theory on the other. What was missing was a combined Critical Theory of politics, the state, and law with a strong normative perspective. As Habermas stated in the preface to *Transformation*:

> The public sphere ... [is an] object whose complexity precludes exclusive reliance on the methods of a single discipline.... [T]he category "public sphere" must be investigated within the broad field formerly reflected in the perspective of the science of "politics" [*Politik*]. When considered within the boundaries of a particular social-scientific discipline, this object disintegrates.[5]

Along the same lines, Habermas added that the "... object that public-opinion research was to apprehend has dissolved into something elusive"[6]; it "[leads] the life of a recluse not quite taken seriously by sociologists: precisely as a fiction of constitutional law."[7] However, because public opinion was not an explicit legal norm, it was not important to the jurists either. As Habermas's contemporary, Wilhelm Hennis, wrote in 1956, "The problems which the rise

[4] Author's private correspondence with Habermas, October 24, 2008. Habermas is referring to William Kornhauser, author of *The Politics of Mass Society* (Glencoe, IL: Free Press, 1959), and Seymour Martin Lipset, author of *Political Man: The Social Bases of Politics* (New York: Doubleday, 1960).

[5] Habermas, "Vorwort zur ersten Auflage," *Strukturwandel der Öffentlichkeit: Untersuchungen zu einer Kategorie der bürgerlichen Gesellschaft. Mit einem Vorwort zur Neuauflage 1990* [original edition, Neuwied: Luchterhand, 1962] (Frankfurt/Main: Suhrkamp, 1990), 51 (emphasis added); *Structural Transformation*, xvii. (*Transformation* hereafter).

[6] Habermas, *Strukturwandel*, 54; *Transformation*, 1.

[7] *Strukturwandel*, 351; *Transformation*, 242.

of opinion research pose for *Staatslehre* [state theory] and political science – at least in Germany – have not customarily been taken up by the *staatswissenschaftlichen* [sciences of state] faculties."[8] Thus Habermas noticed what he called a "gap" opening between the academic disciplines: "The feedback [obtained from opinion research and through its categories] cannot close the gap between public opinion as a fiction of constitutional law and the social-psychological decomposition of its concept."[9] Public opinion was a topic that had fallen, as it were, through the cracks in the intellectual field.

Habermas's critique of the "positivistic" character of contemporary political science cohered with the Frankfurt School tradition of critiquing positivist distortions of social science. But his valorization of the tradition of *Staatsrechtslehre* introduced an element alien to the Frankfurt School traditions of which he was most aware. As he explained:

> In contemporary political science, in contrast to classical social philosophy and the older *Staatsrechtslehre*, democracy is not derived from principles; they replace the objective meaning of institutions with their abstract determinations. Instead of deducing democracy from principles of legality [*Rechtsstaatlichkeit*] and popular sovereignty, it is defined by its actual apparatuses.[10]

Habermas's contrast between a concept of democracy derived from principles and a concept defined by its apparatuses was his way of critiquing what he saw as the strongly negative influence of the positivist trend in American political science on the newly refounded German discipline. Interdisciplinary social science with an emancipatory intent was part of Horkheimer's original vision of Critical Theory, but American political science seemed to Habermas to hold no resources to arrest the decline of the public sphere.

THE PLEBISCITARY DISTORTION OF DEMOCRACY

The first major theme of *Transformation* is: Was democracy really only about the periodic "plebiscitary acclamation" of elite decisions?

---

[8] Wilhelm Hennis, *Öffentliche Meinung und Repräsentative Demokratie* (Tübingen: J. C. B. Mohr, 1956), 13.

[9] Habermas, *Strukturwandel*, 353; *Transformation*, 244 (emphasis added).

[10] Habermas, "Reflexionen über den Begriff der Politischen Beteiligung," in *Student und Politik*, eds. Ludwig von Friedeburg, Jürgen Habermas, Christoph

Habermas interpreted the 1957 elections as an example of how a form of social science – market research – supported the "managed integration" of society from above.[11] Once a "... critical principle wielded by the public, publicity has been transformed into a principle of managed integration (wielded by staging agencies)."[12] Of these "staging agencies," Habermas singled out "... the administration, special-interest groups, and above all, the parties."[13] To Habermas, "the manipulative use ... of the empirical results of survey research"[14] was responsible for the Christian Democratic Union's (CDU's) victory. The CDU expanded its proportion of the vote from 45.2 percent in 1953 to 50.2 percent in 1957.[15]

In a magazine article, "The Federal Republic – An Elective Monarchy?" Habermas argued that independent voters tend to be those who know and care the least and that the CDU in its 1961 campaign was exploiting the latest marketing and advertising techniques to mobilize these "unpolitical" voters.[16] "Scientifically-led marketing makes political advertising into a component of a consumer culture for the un-political [citizen]."[17] Compared with Social Democratic Party (SPD) voters, CDU voters were in his estimate "...to a higher degree pre-politically or wholly unpolitically motivated."[18] Habermas was wrestling with a trend common to all the Western democracies at this time, namely, the splitting of the electorate into an active minority and an apathetic majority.[19] In the context of declining ideological differences between the major parties, "... each party tries to draw as much as possible from this reservoir of the

Oehler, Friedrich Weltz (Neuwied: Luchterhand, 1961), 14; "On the Concept of Political Participation," in *Student und Politik* (Students and Politics hereafter).

11 Habermas, *Strukturwandel*, 307; *Transformation*, 207.

12 Ibid.

13 Ibid.

14 Habermas, *Strukturwandel*, 323; *Transformation*, 219–20.

15 U.W. Kitzinger, *German Electoral Politics: A Study of the 1957 Campaign* (Oxford, England: Clarendon Press, 1960), 67ff.

16 Habermas, "Die Bundesrepublik – ein Wahlmonarchie?" *Magnum: Die Zeitschrift für das Moderne Leben. Sonderheft: Woher-Wohin. Bilanz der Bundesrepublik* (Köln: 1961), 26–9.

17 Ibid.

18 Ibid.

19 He cites in this connection Lipset, *Political Man*, especially part 2; Morris Janowitz et al., eds. *Political Behavior: A Reader in Theory and Research* (Glencoe, IL: Free Press, 1956); and Paul Lazarsfeld et al., eds. *Voting: A Study of Opinion-Formation in a Political Campaign* (Chicago: The University of Chicago Press, 1954).

undecided."[20] The waning of political ideologies and the tendency toward social leveling stood at the center of sociological research at mid-decade. Politicians noticed a loosening of party political affiliation that corresponded with the greater flexibility of parties to form coalitions with different partners.[21] Since voters could expect more or less the same level of welfare-state provision from each of the leading parties, voters' judgments were coming to turn more and more on perceptions of a more personal or emotional type.[22] A 1960 election study Habermas cited had concluded how best to exploit this social phenomenon: "How advantageous it is for a party to have no members, but rather to come to life only at election time with the centralized freedom to maneuver that characterizes an advertising firm existing [solely] for the purpose of the campaign."[23] However, Habermas was dismayed by the manufacture of temporary, ersatz public spheres[24] because political parties merely

> ... "took hold" of the voters temporarily and moved them to acclamation, without attempting to remedy their political immaturity.... For such parties the decisive issue is who has control over the coercive and educational means for ostentatiously or manipulatively influencing the voting behavior of the population.[25]

The state of democracy in the modern Western parliamentary state was deficient and regressive: "This kind of consensus formation would be more suited to the enlightened absolutism of an authoritarian welfare regime than to a democratic constitutional state committed to social rights: everything for the people, nothing by the people – not accidentally a statement stemming from the Prussia of Frederick II."[26] Habermas paints a portrait of a rational public sphere in eclipse: In the place of reasoning and decision-making, propaganda and acclamation hold sway.

In "On the Concept of Political Participation," Habermas came to the conclusion that contemporary international political science contained few valuable resources for countering this multifaceted

[20] Habermas, *Strukturwandel*, 317–8; *Transformation*, 215.
[21] Hennis, *Öffentliche Meinung*.
[22] Ibid.
[23] Kitzinger, *German Electoral Politics*, cited in Habermas, *Strukturwandel*, 312; *Transformation*, 210.
[24] Habermas, *Strukturwandel*, 312; *Transformation*, 210.
[25] Habermas, *Strukturwandel*, 303; *Transformation*, 203.
[26] Habermas, *Strukturwandel*, 323; *Transformation*, 219.

plebiscitary distortion of democracy. Habermas's critique was aimed at what he called the "social-technical" view of democracy, of which U.S. political science was its "prototypical" version.[27] Habermas argued that the "new [American] democracy research" reduced democracy to a method for securing social equilibrium.[28] His examples included the arguments of Morris Jones, David Riesman, and Nathan Glazer that a certain measure of apathy was a stabilizing force in democracies. By isolating political participation as simply one factor in achieving a stable polity, he argued, they missed its normative centrality: "Therein is forgotten the idea of the rule of the people in the form of direct democracy."[29] The hegemony of American political science left a gap that the postwar writings of Franz Neumann seem to have filled for Habermas.

Habermas's efforts to rethink the meaning of democracy show clear debts to Neumann's essays, especially his "The Concept of Political Freedom" [1954]. Habermas's critique of Harold Lasswell's writings, for example, is clearly anticipated by Neumann's views, expressed just five years earlier: "The dominant path in American political science, but modern political science in general, is the … tendency to equate politics with power politics (*Machtpolitik*) … and to conceive politics as a purely technical affair."[30] Neumann had argued that this view stemmed from Machiavelli: "Values appear as subjective preferences, valid when they bring success, invalid when they don't," with the result that history appears meaningless, an "… indifferent repetition of endless struggles between 'in groups' and 'out groups.'"[31] Habermas's critique also echoed Neumann's critique of the elitism and cynicism of much democratic theory:

> … [P]essimistic theories [such as] Machiavelli's view of politics [or] Metternich's conception of foreign relations are … unquestionably fashionable today, and if contrasted with a shallow misinterpretation of Enlightenment philosophy they are certainly more realistic.

---

27 Habermas, *Students and Politics*, 11.
28 Ibid.
29 Ibid.
30 Franz Neumann,"Ansätze zur Untersuchung politischer Macht," in *Demokratischer und autoritärer Staat: Studien zur politischen Theorie*, ed. Herbert Marcuse (Frankfurt/Main: Fischer, 1967), 83; *The Democratic and Authoritarian State: Essays in Political and Legal Theory*, ed. and trans. Herbert Marcuse (Glencoe, IL: Free Press, 1957).
31 Ibid.

> Modern sociology and political science do not weary of stressing that politics is about the manipulation of masses by elites, particularly through clever use of symbols; in order to beat an enemy, one must merely be cleverer.[32]

Neumann's linking of Lasswell to Machiavelli exemplifies the types of arguments Habermas encountered as he eschewed political science and began to investigate the emancipatory resources of constitutional law. Habermas concluded his 1961 magazine article by indicting what he called the "recent Machiavellianism between market-research and emergency-law," which has caused an "anti-Communist desiccation of democracy – for democracy."[33] By "Machiavellianism," Habermas meant that the anticommunist rhetoric deployed by the CDU in the elections echoed a central question of Machiavelli's political theory – "How can … life be made more secure politically?"[34]

Neumann had written that democracy "is not a state-form like any other" because its essence consists in its ability to promote human freedom. Similarly, Habermas wrote, "Democracy works for the self-determination of humanity, and only when this is real, is it true. Political participation then becomes identical with self-determination."[35] Habermas has since repudiated the Abendrothian program of a socialist democracy, but his ideal of democracy remains consistent with much of Neumann's.[36]

THREE DIMENSIONS OF THE RULE OF LAW: SEPARATION OF POWERS, GENERALITY OF THE LEGAL NORM, AND FUNDAMENTAL RIGHTS

In "Political Participation," Habermas portrayed the West German *Rechtsstaat* as a hollow institutional framework beset by contradictions, but one that nonetheless contained an "intention" that pointed

[32] Franz Neumann, "The Concept of Political Freedom" [1954], in *Democratic and Authoritarian State: Essays in Political and Legal Theory* (Glencoe: The Free Press, 1957), 61.

[33] Habermas, "Die Bundesrepublik – Ein Wahlmonarchie?"

[34] Habermas, "Die Klassische Lehre" [1961], *Theorie und Praxis*, 42.

[35] Habermas, *Student und Politik*, 11

[36] And this despite Habermas's pronounced lack of interest in Neumann's work in the 1990s. William Scheuerman encouraged Habermas to revisit Neumann without success. For Habermas's repudiation of Abendroth's version of socialist democracy, see Chapter 5.

beyond capitalism. In its current form, the Basic Law appeared to serve the interests of the bourgeoisie above all, leading Habermas to argue that there could be no real democracy without a socialist transformation of society and the economy. As he explained:

> Under present social relations, the political control of the functions of private capitalist property is the necessary precondition for securing an equal distribution of opportunities for political self-determination and for extending legal security to all spheres of society.[37]

Here Habermas followed Abendroth and Hermann Heller before him: The contradictions of liberal democracy could be resolved in only one of two ways: by evolving into either an authoritarian capitalist state or a democratic socialist one.[38] But what distinguishes Habermas's essay from the writings of Abendroth and Heller is the emphasis on the immanent critique of liberalism. Liberal constitutionalism could not be completely discounted because it contained an "intention" that pointed beyond capitalism, leading Habermas to warn: "Unequal division of property is not compatible with democratic equality, strictly speaking. Either the liberal *Rechtsstaat* fulfills its own *intentions* to become a democratic and social constitutional state," or it will reverse and take on a more or less authoritarian shape, as it had in 1933.[39]

In the same vein of immanent critique, Habermas used Montesquieu's *The Spirit of the Laws* (*Esprit des Lois*, 1751) as a foil for his anatomy of the *Rechtstaat* as an ideal institution.[40] The recourse to Montesquieu probably was suggested by his reading of Franz Neumann's "Montesquieu"(1949), which anticipated Habermas's own conclusions that liberal constitutionalism and democracy were antitheses, as well as Forsthoff's 1951 translation of the *Esprit des Lois* into German.[41] Neumann had described Montesquieu as a naif whose model of liberalism functioned trivially as a "Baedeker's

---

[37] Habermas, *Student und Politik*, 47.

[38] Hermann Heller, *Rechtsstaat oder Diktatur?* [1930], enlarged version of 1929, in Heller, *Gesammelte Schriften*, Bd. 2, *Recht, Staat, Macht*, eds. Hermann Heller, Gerhart Neimeyer, Martin Drath (Leiden: A.W. Sijthoff, 1971).

[39] Habermas, *Student und Politik*, 45 (emphasis added).

[40] See Neumann, "Montesquieu" [1949], in idem, *Demokratischer und Autoritarer Staat*, 142–94.

[41] Ernst Forsthoff, trans. and ed., *Vom Geist der Gesetze* (Tübingen: Laupp, 1951).

guide" to the English constitution for the "antidemocratic wing" of German liberalism in the Empire. Habermas questioned whether the three features Montesquieu considered liberal constitutionalism's signature actually existed in contemporary West Germany. The three were the separation of governmental functions, the generality of application of the legal norm, and the guarantees of basic rights. How relevant were those liberal *Rechtstaatlich* ideals under contemporary conditions of mass democracy and the social welfare state? Habermas asked. The answer common to all his works from the years 1958–63 was that under the new social conditions, liberalism's principles had "... forfeited their original meaning." The only important question that remained, therefore, was "whether or not the realization of these principles" was still possible.[42] In all his works, Habermas advanced the same answer to this question: Yes, but only through socialist transformation.

Habermas did not intend to argue for a new equilibrium among the executive, legislative, and judicial branches of the government in Bonn but rather for the priority of the democratic legislative branch over the other two. His preference for the legislator reflected a Rousseau-influenced notion of the general will. Habermas believed that the Basic Law had produced a lopsided state of affairs: Strong guarantees of basic rights were juxtaposed with the weakest of mechanisms for achieving popular sovereignty. In "Political Participation," Habermas asserted that the drafters of the constitution had produced a document that displayed "... mistrust of the parliament and the bureaucracy."[43] Here he followed Drath, who bemoaned the "remarkable" contrast between the expansive basic rights section of the Basic Law, on the one hand, and the lack of trust placed in the political judgment of the populace, on the other.[44] Plebiscites and referenda were excluded from the Basic Law. "One can say that with us," Drath wrote, "Montesquieu's idea of representation has defeated Rousseau's idea of democracy."[45] Nonetheless, Drath argued, one could not speak of a division of powers in the classical sense. First, the courts intervened too often in legislative

[42] Habermas, *Student und Politik*, 34–5.

[43] Ibid.

[44] Martin Drath, "Die Gewaltenteilung im heutigen deutschen Staatsrecht," in *Faktoren der Machtbildung*, ed. A. R. Gurland (Berlin: Duncker & Humblot, 1952), 27, fn. 57.

[45] Drath, "Die Gewaltenteilung," 27.

and executive actions. He also criticized the fact that the Federal Constitutional Court had arrogated legislative functions to itself when it banned the Socialist Reich Party in 1952 and the Communist Party in 1956.[46] Abendroth also attacked the Court's proceedings against the Communist Party, arguing that by removing an essential right of resistance (*Widerstandsrecht*), the Court failed to learn the lessons of Weimar: "Democracy depends on the readiness of the democratic forces of the nation to protect it."[47] Reflecting on its powers of judicial review, which were unprecedented in German history, Abendroth intoned: "It is not higher-ranking than the Basic Law, rather it is subordinate to it."[48]

From the experience with the plebiscite, and with the Court's ban on the Communist Party, Habermas appears to have formed a view of the highest court as an antidemocratic and antisocialist institution, consistent with both Abendroth's and Drath's assessment of it. The Federal Constitutional Court's emphasis on basic rights, Habermas believed, was neither an adequate substitute for the missing second half of the Weimar constitution (which had guaranteed social rights) nor sufficient compensation for the Court's role in effectively negating popular sovereignty.[49] The West German "economic miracle" had produced both a paternalistic state and an ethos of consumption, Habermas believed. Each exacerbated the weaknesses of the other. As he put it in 1958:

> If one compares the superficiality of the opportunities for political self-determination with the personal protection and personal freedom which are secured to individuals by the liberal basic rights, one gets the impression that citizens of the so-called consumer society are also viewed juristically as customers.... Outfitted with these rights, and as good as excluded from real political power (*Mitbestimmung*), the people become a mere object of care (*Fürsorge*).[50]

Having concluded that the judiciary and administrative bureaucracy were too conservative to promote social reform, Habermas gravitated toward intellectual positions that helped him to buttress his

[46] Ibid.
[47] Abendroth, "Bundesverfassung und Widerstandsrecht," in *Antagonistische Gesellschaft und Politische Demokratie: Aufsätze zur Politische Soziologie* (Neuwied: Luchterhand 1967, originally 1955), 124–7.
[48] Ibid., 123.
[49] Habermas, *Student und Politik*, 36.
[50] Ibid., 39.

case for legislative supremacy. Thus, before 1959, Habermas viewed the Federal Constitutional Court as a paternalistic and repressive force of conservative restoration; afterwards, as discussed below, his view of the Court changed somewhat.

From the left constitutional-legal tradition embodied by Abendroth, Habermas adopted the strategy of a parliamentary road to socialism, buttressed by legal positivism, that is, a narrow and literal reading of statute. Despite the history of legal positivism's long association with constitutional monarchism, Social Democrats had put their trust since the Weimar Republic in a democratic version of a legal positivist approach to the constitution. This followed logically from the fact that both the Weimar constitution and the Bonn constitution contained broad commitments to social rights and welfare.[51] Legal positivism therefore could help to protect the expressed will of the sovereign legislature from interference by an activist judiciary. Thus the clauses of the Basic Law concerning social welfare could be taken as broad mandates for a socialist economy. From Abendroth, Habermas borrowed a critique of the notion that constitutional rights were merely "negative" liberties (in Isaiah Berlin's sense). When Habermas observed that "our constitutional lawyers" have the "inclination" to treat the *Rechtsstaat* and *Sozialstaat* as "opposites," he did not aim to complement negative rights with positive ones but rather to transcend the antinomy altogether.[52] Clearly echoing the interwar Heller's *Rechtsstaat or Dictatorship?* Habermas struck the same chord: "Where the liberal *Rechtsstaat* does not evolve into a *sozialer Rechtsstaat*, it remains in contradiction with itself."[53] The contradiction demanded the "transformation" (*Umfunktionnierung*) of negative rights into rights of participation. As explained in Chapter 1, Habermas moved to the left of the positions articulated by the reform wing of the party at Bad Godesburg.

THE SEPARATION OF POWERS AND LEGAL NORMS

From Schmitt's students, Ernst Forsthoff and Werner Weber, Habermas appropriated a radical critique of the welfare state

[51] See Peter Caldwell, "Is a Social *Rechtsstaat* Possible? The Weimar Roots of a Bonn Controversy," in *From Liberal Democracy to Fascism*, eds. Peter C. Caldwell and William E. Scheuerman (Leiden: Humanities Press, 2000), 142.
[52] Habermas, *Student and Politik*, 37.
[53] Ibid., 36–7.

but used it for a socialist rather than a statist and capitalist end.[54] Habermas thus combined positions from the legal left and right in a unique synthesis. Specifically, he borrowed the insight that the welfare state's class-specific measures had rendered the classical liberal insistence on the "generality" of the legal norm a fiction. While they had taken this trend as indicative of the need to concentrate powers in the executive branch, Habermas considered the breakdown of the traditional separation of powers empirical support for his theoretical preference, namely, that the legislative branch should rule supreme.

Habermas's appropriations from the Abendroth and Schmitt schools yielded an entirely original synthesis. In Forsthoff's writings on the welfare state and administrative law, Habermas found an expert witness to the breakdown of the separation of powers in general and the state-society distinction in particular. With enabling laws and supplementary legislations, the legislator handed over powers to administration. Thus legislation and administration, deemed separate in Montesquieu, began to appear indistinct. If the line between state and society was becoming ever blurrier, then the idea that a private, prepolitical sphere clearly could be demarcated from a public one was equally fictitious. As Habermas concluded in "On the Concept of Political Participation," when "... organized interests exert influence on the organs of state ... [s]ocial power is *eo ipso* political."[55] Social law, he had learned from reading the German experts in constitutional law, was neither public nor private. Habermas's initial insight in *Students and Politics* – "Fused into a single functional complex, the new law reveals the face of the future"[56] – was amplified in his *Transformation*: "Between (state and society) and out of the two ... a repoliticized social sphere emerged to which the distinction between 'public' and 'private' cannot be usefully applied."[57] On the basis of Forsthoff's reading of the "deformalization of law," Habermas concluded that a unified state-society had arrived. What remained was to recognize the already-politicized character of the social sphere.

---

54 Compare Kennedy, "Carl Schmitt and the Frankfurt School."

55 Habermas, *Student und Politik*, 22.

56 From *Students and Politics*. Cited in Jean Cohen and Andrew Arato, *Civil Society and Political Theory* (Cambridge, MA: MIT Press, 1990), 247.

57 Habermas, *Strukturwandel*, 226; *Transformation*, 142.

Habermas, aware of the brown pasts of the Schmitt students, held them at arm's length. Nevertheless, he appropriated their radical critique of the welfare state against the grain of their intention. Like them, Habermas was repelled by the influence of powerful interest-groups. But where they criticized a "vacuum" of state authority, he did not seek to reconstruct a strong executive branch and instead saw the legislative branch as his preferred guardian of the constitution. Habermas learned from the Schmittians that the spheres of "state" and "society" had interpenetrated each other. If public and private spheres were collapsing in on one another, Habermas reasoned, the idea of prepolitical, negative liberties had ceased to be meaningful. Negative liberties could be reinvented only as positive guarantees of participation with a unified state-society. Only by becoming a truly "political society" could the tension between *homme* and *citoyen* be overcome.[58] This is the meaning of Habermas's statement that

> The state-form, which essentially presupposes the division of state and society, still remains, though no longer in its older form. Although society no longer stands opposite the state as an independent entity (as in the liberal model), society is equally not political in an actual sense. This ambivalence stamps the essence of the constitution.[59]

Habermas resolved the "ambivalence" of the constitution with an embrace of a statist solution. With this conclusion, Habermas gambled that *Rechtsstaat* would not be a casualty of democracy. Like Abendroth, Habermas elided the tensions between liberalism and democracy. Abendroth had simply trusted that the democratic legislator would secure the traditional legal guarantees of civil rights to citizens. Similarly, Habermas argued vaguely that the idea of democracy was "co-institutionalized" with the idea of the *Rechtsstaat* but could be realized only in the shape of a "political society." This potentially illiberal feature of Abendroth's positions migrated into Habermas's synthesis. But a seed of doubt remained: "The political control of social power is the necessary condition for the realization of democracy in this sense; whether it is sufficient we will see."[67] In sum, Habermas believed that the resurrection of the public sphere did not require reestablishing the boundary between the state

[58] Habermas, *Student und Politik*, 22.
[59] Ibid., 21.

and civil society. As two political theorists in the Critical Theory tradition observed in 1989, "Paradoxically, the analyst who has done most to identify the normative ideal of the public sphere with the differentiation of state and civil society came to the conclusion (in *Structural Transformation*) that the ideal could only be saved by accepting that the abolition of civil society had already occurred."[60]

FUNDAMENTAL RIGHTS

Between 1958 and 1961, a dramatic change occurred in Habermas's view of the fundamental rights guaranteed by the Basic Law. As important as it is for understanding Habermas's contribution to the reorientation of the Critical Theory tradition, it has never been discussed in the literature on Habermas. Recall that in 1958 Habermas dismissed the basic rights as a paternalistic grant of the state – a poor substitute for real political power: "One gets the impression that citizens of the so-called consumer society are also viewed juristically as customers.... Outfitted with these rights, and as good as excluded from real political power (*Mitbestimmung*), the people become a mere object of care (*Fürsorge*)." By 1961, however, Habermas arrived at a new argument: Rights were not purely ideological but potentially redeemable:

> [It] ... has to be demonstrated that those basic rights guaranteeing the effectiveness of a public sphere in the political realm (such as freedom of speech and opinion, freedom of association and assembly, and freedom of the press) that in their application to the ... structurally transformed public sphere they must no longer be interpreted merely as injunctions but positively, as guarantees of participation, if they are to fulfill their original function in a meaningful way.[61]

Immanent critique could turn rights from injunctions into guarantees – or, in the more familiar language of liberal political theory, from negative to positive liberties.

What accounts for the shift? Concurrent with the years in which Habermas's position changed, a revolutionary series of decisions was

[60] Cohen and Arato, *Civil Society*, 254.
[61] Habermas, *Strukturwandel*, 331–2; *Transformation*, 227.

handed down by the Federal Constitutional Court. The cumulative impact of these decisions was to alter Habermas's view of the Court and with it his understanding of the potential of basic rights jurisprudence. Habermas's lifelong project of rebuilding the normative foundations of Critical Theory began with *Structural Transformation*. Changes in the high court's jurisprudence are a hidden source of this major development in the history of Critical Theory.[62]

Habermas confirmed in an interview that law professor Helmut Ridder's writing on an "objective right to press freedom" was an important influence on his thinking at that time.[63] This was consistent with what he had acknowledged over forty years earlier in a footnote to *Transformation*:

> Pushing the interpretation of the social function of the freedom of private opinion to its logical conclusion, Ridder arrived at the formulation of a "freedom of public opinion" [*Meinungsfreiheit*] aimed at providing citizens with the equal opportunity to participate in the process of public communication to begin with.... Equal access to the public sphere is provided to all other private people only through the state's guarantee of active interference to this end; a mere guarantee that the state will refrain from intrusion is no longer sufficient for this purpose. In the same sense we can interpret the jurisprudence of the *Bundesverfassungsgericht* especially the Lüth/Harlan judgment (1958), the Nordrhein-Westfalen press judgment (1959), the Schmid/*Spiegel* judgment (1961), and the television decision of 1961.[64]

In particular, the *Lüth* case is regarded by legal historians not only as a watershed for the jurisprudence of fundamental rights but also as a turning point in the evolution of a liberal political culture in the Federal Republic.[65] Indeed, the decision generally is regarded today as a landmark effort free speech case. The other three cases are also

[62] The change is evident in a comparison of "On the Concept of Political Participation" (1958), on the one hand, with *Transformation* (1961) and "Natural Law and Revolution"(1963), on the other. Despite a preponderance of continuities with *Student und Politik*, a quiet revolution in Habermas's thought occurred in *Transformation*.

[63] Author's private correspondence with Habermas, June 7, 2005.

[64] Habermas, *Strukturwandel*, 334; *Transformation*, 228.

[65] A comprehensive and enlightening discussion is in Thomas Henne, ed., *Das Lüth-Urteil aus (rechts-)historischer Sicht: die Konflikte um Veit Harlan und die Grundrechtsjudikatur des Bundesverfassungsgerichts* (Berlin: BWV, 2005).

celebrated, classic precedents. Below we examine how and why the four cases influenced Habermas.

The *Lüth-Harlan* decision of 1958 was six and a half years in the making. The case involved a filmmaker popular during the Third Reich, Veit Harlan (1899–1964), who had directed the notoriously anti-Semitic *Jud Süss* (*The Jew Süss*, 1940). The film fictionalizes the eighteenth-century life of Joseph Süss-Oppenheimer (1698–1738), a Jewish financial advisor and tax collector for the Duke of Württemberg. It depicts Süss as a rapist and torturer of a Christian woman who was brought to justice by an Aryan-Christian German community. Joseph Goebbels strongly supported the making of the film, which was hugely popular in the Third Reich. Eric Lüth, Hamburg's director of information, was an activist working for reconciliation between Christians and Jews. In 1951, before an audience of movie producers and distributors, he called for a boycott of Harlan's first postwar film, *Immortal Lover* (*Unsterbliche Geliebte*) on ethical and pragmatic grounds: The reemergence of Harlan was a scandal that would be harmful to the German film community and to Germany generally. Concurrently, student groups throughout Germany protested the theatrical release of two new Harlan films, *Immortal Lover* and *Hanna Amon*.[66]

The producer and distributor of Harlan's film filed a complaint with the Hamburg Superior Court requesting that Lüth cease and desist from his call for a boycott. The court ruled for the distributor and against Lüth. Lüth was deemed to have violated Article 826 of the Civil Code, which read, "Whoever causes damage to another person intentionally and in a manner offensive to good morals is obligated to compensate the other person for the damage."[67] Lüth, in turn, brought a constitutional complaint to the Federal Constitutional Court stating that his basic right to freedom of speech – guaranteed by Article 5 of the Basic Law[68] – had

66 For Horkheimer's support of the student protests, see Max Horkheimer, "Gegen Veit Harlan. Entwurf einer Resolution" (March 19, 1951), in Wolfgang Kraushaar, ed., *Frankfurter Schule und Studentenbewegung*, Bd. 2, 60.

67 Kommers, *Jurisprudence*, 368.

68 Ibid., 366. Article 5, 1 reads: "Everyone has the right freely to express and disseminate his opinion orally, in writing and in pictures and to inform himself without hindrance from all generally accessible sources. The freedom of the press and the freedom of reporting through radio and film are guaranteed. There is to be no censorship."

been violated by the lower court decision prohibiting the boycott. The Court overturned the judgment of the Hamburg court as an unconstitutional infringement of Lüth's basic right to freedom of opinion (*Meinungsfreiheit*). The first sentence of the *Lüth* judgment is its most famous. It reads:

> The basic rights are in the first place defensive rights of the citizen against the state; in the basic rights determinations of the Basic Law are also however an objective value-order, which, as a fundamental constitutional decision is valid and binding on all realms of the law.[69]

Here was outlined for the first time the principle that values embodied in constitutional law henceforth would have a "radiating effect" (*Ausstrahlung*) or "third party effect" (*Drittwirkung*) on areas hitherto governed by private law. Prior to this case, civil rights were considered "vertical"; that is, they protected citizens from their infringement or encroachment by the government. The new dimension opened by the *Lüth* judgment was that fundamental rights were held to have "horizontal" application, that is, that civil or private law (the provisions of the *Bürgerlichen Gesetzbuches*) had to be modified by the basic rights. The Court determined that fundamental rights were at the same time "subjective rights" against government intrusion – that is, rights held by individual citizens – and "objective values" with a "radiating effect" on private law. Wherever the application of a private law limits a fundamental right, this fundamental right has to be taken into account in the interpretation and application of that law. The Hamburg Superior Court thereby erred in its failure to consider Harlan's constitutional right to free expression. *Lüth* was the first in a line of jurisprudence that claimed to protect citizens from both vertical and horizontal risks to their fundamental rights. The "pivotal importance" of *Lüth*, as summarized by one leading authority, is that the decision

> … emphasizes the individual and social dimensions of speech.… Speech, like other basic rights, is both negative and positive in character. Its negativity protects the individual against official restraints on speech; its positivity obliges the state and its agents to establish the conditions necessary for the effective exercise of speech rights.[70]

[69] Cited in *BVerfGE* 7:198: "Objective value-order" is the translation of "*objective Wertordnung*."
[70] Kommers, *Jurisprudence*, 376.

In the reasoning of the Federal Constitutional Court in *Lüth*, it is likely that Habermas heard a victory for the kind of reasoning that he and Abendroth had supported – without avail – on the social welfare state. The result of *Lüth* was a much-widened role for the judiciary as a whole in the shaping of society.

Two other cases – the first *Television* case and the *Schmid-Spiegel* case – must have caught Habermas's attention for the same reason *Lüth* did: They illustrated the state's positive obligations under Article 5 to support the public sphere. The *Schmid-Spiegel* case was important for underscoring the new interpretation of Article 5 as bestowing rights of an "objective" character (in contrast to the "subjective" rights of the press against encroachment by the state). By "objective right," the Federal Constitutional Court meant "… an affirmative constitutional right to institutional autonomy and independence."[71] Print media, as in the *Schmid-Spiegel* case, and television earn this objective right from the "public function" they perform in a liberal democracy.[72]

The first *Television* case resulted from the decision of Adenauer to establish a second federally operated television station on July 25, 1960.[73] States led by the SPD brought a constitutional complaint based on Basic Law Articles 30 and 70, Section 1. The Federal Constitutional Court held that Adenauer's action violated the reserved powers of the states, finding that "… this modern instrument of opinion-formation should neither be at the mercy of the government nor of one single group."[74] The governing boards of broadcasting stations henceforth would include broad-ranging representatives, including from political parties, religious denominations, trade unions, and employer groups.

The *Schmid-Spiegel* case originated with the complaint of a high-ranking state judge, Richard Schmid, who in 1953 was accused by the newsmagazine *Der Spiegel* of having communist sympathies, even though the magazine had information that proved otherwise. Schmid responded aggressively to the libel in a newspaper article but was in turn accused of libel by *Der Spiegel*. The decision of the

71 Ibid.
72 Ibid., 403.
73 *BVerfGE* 12:205 (1961).
74 Kommers, *Jurisprudence*, 406. While the Court endorsed the existing monopoly of broadcast media, it did not rule out the entrance of privately owned media in future.

Göttingen Superior Court was for *Der Spiegel* and against Schmid and was affirmed on appeal. Schmid filed an Article 5 complaint with the Federal Constitutional Court, which ruled in his favor.

The *Nordrhein-Westfalen* case of 1959 involved the legislative effort of that state to bar publishers and editors who disseminated materials advocating socialism, militarism, totalitarianism, or racial discrimination.[75] The Federal Constitutional Court found that the law violated the Article 5 right of a free press to perform its public function – as established in the *Lüth* case. But it also found that the state had effectively usurped the prerogative of censorship reserved by Article 18 to the high court itself.[76] Free speech was not absolutely protected in West Germany; it was guided by the doctrine of "militant democracy"(*streitbare Demokratie*), which limited speech deemed inimical to the "free democratic basic order"(*freiheitliche-demokratische Grundordnung*).[77] The concept of a "militant democracy" – or democracy that would set limits to free speech and political action in order to protect that same order – originated with an essay political scientist Karl Loewenstein wrote from exile: "The most perfectly drafted and devised statutes are not worth the paper on which they are written unless supported by the indomitable will to survive ... Democracy becomes militant."[78] In 1931, Loewenstein argued before the Association of *Staatsrechtslehrer* that the state has a "duty of self-preservation."[79]

[75] *BVerfGE* 10: 118, 121 (1959).

[76] Kommers, *Jurisprudence*, 43: "According to Art. 18, persons who abuse the basic freedoms of speech, press, teaching, assembly association, privacy of the mail and telecommunications, property, or the right of asylum in order to combat the 'free democratic basic order' shall forfeit these rights."

[77] The doctrine is an interpretation of the combined significance of Articles 18 and 21, Section 2. Article 21, Section 2, states that political parties who seek "... by reason of their aims or ... behavior to endanger the existence of the Federal Republic of Germany shall be unconstitutional." For the scholarly discussion, see Jürgen Becker, "Die Wehrhafte Demokratie des Grundgesetzes," in *Handbuch des Staatsrechts des Bundesrepublik Deutschland*, vol.VII: Normativität und Schutz der Verfassung-Internationale Beziehungen (Heidelberg: C.F. Müller,1992), 309–59; Hans-Jürgen Papier, Wolfgang Durner, "Streitbare Demokratie," *Archiv des Öffentlichen Rechts* 128 (2003), 340–71.

[78] Karl Loewenstein, "Militant Democracy and Fundamental Rights, II," *American Political Science Review* 31:4 (August 1937), 638–58.

[79] A 1941 essay by Karl Mannheim is generally regarded as the source of the German translation of the concept "*streitbare Demokratie*." See Mannheim, *Diagnosis of Our Time* (New York: Oxford University Press, 1944).

Habermas's description of the *Nordrhein-Westfalen* case as a progressive one is intriguing. The Federal Constitutional Court had affirmed the freedom of the press according to Article 5 but did nothing to challenge the doctrine of militant democracy: It rejected the state's right to censor the press because the right to censor belonged at the federal level. Habermas's reading of the first *Television*, *North Rhine-Westphalia*, and *Schmid-Spiegel* cases reveals the influence of the Abendroth school on his thinking about the public sphere.

The influence of both the Schmitt and Abendroth schools on Habermas's thought in the 1957–63 period is clear, abundant, and direct. With the third major school of constitutional theory, that of Rudolf Smend, however, the influence is less direct but equally significant. Habermas must have known Smend's writings from Abendroth, who regularly taught his texts in his seminars.[80] Nevertheless, Habermas practically never cited Smend in his writings. There are only two exceptions: One is a citation to an encyclopedia article of Smend's in his "Natural Law and Revolution" (1963) and the other a sole reference in *Transformation*.[81] But Smend's thought nonetheless had a major impact on Habermas through Smend's students and intellectual network, on the one hand, and the hegemony of Smend's constitutional theory on the high court throughout the 1950s, on the other. Gerhard Leibholz, an influential jurist on the high court from 1951, had written his *Habilitation* under Smend, and Smend invited Leibholz to take over his chair in Göttingen.[82] Leibholz opened the door for Smend's influence on the Court.[83] Leibholz brought Horst Ehmke, a student of Smend's, to the Court as his assistant in 1956. Ehmke had worked with SPD delegate Adolf Arndt (1904–74) from 1952–6. Arndt subsequently brought another Smend student, Wilhelm

[80] Abendroth *Nachlass*, Institute for Social History, Amsterdam.

[81] Habermas made reference to Smend's 1956 lexicon article, "The Theory of Integration" in order to critique it, but there is no sustained argument. See Habermas, "Natural Law and Revolution," in *Theory and Practice*, 117; orig. "Naturrecht und Revolution," in *Theorie und Praxis: Sozialphilosophische Studien*, 5th ed. (Frankfurt/Main: Suhrkamp, 1988), 123. The reference in *Transformation* is to a 1955 essay by Smend on the concept of public opinion. See *Strukturwandel*, 137; *Transformation*, 70.

[82] Günther, *Denken*, 191.

[83] Peter Badura, "Staat, Recht und Verfassung in der Integrationslehre. Zum Tode von Rudolf Smend," *Der Staat* 16 (1977), 304. Cited in Henne, *Lüth-Urteil*, 214.

Hennis, to work with him. In major decisions of which Habermas took note – particularly the 1952 and 1956 decisions to ban the Communist Party (KPD) and Socialist Reich Party (SRP) and the 1958 *Lüth* judgment – Smend's integrative theory of the constitution supplied the essential rationale. Furthermore, Habermas learned from, and cited, several of Smend's students who went on to prominent careers in political science and law, including Martin Drath and Gerhard Leibholz, both of whom sat on the Federal Constitutional Court, and Horst Ehmke, Konrad Hesse, and Wilhelm Hennis.[84]

The decisions to ban the political parties, made in the name of "militant democracy," rested on a combination of natural law reasoning and Smend's legal theories; the two influences are very hard to disentangle. For Smend, the legitimating power of law derived from natural law, not from democratically generated law.[85] In the early 1950s, the Federal Constitutional Court described the free, democratic basic order as a "value order" or "value system,"[86] a formulation that revealed clearly the influence of Smend's central Weimar-era text, *Constitution and Constitutional Law* (1928). There, Smend described the basic rights catalogue of the Weimar constitution as a "value system" rather than a programmatic guide for legislators.[87] In its 1952 ban on the SRP, the Court followed Smend by using the language of "basic values" (*Grundwerte*) instead of basic rights (*Grundrechte*).[88] Similarly, in its ruling banning the KPD in 1956, the Court described the "free democratic order" as a system of "absolute values" that must be defended: The Basic Law would be "no value-neutral order" but rather a "value bound order."[89] Smend's doctrine of integration thereby dominated the Court in the 1950s through shared constitutional values:

> In a series of decisions, the federal criminal and civil court explicitly used natural law as a gauge. The federal constitutional court took

[84] Leibholz was on the Federal Constitutional Court from 1951–71; he had no party affiliation. Hesse was elected once by the SPD and once by the FDP and served from 1975–87.

[85] See Smend, *Verfassung und Verfassungrecht*, 210; and Ilse Staff, "Das *Lüth*-Urteil. Zur demokratietheoretischen Problematik materialer Grundrechtstheorie," in Henne, *Lüth-Urteil*, 317.

[86] *BVerfGE* 2:1, 17ff; 5:85, 134, 204–7.

[87] Henne, "'Von 0 auf Lüth in 6½ Jahren.' Zu den prägenden Faktoren der Grundsatzentscheidung," in Henne, *Lüth Urteil*, 213.

[88] Henne, "Von 0 auf Lüth," 208.

[89] *BVerfGE* 5, 138–9.

> care not to be too explicit about it, but its understanding of basic rights as values comprising a system of values and of free action as more or less value-laden was rooted in the natural law renaissance of the time. This understanding … also undergirds the current view that basic rights are elements of an objective order, which is to say, they are not merely subjective individual rights but objectively obligate the government to ensure conditions of freedom and equality. Smend's was the constitutional theory accompanying these developments. Again the Federal Constitutional Court cautiously avoided express references to it. But its presupposition that basic rights form a value system found an obvious second root in Smend's concept of a basic rights value system as a national system of moral values and cultural goods.[90]

As explained in Chapter 1, Smend's theory was the most congenial theory available after Schmitt's decisionism and the positivism of Hans Kelsen, Richard Thoma, and Gerhard Anschütz had been discredited. Its need for an antipositivist doctrine led the Court to varieties of value jurisprudence. But the Court eschewed explicit reliance on Smend's ideas because Smend's democratic credentials were not entirely in order. Thus, when the Court decided that the international reputation of Germany was at stake in the *Lüth* case, it took care not to explicitly rely on Smend, whose sympathies for Mussolini in the 1920s were well known. In 1956, Smend complained about his reputation: "The theory of integration is denounced from the conservative side as ultrademocratic, and from the liberal and socialist [sides] as fascist."[91]

But the evidence of Smend's influence on the *Lüth* judgment is overwhelming. Scholars agree that the case was clearly connected to the material, value-oriented theory of Smend and that it relied on Smend's emphasis on the social dimensions of freedom of expression.[92] Ironically, the Smend school distanced itself from the *Lüth* judgment. While the Court clearly reached back to the integration language of Smend's 1928 work, the Smend school had since moved in a different direction. Indeed, Smend dropped the words "value" (*Wert*) and "value order" (*Wertordnung*) from his 1958 lexicon article

[90] Bernhard Schlink, "Why Carl Schmitt?" *Constellations* 2:3 (1996), 429–44.
[91] Smend, "Integrationslehre," 301.
[92] See Henne, *Lüth Urteil*, 220; Staff, *Lüth-Urteil*, 319; Stefan Ruppert, "Geschlosenne Wertordnung? Zur Grundrechtstheorie Rudolf Smends," in Henne, *Lüth-Urteil*, 342–6.

on the theory of integration.[93] As the leading scholar of the case summarizes it, "An astonishing path: the theories and theses of the antipositivist Smend, genuinely antiparliamentary and antiliberal, served now ... as the keyword for the basic rights jurisprudence of a parliamentary and liberal democracy."[94] Thus the defining decision of postwar West German jurisprudence was bathed in a number of ironies.

The *Lüth* decision shared with the earlier "militant democracy" decisions a description of the constitutional order as the repository of fundamental values. But whereas in the judgment against the SRP in 1952 the Court had spoken of "highest fundamental values" (*oberste Grundwerten*) and a "value-bound order" (*wert-gebundenen Ordnung*), the *Lüth* Court now spoke of a "value system" (*Wertsystem*) and "objective value order"(*objektiven Wertordnung*).[95] Concealed within these scintilla of linguistic difference was a revolutionary sea change. Smend had appropriated the concept of "values" from fellow Weimar philosopher Max Scheler (1882–1950) and his student Nicolai Hartmann (1874–1928).[96] Their "material value ethics" was a variant of natural law. The Court's invocation of an "objective value-order" meant something different than it had meant for Smend, Scheler, and Hartmann. By 1958, a retreat from the natural-law renaissance of the first half of the decade was under way; *Lüth* was its death blow.[97] The Court moved away from the "value philosophy" of Hartman and Scheler and toward a reliance on the concrete constitutional text.[98] As one scholar of the case explains, "... 'objective value order' was *Verfassungsimmanent* – and therefore marks a break with arguments from natural law."[99] In other words, the value system of the constitution was no longer thought to be anchored in transcendental truths; its "objectivity" referred only to its immanence in the constitutional text itself. In another scholar's words, "The formula of value-order (*Wertordnung*) was the means of transport, the catalyst of the new. Once executed – and this happened relatively quickly – one didn't need the impulse anymore."

93 Günther, *Denken*, 167–71.
94 Henne, "Von 0 to *Lüth*," 220.
95 Ibid., 218
96 Ruppert, "Geschlossene Wertordnung," 334.
97 Günther, *Denken*, 194; Henne, *Lüth-Urteil*, 207–9.
98 Günther, *Denken*, 195.
99 Ruppert, "Geschlossene Wertordnung," 346.

The value language employed by the Court in *Lüth* therefore was an old medium, but it carried a fundamentally new message.[100]

The Schmitt school despaired of the high court's high-profile decision, which they believed would erect an illegitimate "tyranny of values" over West German society.[101] Schmitt decried, "Value-philosophizing jurists in 1958 cannot escape the charge of anachronism.... [W]e don't live in 1928 anymore."[102] As Forsthoff wrote to a colleague privately, "[Schmitt] ... is allergic to hearing the word 'value.'"[103] Given that the Smend school distanced itself from the *Lüth* judgment, it was ironic that Forsthoff and Schmitt saw in it a great victory for their long-time rival.[104] In a rebuttal of Forsthoff's critique of the new "tyranny of values," Smend's student, Alexander Hollerbach, defended *Lüth's* conclusion but also emphasized the differences between *Lüth* and the current position of the Smend school. The contemporary jurists' talk of a "value system" was not, according to Hollerbach, an "abstract, crypto-natural law ... schema of intransigent closedness" but simply a method for producing hermeneutic coherence.[105]

For Habermas in 1961, the *Lüth* judgment was not the progressive landmark most of today's legal scholars would have it be. While he appreciated the high court's embrace in *Lüth* of an "objective right" to freedom of the press, he seems to have retained his Abendrothian skepticism toward the paternalism of the Federal Constitutional Court. The Court used the same language in its 1956 ban on the Communist Party, a decision of which Abendroth was strongly critical.[106] Habermas's skepticism is apparent in the essay, "Natural Law and Revolution" (1963), in which he takes a view of basic rights

---

[100] Rainer Wahl, "*Lüth* und die Folgen: Ein Urteil als Weichenstellung für die Rechtsentwicklung," in Henne, *Lüth-Urteil*, 371–97.

[101] Schmitt, "Tyrannei der Werte – Überlegungen eines Juristen zur Wert-Philosophie" [1960], in *Säkularisierung und Utopie – Ebracher Studien. Ernst Forsthoff zum 65. Geburtstag* (Stuttgart, 1967), 37–62.

[102] Ibid, 40.

[103] Böckenförde to Schnur (October 11, 1962), *Nachlass* Schnur. Cited in Günther, *Denken*, 129.

[104] Forsthoff, "Umbildung des Verfassungsgesetzes,"[1959], in *Verfassung: Beiträge zur Verfassungstheorie*, ed. Manfred Friedrich (Darmstadt: Wissenschafliche Buchgesellschaft, 1978), 117–52.

[105] Alexander Hollerbach, "Auflösung der Rechtsstaatlichen Verfassung? Zu Ernst Forsthoffs Abhandlung 'Die Umbildung des Verfassungsgesetzes' "[1960], in *Verfassung: Beiträge zur Verfassungstheorie*, ed. Manfred Friedrich (Darmstadt: Wissenschafliche Buchgesellschaft, 1978), 171.

[106] Abendroth, "KPD Urteil," 139ff.

more critical than that articulated by the Court. That Habermas would find it necessary in 1963 to argue against the natural-law grounding of rights reveals a dramatic gap in Habermas's understanding of what had occurred recently in West German jurisprudence. He must not have grasped the extent to which *Lüth* marked the end of the natural-law renaissance of the 1950s. It is surprising, therefore, that Habermas described the discussion of human and civil rights in Germany as "peculiarly ambivalent."[107] He deemed the discussion of rights in the advanced democratic welfare states to be "paradoxical" because

> On the one side, the guarantee of fundamental rights is the foundation of constitutionality.... On the other side, Natural Law is devoid of any and every convincing philosophical justification.... They have lost their credibility in the pluralism of attempts to justify them and in general have remained far below the level of contemporary philosophy.[108]

His main example is the philosophers Nicolai Hartmann and Max Scheler.[109] But *Lüth* had shown that the discussion of rights in Germany had moved beyond the natural law argumentation of the early 1950s, and Scheler and Hartmann were no longer relevant to the discussion.

For this reason, Habermas's characterization of the Cold War as a clash between the party of natural law (the West) and the party of revolution (the Eastern Bloc) seems anachronistic. Habermas suggested that Marxism had gone too far in "discrediting the idea of legality" and that the inherent "link" between natural law and revolution thus had been broken:

> Marx, with his critique of ideology applied to the bourgeois constitutional state...went beyond Hegel to discredit so enduringly for Marxism both the idea of legality itself and the intention of Natural Law as such, that ever since the link between Natural Law and revolution has been dissolved. The parties of the internationalized civil war have divided this heritage between themselves with fateful unambiguity: the one side has taken up the heritage of revolution, the other the ideology of natural law.[110]

---

[107] Habermas, "Natural Law," 113.
[108] Ibid.
[109] Ibid.
[110] Ibid.

Perhaps the anachronism is less acute if the interpretation is reframed: Given that Habermas was impressed by the progressive trend initiated by *Lüth* in 1958, it is possible that he was frustrated by the ideology of the Cold War that appeared to reinscribe the very dichotomy that a radically reformist jurisprudence challenged. In other words, the jurisprudence of the high court signified the potential of a constitutional state to redeem the promises of the basic rights and, with them, the broader "validity-claim" of the *Rechtsstaat*. Negative injunctions were being reconceived as positive guarantees, just as he and Abendroth had hoped earlier. *Lüth* modeled a radical reform of German political institutions that suggested exit routes from the antinomy of natural law or revolution.

The openness of the Smend school to influences from Anglo-American jurisprudence also resulted in a dialogue with the émigré Social Democratic–republican tradition in Weimar theory. By the time of *Lüth*, the Smend school had built bridges to Anglo-American jurisprudence. This resulted in a dialogue with the Social Democratic–republican tradition in Weimar theory, representatives of which had taken refuge in the United States. Smend's student, Horst Ehmke, for example, built personal and intellectual connections to Otto Kirchheimer and Ernst Fraenkel before Fraenkel returned to Germany in 1951. Smend offered Kirchheimer a chair in Göttingen, but Kirchheimer declined, opting instead to remain in the United States. Despite the exonerating function of the myth of judicial positivism, the high court's adoption of Smend's theory of integration led to a convergence between representatives of the Smend school and the Abendroth school around the idea of "objective rights." The convergence also can be described as a rapprochement between the positions of Weimar antagonists Smend and Heller. Similarly, Peter Häberle's 1962 dissertation, written under Smend's student, Konrad Hesse, in Freiburg, emphasized the institutional, that is, "objective," side of basic rights.[111]

German constitutional theory was the decisive influence shaping Habermas's political thought in the years 1958–63. The politics of the constitutional lawyers after World War II led to a division of their professional association into three main groupings around the figures of Schmitt, Abendroth, and Smend. Each position sought to reconnect with the debates in constitutional theory that had

[111] See Günther, *Denken*, 253.

broken off in 1933. Both the Abendroth and Schmitt schools were marginalized, leaving the field dominated by Smend and his students. Absorbing impulses from the Abendroth and Smend schools enabled Habermas to reconnect threads of discourse that had been cut by the Third Reich. Habermas's early political writings shows the imprint of the Abendroth school first and foremost, the Smend school through the decisions of the Federal Constitutional Court and his extensive intellectual network, and lastly the Schmittians.

3 1961–1981: From the "Great Refusal" to the Theory of Communicative Action

The political protest campaigns of the 1960s were the crucible in which Habermas's theoretical commitments of the 1970s were forged, but not in the way it is usually imagined. The received picture of the impact of 1968 on Habermas is the following: "[As] … the student movements overtake the mainstages of Paris, Berlin [and elsewhere], … [Habermas] gradually devolves from an intellectual leader of the progressive German left into a reform-minded German professor, formal philosopher (more neo-Kantian and Hegelian than Marxian), and legal scholar."[1] Burned by encounters with leftist students who saw him as a betrayer of their movement, Habermas thus is supposed to have retreated into the development of a formal theory of communication. The image of a theorist in retreat is nourished by his professional move from the public University of Frankfurt to the more protected ivory tower environment of the Max Planck Institute, an institution devoted solely to academic research. In 1970, he assumed the codirectorship of the Max Planck Institute for the Study of the Scientific-Technical Conditions of the Lifeworld in Starnberg.

However, Habermas did not retreat or recoil from a more leftist theoretical position into the theory of communicative action. The years 1969–70 marked a significant caesura in German politics and intellectual life generally. Habermas's former mentor, Theodor W. Adorno, died in August 1969, and Hans-Jürgen Krahl, Adorno's leading pupil and outspoken theoretician of the student revolution, died in an automobile accident in February 1970. Other close colleagues of Habermas all left Frankfurt: Ludwig von Friedeburg left for a position in the administration of Hesse in 1969, Oskar Negt took an academic position in Hannover, and Claus Offe set off on a

[1] Matustìk, *Profile*, 93.

fellowship to the United States.[2] Habermas's correspondence with Marcuse explains why he went to Starnberg: First, after Adorno's death, "… [t]here was not much left" in Frankfurt; and second, he was offered fifteen coworkers (*Mitarbeitern*) and complete freedom of research.[3] But a strong degree of continuity in Habermas's theoretical and political concerns bridges the caesura of 1969–70.

Habermas is partly responsible for this misunderstanding of the impact the events of 1968 had on his work. In an interview in the late 1980s, he asserted that "… my research program has remained the same since about 1970, since the reflections on formal pragmatics and the discourse theory of truth first presented in the Christian Gauss lectures."[4] One scholar argues that Habermas promoted the interpretation that the "real Habermas" emerges only after 1970 and that this construction of his biography was intended to distance himself from his origins in the Frankfurt School.[5] It seems, therefore, that by downplaying the continuities with his work before 1970, Habermas fueled the myth of a Habermas stung by the '68ers.

Habermas's spring 1971 Christian Gauss lectures at Princeton, "Reflections on the Linguistic (*Sprachtheoretische*) Foundation of Sociology," do announce a new research program for which the label "linguistic turn" is not wrong but also not terribly illuminating. In any event, the political significance of the linguistic turn is overstated for a number of reasons. Since the turn to language dates to at least 1966, when Habermas became one of four editors of a series of books from Suhrkamp called *Theory*, in which Noam Chomsky, Gregory Bateson, John Searle, and others were first translated for the German academic audience, his linguistic turn cannot accurately be deemed the result of Habermas's experiences in the tumultous period 1967–9.[6] While it may seem plausible

[2] Rolf Wiggershaus, *Jürgen Habermas* (Reibeck bei Hamburg: Rowohlt Taschenbuch, 2004), 94–5.

[3] Ibid.

[4] In "Interview with Torben Hviid Nielsen," in Habermas, *Die Nachholende Revolution* (Frankfurt: Suhrkamp, 1990), 116.

[5] See Peter Hohendahl, "The Public Sphere: Models and Boundaries," in *Habermas and the Public Sphere*, ed. Craig Calhoun (Cambridge, MA: MIT Press, 1992), 99–102.

[6] Wiggershaus, *Habermas*, 94. The other editors were Dieter Henrich, Jacob Taubes, and Hans Blumenberg; they published Chomsky's *Aspects of Syntax Theory*, Gregeory Bateson's *Schizophrenia*, and John Searle's *Speech-Acts*.

to contrast the abstractness of the "linguistic turn" he developed systematically in the 1970s with his earlier, more obviously Marxist historical account of the rise and decline of the public sphere, the movement from the one to the other does not signify a movement away from radical reformism.[7] It is not difficult to see why the *Theory of Communicative Action* (1981) has been misunderstood to signify a political retreat. It is written at a level of abstraction that is high, even when measured against the rest of Habermas's oeuvre; its systematic reconstruction of the history of social theory gives it a scholastic air. A 1968 volume entitled, *The Left Answers Habermas*, edited by a former *Assistent* of Habermas, Oskar Negt, had attacked Habermas for betraying the movement. In 1989, however, Negt published an apology for the volume that had left the lasting impression that it was "... as if Habermas no longer belonged to the left." Defending Habemas against the implicit connection between his linguistic turn and his alleged conservative turn, Negt forcefully underscored the opposite: "The original impulse for the language and communicative theory of Jürgen Habermas is a *political* impulse."[8]

Habermas's two-volume *TCA* is the mature statement of his social theory and the culmination of nearly all his work in the 1970s, including *Legitimation Crisis* (1973) and *The Reconstruction of Historical Materialism* (1976).[9] Although the book was written intensively between 1977 and 1980, major characteristics of the theory were developed as early as 1964 9. The outline of *TCA* is already clearly discernible in Habermas's critique of Marcuse in "Technology and Science as an Ideology" (1968). At its core, the impulse to reconstruct

[7] See Hohendahl, "Public Sphere," 100–1.

[8] Oskar Negt, "Autonomie und Eingriff," *Frankfurter Rundschau* (June 16, 1989). With acknowledgments to Matŭstìk for the source. Matŭstìk, *Profile*, 111.

[9] Jürgen Habermas, *Theorie des Kommunikativen Handelns*, Bd. 1: *Handlungsrationalitat und gesellschaftliche Rationalisierung*, and Bd. 2: *Zur Kritik der funktionalistichen Vernunft* (Frankfurt/Main: Suhrkamp, 1981); *The Theory of Communicative Action*, Vol. I: *Reason and the Rationalization of Society*, trans. Thomas McCarthy. (Boston: Beacon Press, 1987); *The Theory of Communicative Action*, Vol. II: *Lifeworld and System: A Critique of Functionalist Reason* (1987); *Legitimationsprobleme im Spätkapitalismus* (Frankfurt/Main: Suhrkamp, 1973); *Legitimation Crisis*, trans. Thomas McCarthy (Boston: Beacon Press, 1973); *Zur Rekonstruktion des Historischen Materialismus* (Frankfurt/Main: Suhrkamp, 1976); partial trans. only in *Communication and the Evolution of Society* (Boston: Beacon Press, 1979).

historical materialism stems from the same political objectives that drove Habermas's critique of technocratic reason and plebiscitary government in the 1960s, namely, an analysis of the obstacles to egalitarian, democratic will-formation in advanced capitalist states. The agenda he set as codirector of the Max Planck Institute extended his preoccupation of the late 1960s with the significance of science and technology for Marxist theory. The relevant query, therefore, is not "What is the significance of Habermas's linguistic turn?" but rather, "What is the significance of Habermas's desire to reconstruct historical materialism?" Understanding Habermas's reconstruction of historical materialism depends first on understanding the West German discourse on technology in the 1960s. Framed by a pervasive discourse on "technocracy," the positions Habermas advocated between 1966 and 1969 have a structural coherence that is apparent only in historical retrospect. Habermas's writings respond to persistent antinomies of the discourse on technocracy, a discourse that encompassed all political tendencies in West German society from the far left to the conservative right. The shape of this intellectual field is the key to explaining the frustrations Habermas encountered and the breakthroughs he devised.

Conceiving of the discourse on technocracy in this way enables us to map the most important tensions in Habermas's position: why, for example, Habermas accepted the radical students' critique of the "technocratic university" but rejected so much of their protest as senseless "action for action's sake." It explains the intensity of his rejection of the Great Coalition – the alliance of Social Democratic Party (SPD) and Christian Democratic Union (CDU) that ruled from 1966 to 1969 – and of the amendment to the constitution passed in 1968 permitting the government to declare a state of emergency. It enables us to see how his proposition of an "emancipatory interest in knowledge" represents a middle position between Marcuse's critique of the technological state, and the embrace of technocratic planning by the leading conservative intellectuals of the 1960s: Hans Schelsky, Hermann Lübbe, and Arnold Gehlen. Finally, it highlights Habermas's inclination to seek a dialectical third path between ideological options.

Initially, Habermas embraced the student movement's chief issues: the critiques of the emergency laws, the politics of the CDU-SPD coalition, and certain reforms of the universities. Common to all three critiques was the label the students applied to the politics they rejected: "technocratic." The technocracy theorists advanced the argument that scientific progress had created a "technical state" in which major decisions would be made by experts rather than politicians and that the state apparatus was sufficient to solve all problems of social conflict and distribution. Like the students, Habermas viewed the organization of research and instruction at German universities as a paradigm case of the technocratic form of "domination." The students also saw Chancellors Ludwig Erhard (1963–6) and Kurt Georg Kiessinger (1966–9) as committed to technocratic Keynesian economic strategies. In the students' critique of technocracy, Habermas heard a kindred analysis of the plebiscitarian distortion of democracy. But soon Habermas realized that the image of the state put forward by student radicals resembled nothing so much as the image of the state put forward by the technocrats themselves. Trapped between a governing regime he saw as technocratic, on the one hand, and an opposition that was too unreflectively activist and antitechnology, on the other, Habermas turned to the question of the relationship of scientific expertise to political practice thematized by Max Weber in his famous lectures of 1917 and 1918. Faced with visions of technological utopia on both the left (Marcuse) and the right (the technocratic conservatives), Habermas sought new ways to think about the relationship of technology and democracy.

In 1970, Habermas's student, Claus Offe, described the recent intellectual convergence between technocrats and students. Political science since Max Weber, Offe wrote, had recognized the dual basis of domination in the "objective" dimension of power and the "subjective" dimension of belief in the legitimacy of rulers. Domination in a democracy was unthinkable without at least the toleration, if not the consent, of the ruled. But this view, according to Offe, "... is now placed in question by some critical perspectives in the analysis of late capitalist societies as also on the other side by the conservative representatives of the technocracy-thesis."[10] Offe's formulations attest to a phenomenon Habermas had seen earlier: The actionism of the students and the technocracy of the intellectuals appeared to be mirror images of each other. Although

[10] See Offe, "Das politische Dilemma der Technokratie," in *Texte zur Technokratiediskussion*, eds. Claus Koch and Dieter Senghaas. (Frankfurt/Main: Europäische Verlaganstalt, 1970), 158. Political scientist Claus Offe completed his doctorate in sociology with Habermas in 1968.

Habermas did not formulate it in these terms, he seems to have sensed that both misunderstood the correct relationship of legality to legitimacy. Attention to this submerged theme enables us to decode Habermas's ambivalent relationship to the '68ers revolution. A major strength of the student movement, Habermas seemed to reason, was its sensitivity to the question of legitimacy: The ideologies that legitimated society were weak. A major weakness of the movement, however, was that the protesting students believed that they could dispense with legality.

FROM DECISIONISM TO TECHNOCRACY: 1961–4

> [A]nyone who is at all sensitive to politics and the political impact of theories is bound to react to changed contexts. In the 1960s, it was necessary to engage the theories of technocracy.[11]

After acceptance of his *Habilitationsschrift* by the Political Science Department at Marburg University in 1961, Habermas gave an inaugural lecture entitled, "The Classical Doctrine of Politics in Relation to Social Philosophy."[12] Habermas's central problematic in the lecture was "the growing scope for pure decision"; he suggested that the greatest obstacle to democracy was the short-circuiting of political praxis by technocratic elites.[13] Continuing the theme sketched in his 1958 essay, "On the Concept of Political Participation," Habermas explained that by modeling itself on the modern experimental natural sciences, Western European political science ceased to pose questions about the nature of the good life. According to Habermas, Max Weber's intervention in the value judgment controversy in German social science marked the culmination of the process in which "... the social sciences ... were completely separated from the normative elements that were the heritage of classical politics." In the seventeenth century, Habermas explained, Thomas Hobbes "completed the revolution" begun by

---

[11] "Interview with Nielsen," 116.

[12] Habermas, "The Classical Doctrine of Politics and Its Relation to Social Philosophy," in *Theory and Practice* [1971], trans. John Viertel (Boston: Beacon Press, 1973), 41–81; orig. "Die Klassische Lehre von der Politik in ihrem Verhaltnis zur Sozialphilosophie" (1961), in idem, *Theorie und Praxis* (Neuwied am Rhein/Berlin: Luchterhand, 1963), 48–88.

[13] Habermas, "Classical Doctrine," 41–2.

Machiavelli and More; with Hobbes, a "social philosophy" modeled on the new ideas of science displaced the "classical doctrine of politics."[14] Since then,

> Human behavior is therefore to be now considered only as the material for science. The engineers of the correct order disregard the categories of ethical social intercourse and confine themselves to the construction of conditions under which human beings, just like objects within nature, will necessarily behave in a calculable manner.[15]

In modeling itself on the natural sciences, a science of politics risks treating the human being more as an object than a subject of historical processes. Concern with the correct epistemology of the social sciences was an important thread in Habermas's work from 1961 through 1968, but it ceased to be the *via regia* in his work after that.[16]

From 1961 to 1964, Habermas was Extraordinary Professor of Philosophy at Heidelberg. In his other work of the early 1960s, "decisionism" became a major category of analysis, as the essays "Dogmatism, Reason and Decision in our Scientific Civilization" (1963) and "Science and Politics" (1964) show. In them, Habermas challenged the "strict division" of scientific knowledge from political decision for which Weber was famous. Weber, he declared, belonged to the Hobbesian tradition because in his system, "[i]n the last instance, political action cannot be rationally grounded."[17]

---

[14] Ibid.

[15] Ibid., 43.

[16] "I no longer believe that epistemology is the *via regia* [royal road]." See "Interview with T. Hviid Nielsen," 216. For comparable remarks on hermeneutics, see Habermas's debate with Gadamer, "Der Universalitätsanspruch der Hermeneutik," in *Hermeneutik und Dialektik. Aufsätze* (Hans-Georg Gadamer zum 70 Geburtstag), (Tübingen: Mohr, 1970). *Festschrift fur H.G. Gadamer*, Pt. 1, eds. R. Bubner et al. (Tübingen: 1970), 73–104; Habermas, *Zur Logik der Sozialwissenschaften* (*On the Logic of the Social Sciences*), first published in the *Philosophische Rundschau* 14:5 (1967); and Habermas, *Erkenntnis und Interesse* (*Knowledge and Human Interests* (Frankfurt/Main: Suhrkamp, 1968).

[17] Habermas,"Wissenschaft und Politik," *Offene Welt: Zeitschrift für Wirtschaft, Politik, und Gesellschaft* 86 (December 1964), 413. Text overlaps with "Verwissenschaftliche Politik und öffentliche Meinung" [1963], in *Humanität und Politische Verantwortung. Festschrift für Hans Barth*, ed. R. Reich (Zurich: Erlenbach, 1964). Revised and reprinted in *Technik und Wissenschaft als "Ideologie"* (Frankfurt/Main: Suhrkamp, 1968), *TWI* hereafter, 120–45. Condensed and translated by Jeremy Shapiro as "The Scientization of Political Opinion," in Habermas, *Towards a Rational Society: Student Protest, Science and Politics* (Boston: Beacon Press, 1970), 62–80.

Habermas named this the "decisionist" model, in which technocratic recommendation was harnessed to a politics unconstrained by ethics. The problem with the decisionist model, Habermas explained, is that in the movement from *technē* (technique) to technology, decisions are "painfully isolated from reason"[18]:

> For when this type of science attains a monopoly in the guidance of rational action, then all competing claims to a scientific orientation for action must be rejected.... Any theory that relates to praxis in any way other than by strengthening and perfecting the possibilities for purposive-rational action must now appear dogmatic ... The goal is to respond to every dogmatic assertion with *the decisionistic thesis that practical questions cannot be discussed cogently and in the final instance must be simply decided upon, one way or another* ... Action still requires orientation ... but now it is dissected into a rational implementation of techniques and strategies and an irrational choice of so-called value-systems. *The price paid for economy in the selection of means is a decisionism set wholly free* in the selection of highest-level ends.[19]

More than many continental thinkers, Habermas was receptive to currents emanating from England and the United States. In this respect, Habermas is best known for adopting aspects of the pragmatism of George Herbert Mead, John Dewey, and Charles Sanders Pierce. Karl-Otto Apel, a philosopher and colleague at the University of Heidelberg, encouraged Habermas to read the American pragmatists when they were translated into German in the early 1960s.[20] But a contextual reading shows that the question of decisionism was the central motivation for Habermas's interest in the pragmatists. As he explained in the 1964 essay: "It was the great discovery of pragmatism to insist upon the analysis and rational discussion of the relationship between available techniques and practical decisions, which were completely ignored in the decisionist model."[21]

---

[18] Habermas, *Theory and Practice*, 216.

[19] Ibid., 317–8 (emphasis added).

[20] See "Interview with the *New Left Review*"[orig. May 1985], in *Die Neue Unübersichtlichkeit* (Frankfurt/Main: Suhrkamp, 1985; *DNU* hereafter), 215; for a broader discussion and interviews with Habermas on his reception of the American pragmatists, see *Habermas and Pragmatism*, eds. Mitchell Aboulafia, Myra Bookman, and Catherine Kemp (London: Routledge, 2002).

[21] Habermas, "Verwissenschaftliche Politik und öffentliche Meinung," 126.

He corroborated this in a 1981 interview, attributing his interest in the pragmatists to an effort to compensate for the "democratic theory deficit in Marxism."[22] Beginning in the early 1970s, some West German scholars began to characterize the conservative ideologies of the 1960s as a new and distinct version of German conservatism.[23] In a 1970 volume explicitly devoted to the topic, the editors wrote that the concept of technocracy had evolved from a concept unknown outside of small sociology circles in 1960 to one frequently used by representatives of the student movement and in reportage.[24] In essays written between 1964 and 1968, Habermas directly engaged these theories.[25] The technocracy thesis provided a new occasion to refine his critique of plebiscitary tendencies within democracy. To recapitulate an earlier piece of the argument about the 1950s made in Chapter 2, Habermas shared the belief of West German legal conservatives such as Huber, Forsthoff, and Weber that the state was "overburdened" by the demands of civil society. The next generation of conservatives creatively converted this pessimistic analysis into an optimistic prognosis: The technocratic state would provide the means for circumventing the consensual dimension of political organization.[26] The decisionist problematic of the 1950s thus metamorphosed into the technocracy discussion of the 1960s.

The discussion began with an influential 1961 lecture, "Man in Scientific Civilization," by sociologist Helmut Schelsky. Schelsky asserted that "[m]odern technology requires no legitimacy; with it,

[22] Axel Honneth et al., "Dialektik der Rationalisierung," in *DNU*, 167–208.

[23] See Martin Greiffenhagen, *Das Dilemma des Konservatismus in Deutschland* (München: Piper, 1971); Helga Grebing, *Konservative gegen die Demokratie: Konservative Kritik der Demokratie in der Bundesrepublik* (Frankfurt/Main: Europäische Verlagsanstalt, 1971); Hans Jürgen Pühle, "Konservatismus und Neo-Konservatismus: Deutsche Entwicklungslinien seit 1945," in *Konservatismus eine Gefahr für die Freiheit?* Festschrift für Iring Fetscher zum 60. Geburtstag, eds. Eike Hennig and Richard Saage (München and Zürich: R. Piper, 1983), 409.

[24] Claus Koch and Dieter Senghaas, eds. *Texte zur Technokratiediskussion* (Frankfurt/Main: Europaische Verlagsanstalt, 1971 [1970]), 5–12. For more on the technocracy debate, see *Technokratie als Ideologie: Sozialphilosophische Beiträge zu einem politischen Dilemma*, ed. Hans Lenk (Stuttgart: Kohlhammer, 1973).

[25] Habermas, "Technischer Fortschritt und soziale Lebenswelt," *Praxis* (Zagreb), Heft 1–2 (1966), 217–28, reprinted in *TWI*, 104–19; "Technik und Wissenschaft als 'Ideologie,'" *Merkur*, Heft 243 (July 1968), 591–610 and Heft 244 (August 1968), 682–93, reprinted in *TWI*, 48–103.

[26] Compare with Thornhill, *Political Theory*, 135.

man 'rules', because it functions. . . . [T]he statesman is not at all 'decision-maker' or 'ruler' but rather analyst, planner, executor. Politics in the sense of normative will-formation falls in principle outside of these realms."[27] For Carl Schmitt's famous epigram – "Sovereign is he who decides on the exception" – Schelsky substituted his own bulkier version: "Sovereign may be called whoever in a given society achieves highest efficiency in the application of scientific and technological measures."[28] Schelsky was arguing that under modern technical conditions, the idea of democracy had lost its "classical" substance. Deliberation was made unnecessary by the objective exigencies of the facts. Schelsky's key concept – "*Sachgesetzlichkeit*" (the law-giving power of things) – vividly encapsulates the "leveling," as it were, of empirical and normative levels of analysis in his thought.[29]

Schelsky's thought strongly reflects the influence of his teachers, Arnold Gehlen and Hans Freyer (1887–1969). Gehlen and Freyer were representative of the "conservative revolution" of Weimar Republic intellectuals who counterposed power, vitality, and action ("the deed") to the decadence of Western civilization in general and German parliamentarism in particular.[30] Gehlen was a part-time colleague of Forsthoff's at the University of Königsberg in the 1930s and was influenced by a concept, "*Daseinsvorsorge*" (roughly, welfare provision), that Forsthoff had introduced in the Third Reich in 1938.[31] Forsthoff, Gehlen, and Schelsky emphasized the ways in which economic growth and technical progress could mitigate class struggle, and their ideas were popularized in books published in 1965.[32] The

[27] Ibid., 456.

[28] Ibid., 455.

[29] Schelsky's prominence as a public intellectual began with the dissemination of his thesis that West Germany was a "levelled, middle-class society," for which a Marxist class-politics was ill-suited. Schelsky, *Der Mensch in der wissenschaftlichen Zivilisation* (Köln: Westdeutscher Verlag 1961).

[30] See Jerry Muller, *The Other God that Failed: Hans Freyer and the Deradicalization of German Conservatism* (Princeton, NJ: Princeton University Press, 1987). *Der Tat* (*The Deed*) was the title of the movement's most significant journal.

[31] Dirk Van Laak, "From the Conservative Revolution to Technocratic Conservatism," in Werner-Müller, *German Ideologies since 1945*, 141. "*Daseinsvorsorge*" comes from Ernst Forsthoff, *Die Verwaltung als Leistungsträger* (Stuttgart/Berlin: Kohlhammer, 1938).

[32] Ibid.,155. Wilhelm Fucks's *Formulas for Power* was a bestseller in 1965; intellectual publicist Rüdiger Altmann's concept of the "formed society" (*formierte Gesellschaft*) made its way into the speeches of Ludwig Erhard in 1965.

conservative political affinities of Schelsky's position would have been apparent to Habermas.[33]

In his 1963 "Scientized Politics and Public Opinion" and the related 1964 essay, "Science and Politics," Habermas began to grapple with how the decisionist problematic had metamorphosed into technocratic conservatism.[34] Habermas argued that Weber's formulation belongs to an *earlier* stage in the "scientization of politics" and that the technocratic model now was more accurate than the Weberian, or "decisionist," account.[35] By the "scientization of politics," Habermas sought to describe two phenomena that were changing the relationship of scientific expertise to political decision: the growing scope of scientific research under government contract and scientific consultation to public agencies. The context for both was an international one.

In France under de Gaulle, as well as in the United States under Kennedy, the term "technocratic" was applied to both trends.[36] As one scholar-activist wrote in 1970, "Above all, the German technocracy discussion stood under the shadow of the reform élan of the Kennedy clan.... Equally influential in these years was the aura attached to the French planning bureaucracy in the flowering of the Fifth Republic."[37] Habermas viewed the United States as the country in which the "scientization of political practice" had most advanced,[38] with government-level bureaucracies and consulting agencies directing research and development.[39] One scholar posits

---

[33] Habermas had already written a critique of Gehlen in 1956: "Der Zerfall der Institutionen," reprinted in *Philosophische-Politische Profile*, 3rd ed. (Frankfurt: Suhrkamp, 1998), 101–6. Habermas linked Schelsky and Freyer in his "Technische Fortschritt und Soziale Lebenswelt," *TWI*, 115–6. In *TWI*, he cited Gehlen, "Anthropologische Ansicht der Technik," from Hans Freyer et al., eds. *Technik im technischen Zeitalter*, (Düsseldorf: Schilling, 1965).

[34] Habermas, "Wissenschaft und Politik," *Offene Welt* (Köln/Opladen, 1964), 414.

[35] Max Weber, "Politik als Beruf," *Gesammelte Politische Schriften* (Tübingen: J. C. B. Mohr, 1958).

[36] Greiffenhagen, *Dilemma des Konservatismus*, 54. Habermas also cites as an influence Jacques Ellul, *The Technological Society* (New York: Knopf, 1967 [1964]).

[37] Senghaas, "Foreword," 6, and idem, "The Technocrats: Ruckblick auf die Technokratie-bewegung in den USA," in *Texte zur Technokratiediskussion*, 282–92.

[38] Habermas, "Verwissenschaftliche Politik," 131.

[39] Ibid.,134.

that the development of a long-term research policy in the Federal Republic of Germany was an important impetus behind Habermas's questioning of the relationship of science and democratic decision-making in this period. Committees and ministries designed to discuss the industrial implementation of scientific research were established in 1957, 1962, and 1963. In the early 1960s, Minister Erhard arranged for regular exchanges between representatives of university and industry to promote useful scientific innovation.[40]

In addition to these trends in German social planning, the challenge posed by nuclear power and weaponry was another key context informing Habermas's first reflections on technocracy. Habermas was an outspoken participant in the movement against the arming of the German Army with atomic weapons in 1957–9. His codirector at the Max Planck Institute was Carl Friedrich von Weiszäcker (1912–2007), a physicist and philosopher with ties to the peace movement. Weiszäcker had signed the Göttingen Manifesto in 1957 against the atomic weapons deployment and was a founding member of the Association of German Scientists.

The leading idea behind the foundation of the Max Planck Institute in Starnberg[41] was "… the danger to humanity posed by the atom bomb."[42] Habermas read the first critiques of Schelsky's lecture in the forum for reform scientists, *Atomzeitalter* (Atomic Age).[43] The mobilization of German and international atomic scientists in the public sphere became Habermas's model for how scientists could challenge technocracy: "Scientists are objectively compelled to go beyond the technical recommendations that they produce and reflect upon their practical consequences." This was especially and dramatically true for atomic physicists.[44] While examples of such

[40] Thornhill, *Political Theory*, 147–8.

[41] Max Planck Institute for the Study of the Life-Conditions of the Scientific-Technical World in Starnberg (*der Lebensbedingungen der wissenschaftlichen-technischen Welt*); the institute's name itself illustrates the discourse under discussion here. Senghaas, *Abschreckung und Frieden. Studien zur Kritik organisierter Friedlosigkeit* [1969], revised ed. (Frankfurt: Europäische Verlagsanstalt, 1981). Senghaas described deterrence as a "technocratic" doctrine.

[42] Cited in Jeffrey Herf, *War by Other Means: Soviet Power, West German Resistance, and the Battle of the Euromissiles* (New York: Free Press, 1984), 93.

[43] Habermas cites, for example, Hans P. Bahrdt, "Helmut Schelskys technischer Staat," *Atomzeitalter* 9 (Frankfurt, 1961), and other essays from issues of *Atomzeitalter* in 1961 and 1963.

[44] Habermas, "Verwissenschaftliche Politik," 143; *Towards a Rational Society: Student Protest, Science and Politics*, 78–9, *TRS* hereafter,

engagement were few and conditions unfavorable, reflection on the practical consequences of science needed to be "... transferred to the broader public forum of the general public."[45] What Habermas judged to be at stake was whether knowledge is "... merely transmitted to men engaged in technical manipulation for purposes of control or is simultaneously appropriated as the linguistic possession of communicating individuals"[46] Unless technical knowledge was "translated" into practical knowledge, political power would remain substantively irrational.[47] The public sphere is the only forum for the translation, and that act of translation is the only way to make a "... scientized society ... a rational one."[48] Technocratic thought, Habermas insisted, dangerously distorted the proper relationship of science to politics.

Habermas located Weber's "decisionistic" description and advocacy of a strict division of labor between expert and politician within a "tradition" that originates with Hobbes and leads up to Schumpeter.[49] Fully echoing his arguments in *Transformation*, Habermas described this tradition as the "unquestioned" orthodoxy of contemporary political sociology.[50] Habermas then identified the "technocratic" tradition – with roots in Bacon and Saint-Simon – and argued that intellectuals such as Schelsky and Jacques Ellul had abandoned the decisionistic model for the technocratic one.[51] With specialists trained to advise on the objective requirements of new technologies and strategies, the sphere of decision remaining to the politician begins to shrink. New techniques, such as systems analysis and decision theory, "... rationalize choice as such by means of calculated strategies and automatic decision procedures."[52] This reverses the pattern announced by Weber in which decision-making power was to remain firmly in the hands of the politician, not his or her scientific advisors. In both models, however, the role of the public is reduced to giving its plebiscitary assent to the managers of administration. The difference is that in the decisionist model, politicians still had real choices to make.

---

45 Ibid., 144; *TRS*, 79.
46 Ibid.
47 Ibid., 145; *TRS*, 80.
48 Ibid.
49 Habermas,"Verwissenschaftliche Politik," 128.
50 Ibid.
51 Ibid., 122; *TRS*, 63.
52 Ibid.

Into this debate stepped Hermann Lübbe (b. 1929), a young conservative whose career eventually would form the mirror image of Habermas's: Lübbe became the most recognized conservative philosopher and public intellectual in postwar Germany. For Habermas, Lübbe's essay, "On the Political Theory of Technocracy"(1962), revealed nascent tensions in the new conservativism.[53] Lübbe followed Schelsky in observing an increase in the power of experts vis-à-vis politicians. Like Habermas, however, Lübbe reproached the advocates of the technocratic model for what Habermas called "camouflaging" political questions with the "logic of reality" (*als Logik der Sachen tarnen*). Ironically, it was from his political opponent Lübbe that Habermas borrowed the insight that while the scope of decision had narrowed somewhat, technocratic rationalization of the procedures of decision, "… [had reduced] the decision to its pure form, purging it of every element that could be made … accessible to rational analysis."[54] In other words, Lübbe saw that the ideology of technical decision-making was poised to become the new ideological justification for the politician's refusal to submit his or her values to discussion. The difference between them, according to Habermas, was that Lübbe "[maintained] … the antithesis between technical knowledge and the exercise of political power as defined by Weber and Carl Schmitt,"[55] whereas Habermas sought to overcome the antinomy.

Habermas's critique of the antithesis of technical knowledge and political power was that it relied on a static concept of values that obscured the way in which values and techniques evolved dialectically over time. Technical progress could produce new interests and values. For a dialectical solution to what he envisioned as a static opposition of values and techniques, Habermas looked to Dewey's pragmatism. In pragmatism, Habermas found a model for the critical interaction of expert and politician. Since the development of new techniques was already governed by a "horizon of needs" and values, this horizon need only be made explicit.[56] Sketching

[53] Hermann Lübbe, "Zur politischen Theorie der Technokratie"[1962], in *Theorie und Entscheidung: Studien zum Primat der praktischen Vernunft* (Freiburg: Rombach, 1971), 32–53. The essay was published originally in *Der Staat: Zeitschrift für Staatslehre, öffentliches Recht und Verfassungsgeschichte*.

[54] Habermas,"Verwissenschaftliche Politik,"124.

[55] Ibid.

[56] Ibid.,136; *TRS*, 74.

a composite model drawing on hermeneutics, pragmatism, and critical social theory that would become the basis for his more extensive treatments of the same subjects, Habermas envisioned the dialogue about the social role of science and technology as a "hermeneutic" conversation between citizens and experts.[57] There is a dialectic, in other words, between what we want to do and what we are able to do, but the "process of translation" between science and politics requires that citizens be included in the discussion.

> [A] ... long term research and education policy ... must enlighten those who take political action about their tradition-bound self-understandings of their interests and goals in relation to socially potential technical knowledge and capacity. At the same time it must put them in a position to judge practically, in the light of these articulated and newly interpreted needs, in what direction they want to develop.... This discussion necessarily moves in a circle.[58]

Habermas's choice of the language of "horizon" appears to be derived from Hans-Georg Gadamer's seminal work, *Truth and Method*, which Habermas read in Heidelberg in 1961.[59] Habermas's early work on decisionism and technocracy is the political matrix from which his other philosophical initiatives in the 1960s related to hermeneutics and pragmatism stemmed.[60]

HABERMAS AND THE STUDENT MOVEMENT, PHASE ONE: AGAINST TECHNOCRACY

The history of West German student protest in the 1960s can be divided neatly into the before and after of a crucial event, namely, the shooting by Berlin police of a student peacefully demonstrating against a visit by the Shah of Iran in June 1967. After the death of the student, Benno Ohnesorg, the pace of protest accelerated markedly. June 1967 was also a significant turning point in Habermas's career: Before it, Habermas was the recognized leader of the student left; afterwards, he was viewed by it with suspicion and distrust. Shortly after Ohnesorg's funeral, Habermas charged student leader

---

[57] Ibid., 136–9; *TRS*, 74–6.
[58] Ibid., 136; *TRS*, 74.
[59] "Interview with *New Left Review*," *DNU*, 214.
[60] Ibid.

Rudi Dutschke with advocating a dangerously voluntaristic approach to revolution that Habermas labeled a fascism of the left. While Habermas was not the only member of the older generations of theorists at the Frankfurt School who worried about the tactics of radical students, Habermas's reputation suffered disproportionately.[61] Adorno had been the victim of student disruptions of his lectures on July 7, 1967, and joined Habermas and von Friedeburg in rejecting the demands for university restructuring during the Frankfurt student strike of December 8–18, 1968. Adorno and Horkheimer stood behind the rector's decision to call the police to expel the students from the Institute of Social Research, to which they had retreated after the rooms and offices of the sociology department the students had occupied between January 24 and 31, 1969, were closed. Already depressed by the students' actions, until his death in August 1969, Adorno remained traumatized by one aggressive stunt on April 12 involving female students who bared their breasts to him in his classroom. The correspondence between Marcuse and Adorno from January and August 1969 focused on the differences between the two mens' perceptions of the students. Like Habermas, Adorno saw them as "actionists."[62] Habermas thus was not alone in his diagnosis.

In the years 1965–7, Habermas embraced the students' causes for two reasons: first, because they shared his critique of technocratic governance, and second, because they seemed to hold the *Rechtsstaat* to its own declared constitutional principles. After June 1967, Habermas continued to support many of the students' goals, but this fact was overshadowed by the inflammatory tenor of his criticisms of their methods. He used language that pathologized their worldview and tactics: left-wing disorders, infantilism, projection, playing at revolution.[63] Despite this provocative language, Habermas felt misunderstood by the students, who deemed him a betrayer, preferring to regard himself as a sober analyst of a delicate historical moment in which the project of radical reform hung in the balance.

---

[61] See *Die Linke antwortet Jürgen Habermas*, ed. Oskar Negt (Frankfurt/Main: Europäische Verlagsanstalt, 1968).

[62] Adorno, "Marginalien zu Theorie und Praxis"(June 1969), in *Stichwörte* (Frankfurt/Main: Suhrkamp, 1969), 180–2, 186–91.

[63] See the essays compiled in Habermas, *Protestbewegung und Hochschulreform* (Frankfurt/Main: Suhrkamp, 1969), *PuH* hereafter.

Later, showing contrition, Habermas explained his position as an emotional "overreaction" that reflected the traumatic experiences of his "generation," that is, the '58ers' firsthand experience of the Third Reich and consequent reflexive rejection of violence in any form.[64] But this stance obscures the fact that his allegation of "leftist-fascism" was not an outlier but consistent with the broader critique of actionism he repeated over and over during the years 1967–9. In the context of the student-led opposition to technocracy, Habermas's critique of actionism was both predictable and consistent. To be precise, until the tripwire of legality was crossed, Habermas remained sympathetic to the students' position, but once the students crossed the line, Habermas turned their shared critique of technocracy against the students themselves. The ways he characterized student activism as "actionism" clearly illustrate his projection of his own preoccupation with the technocratic distortion of the link between theory and praxis.[65]

Several major issues occupied the energies of the West German student movement between 1965 and 1969. The students favored major reform of the university and the development of an extra-parliamentary opposition (*Ausserparlamentarische Opposition*, or APO); they opposed press concentration generally and the Springer publishing company in particular, West German support for the United States' war in Vietnam, the SPD's entrance into coalition with the CDU/Christian Social Union (CSU), and the amendment of the German constitution to permit the government in Bonn to declare a state of emergency. Habermas actively supported the students as long as he interpreted their positions as an articulation of a coherent worldview – one that was pro-*Rechtsstaat* and antitechnocracy.

To understand why these positions cohered in Habermas's framework, we need to review the historical context of the emergency laws in particular. Even after returning sovereignty to West Germany in 1955, the Allies reserved the right to restore domestic order. German politicians were eager to fill this gap in German sovereignty. In the early 1960s, a movement of intellectuals and trade

[64] See Habermas, "Deutscher Herbst," in *Kleine Politische Schriften I-IV* (Suhrkamp: Frankfurt/Main, 1981), 364. With acknowledgments to Matůstík's work for the reference.

[65] The concept of "actionism" was first developed by Adorno, however.

unionists developed a campaign against the introduction of emergency legislation. The first conference held by the opposition to the planned laws was held at the University of Bonn on May 30, 1965, under the title, "Democracy and the State of Emergency."[66] The campaign was led by a group called "Emergency of Democracy" (*Notstand der Demokratie*). The proposed emergency laws became the central focus of the APO in the latter half of 1967 and the subject of public hearings in the *Bundestag* in November. That month, the German Socialist Students' League (SDS) in Frankfurt called students to a "go-in" protest of the lecture of Frankfurt professor of political science Carlo Schmid, selected because he had as an SPD minister in the coalition government helped author the proposed emergency laws.[67] On May 11, 1968, 30,000 demonstrators, most of whom were students, marched on Bonn.

Between the first parliamentary discussions of the laws in mid-May and their adoption on May 30, Horkheimer, Adorno, Hans-Jürgen Krahl, and Oskar Negt all wrote or spoke against the amendment. Habermas signed a statement on May 17 declaring the future of democracy in Germany to be in danger.[68] Legal scholars Helmut Ridder, Jürgen Seifert, and Abendroth also played prominent roles in the opposition campaign. In retrospect, the concern over the emergency laws may seem overblown, given that once passed, the provisions were never invoked in the subsequent history of the Federal Republic. But this neglects the sentiments of the time: The relative proximity to the Nazi period meant that the public memory of how Article 48, the emergency clause of the Weimar

[66] Vol. 1, 220.

[67] SDS Gruppe Frankfurt, Flugblatt-Anruf zur Teilnahme am *Go-in* in die Vorlesung von Carlo Schmid (November 16, 1967), in Wolfgang Kraushaar, ed., *Frankfurter Schule und Studentenbewegung. Von der Flaschenpost zum Molotowcocktail, 1946–1995*, Vols. 1–3 (Hamburg: Digital Edition, 2003 [orig. 1998]), Vol. 2, No. 162.

[68] Max Horkheimer, "Gedanken zum Notstandsgesetz, mit grosser Mehrheit angenommen am 15 Mai 1968," Kraushaar, *Frankfurter Schule* 2:207; Theodor Adorno, "Gegen die Notstandsgesetze. Ansprache auf der Veranstaltung 'Demokratie im Notstand' im Grossen Sendesaal des Hessischen Rundfunks" (May 28, 1968), Kraushaar, *Frankfurter Schule* 2:212; Oskar Negt, "Fernsehrede im Hessischen Rundfunk" (May 28, 1968), Kraushaar, *Frankfurter Schule* 2:213; Hans-Jürgen Krahl, "Romerbergrede. Gegen die Verabschiedung der Notstandgesetze," Kraushaar, *Frankfurter Schule* 2:209; see also Abendroth, "Die Gefahren einer Notstandsverfassung," Rede in der Anhörung des Deutschen Bundestages zur Notstandsgesetzgebung, (November 9, 1967).

constitution, had been used to facilitate the Nazi takeover of the German state was still fresh.[69]

The statements of Horkheimer and Adorno illustrate that they too valued the legal guarantees afforded by the Basic Law. Horkheimer declared his "scorn" for those who considered the free constitution (*freiheitliche Verfassung*) an illusion.[70] Adorno declared that other countries might be able to have emergency laws, but the German experience with Article 48 made that unthinkable. This high degree of consensus on the left about the importance of defending the German constitution is often neglected in the narrative about Habermas and 1968, which depicts him as outside the mainstream of the movement. The defense of legality was not a position monopolized by conservatives.

The terms in which Habermas affirmed the student movement illustrate his own concerns with the principles of legality and the constitution generally. Habermas was one of many signatories to a letter to Chancellor Adenauer expressing outrage about the government's raid on *Der Spiegel* in 1962.[71] The incident was provoked by an article in *Der Spiegel* about defense policy that the government alleged disclosed important national security secrets. In a November 1967 lecture sketching the history of protest in West Germany, Habermas wrote that the response to the *Spiegel* affair "… is the model case of defensive mobilisation of the public in the name of violated constitutional rights."[72] Similarly, Habermas viewed the state's actions leading up to Ohnesorg's shooting as illegitimate: Student protests against the Shah of Iran's visit were met with "… illegal prohibitions of demonstrations, dubious confiscations and problematic arrests, indefensible court proceedings, open police terror."[73] At a teach-in on June 5 attended by 3,000 students and the university rector only three days after the Ohnesorg shooting, Habermas warned that there was a real "… danger that the democratic and lawful state silently turns into a police state."[74]

---

[69] See Russell Miller, John LaMont, et al., "40/68 – Germany's 1968 and the Law," *German Law Journal* 10:3 (1969), 223–60. Available at www.germanlawjournal.com/.

[70] Horkheimer, "Gedanken zum Notstandgesetz."

[71] "We are disturbed Mr. President," Kraushaar, *Frankfurter Schule* 1:194.

[72] Habermas, "Studentenprotest in der Bundesrepublik: Ein Vortrag im New Yorker Goethehaus" (November 1967), in *PuH*, 169.

[73] Ibid., 162.

[74] Kraushaar, *Frankfurter Schule* 1, 256.

Conversely, Habermas characterized the early student movement's values in terms that so closely resembled his own that a type of projection must have been involved: "The task of the student opposition was and is to compensate for the lack of theoretical perspective … the lack of radicality in the interpretation and practice of our social and democratic constitution [*sozialrechtstaatlichen und demokratische Verfassung*]."[75] His characterizations seem to attest to his values as much as those of the students: "Today's protest is directed against a society that has lent the emancipatory ideals of the eighteenth century the force of constitutional norms and has accumulated the potential for their realization."[76]

When a sharp recession hit the West German economy in the summer of 1966, public reaction was nearly hysterical.[77] Within months, cracks in the coalition of the CDU/CSU with the Free Democratic Party (FDP) were exacerbated, and the CDU made overtures to the SPD to join it in what came to be known as the "Great Coalition." On November 21, Habermas composed a letter to Willy Brandt that was co-signed by other professors and assistants at the University of Frankfurt. Entitled, "Theses Against the Coalition of the Despondent with Dictators," the letter argued that the SPD betrayed its best traditions by rehabilitating the *Spiegel* affair–discredited CSU politician Franz-Josef Strauss and going "arm in arm" with the CDU's Georg Kiessinger, a former member of the Nazi Party who had worked for the Ministry of Propaganda.[78] In a strongly worded critique, Habermas wrote, "We have more reason to fear the new coalition than the old" because the former "endangers the foundations of parliamentarism."[79] Disregarding these concerns, the coalition formed and quickly installed Karl Schiller as Minister of Economics and Strauss as Minister of

---

[75] Habermas, "Rede über die politische Rolle der Studentenschaft in der Bundesrepublik," in *PuH*, 141; orig. address at the Congress, "University and Democracy," Hannover, June 9, 1967.

[76] Habermas, "Studentenprotest," *PuH*, 170.

[77] Thomas Ellwein, *Krisen und Reformen. Die Bundesrepublik seit den sechziger Jahren* (München: Deutscher Taschenbuch, 1993), 17; Anthony Nicholls, *The Bonn Republic: West German Democracy, 1945–90* (New York: Longman, 1997), 187.

[78] "Thesen gegen die Koalition der Mutlosen mit den Machthabern," Kritik an der Grossen Koalition auf einer vom Sozialdemokratischen Hochschulbund veranstalteten Podiumsdiskussion (November 1966), Kraushaar, *Frankfurter Schule* 2:108.

[79] Ibid.

Finance. Together they pursued a macroeconomic policy combination of tax cuts and public expenditures on infrastructure that they called "global steering." This required "concerted action" among trade unions, business leaders, and the state. Social policy began to shift from a reactive and compensatory approach to economic problems to an "active, society-shaping policy."[80] For Habermas, the most problematic aspect of this corporatism was its paternalistic features. Also, the prospect of a neutralized SPD eager to cooperate in reasserting German sovereignty by means of emergency legislation was frightening for Habermas. Immediately after passage of the emergency laws, Habermas took his case to the students at the Frankfurt cafeteria:

> A stability and growth-securing politics can today only guard the illusion of an expert-led execution of administrative and technical tasks, because the public sphere is depoliticised. The technocratic illusion, which justifies the depoliticization of wide layers of the population as inevitable, is itself only possible as a result of this depoliticization.[81]

Habermas's counterposition of technocracy and democracy was further reinforced by an additional factor: the position of the university during the Vietnam War. David Halberstam and other observers in the late 1960s described the United States' moral and political blindness in Vietnam as the product of a technocratic outlook, of whom Defense Secretary Robert McNamara was the archetype.[82] Habermas was an early and outspoken critic of the U.S. war in Vietnam, attending teach-ins such as the conference held in Frankfurt on May 22, 1966, "Vietnam: Analysis of a Model," at which Herbert Marcuse also was present. In 1967, Habermas elaborated the interconnection of Vietnam, technology, and student protest in these terms:

> Today's protest is directed against a society that... has not abolished hunger in a world of potential abundance, while it has widened the

[80] F. X. Kaufmann, *Sozialpolitische Denken: Die Deutsche Tradition* (Frankfurt/Main: Suhrkamp, 2003), 160.

[81] Habermas, "Die Scheinrevolution und ihre Kinder: Rede auf dem Kongress des VDS am 2 Juni 1968," in *PuH*, 188; orig. *Frankfurter Rundschau* (June 5, 1968).

[82] John McDermott, "Technology: The Opiate of the Intellectuals," *New York Review of Books* 23:2 (July 31, 1969), 25–35.

> gap between industrial and developing nations, exporting misery and mass violence along with mass hygiene. This is the symbolic meaning American intervention in the Vietnamese civil war has taken on in the eyes ... of most German students.[83]

The subsumption of the university into the military-industrial complex, he argued, had warped the relationship between science and politics:

> A university divested of its apolitical self-understanding could have an effect in ... preventing research ... from migrating to social sectors outside of the university where it is used for repressive ends ... *If the university were enlightened about the politics of science* ... it could make itself an advocate [of evaluation of the practical implications of scientific-technological development] instead of leaving [it] to the criteria of the military-industrial complex.[84]

The organization of teaching and research provided many examples of how universities were "interlocked" with the state: "This fusion is the soil in which the concept of technocracy – and hatred of it – grows and confirms itself."[85] Habermas's statement illustrates that he saw the German university as the technocratic institution par excellence. Because he viewed the war, the extra parlimentary opposition (Äusserparlimentariche Opposition, or APO), the emergency laws, and the university through the lens of the modernization of German conservatism – that is, as technocratic conservatism – Habermas developed an integrated set of theoretical and practical commitments.

In numerous essays written between 1965 and 1969, Habermas joined the student movement for university reform, authoring concrete proposals and responses to governmental recommendations that he published in high-profile venues such as *Die Zeit*, *Frankfurter Allgemeine Zeitung*, and *Der Spiegel*. Habermas clearly supported the cause of university reform, writing of "catastrophic study conditions and an inadequate organization of university instruction."[86] He declared the students' calls for a "democratization" of the university "logically persuasive."[87] Habermas provided the foreword to a 1965

[83] Habermas, "Die Scheinrevolution," *PuH*, 170.
[84] Habermas,"Einleitung," in *PuH*, 47 (emphasis added).
[85] Ibid., 16.
[86] Habermas, "Studentenprotest," in *PuH*, 158.
[87] Ibid.

collection of essays arguing in favor of university reform. Arguing in a manner analogous to his interpretation of the *Sozialstaat* clauses half a decade earlier, Habermas wrote that the freedom of scholarship guaranteed by the German constitution "... must be interpreted today in the sense of subjective rights to participation."[88] In May 1966, the debate entered a new phase when the Federal Council on Education and Culture (*Wissenschaftsrat*) proffered its recommendations for change. Habermas agreed with the students who were "rightly outraged" by the "cosmetic" recommendations.[89] Habermas rejected both the suggestions for a mandatory limit of four years' study time and the exclusive orientation of studies to preparation for career, asking, "Do we really want the university in streamlined form?"[90] Habermas notes that the Federal Council's proposals were a clear turning point in student perceptions of the reforms, leading the students to "conceive of university reform as technocratic" in nature.[91]

In a January 1967 lecture, Habermas suggested that conservative professors most likely would read the latest recommendations "... as a technologically conceived strategy for adaptation and adopt it"; alternatively, they could "... interpret it ... in accordance with the so-called progressives."[92] In the summer of 1968, Habermas declared the proposals of the Federal Council to be "old wine in new bottles."[93] In November, the Education Ministry adopted the Federal Council's recommendations on the administrative reorganization of the universities. In a February 1969 essay entitled, "Recommendations for a Technocratic University Reform?" Habermas rejected the ministry's reforms in favor of a counterproposal developed by the Hessian Culture Minister Ernst Schütte.[94]

Habermas's writings on university reform drew extensively on the discourse on technocracy of the middle to late 1960s. He

[88] Habermas, "Vorwort zu Hochschule in der Demokratie" (January 1965), in *PuH*, 91.
[89] Habermas, "Studentenprotest," in *PuH*, 158.
[90] Habermas "Zwangsjacke," in *PuH*, 107; orig. *Der Monat* (November 1966).
[91] Ibid., 92.
[92] Habermas, "Universität in der Demokratie," in *PuH*, 121; conference at the Free University, Berlin, (January 20, 1967).
[93] Habermas, "Heilige Kühe der Hochschulreform," in *PuH*, 217; orig. *Die Zeit* (September 27, 1968).
[94] Habermas, "Empfehlungen zur technokratischen Hochschulreform?" in *PuH*, 235; orig. Festschrift fur Ernst Schütte (February 1969).

inveighed against the technocratic model and the notion that "technical necessities"(*Sachzwänge*) could obviate the need for discussion of the standards by which decisions are made. "*Sachzwang*" is the key word Habermas borrowed from the technocratic conservative discourse represented by Schelsky. Habermas argued that the Education Ministry's reforms would reinforce social elitism; merely establishing committees of students, professors, and assistants with equal representation was not an adequate substitute for more substantial "democratization."[95] Moreover, Habermas named the ministry's proposal a "decisionist" model, in which the decision-making powers of the university president remained "extraordinarily strong" and the role of the Senate merely advisory: "As long as the President can secure cover from the *Kuratorium* [Board of Trustees], his position reminds us of a constitutional monarch, whose real power is based on the army, nobility and state bureaucracy."[96] As late as 1969, therefore, Habermas employed the categories of technocracy and decisionism to frame his understanding, analysis, and polemic against the state-led proposals for university reform.

But Habermas had to share the category of "technocratic university reform" with radical student groups who had long since parted company with him. Contemporary articles in the German Socialist Students' League (SDS) journal *Neue Kritik* and SDS leaflets make this clear. In a January 1969 leaflet, for example, the SDS argued that "... the technocrats around Löffler, Stein, [and] Korber" hoped to meet the demands of students seeking university reform with a "technocratic reform program" and thereby isolate the SDS from the mass of "reform-willing" students.[97] The SDS believed that *Drittelparität* – the addition of student and administrative representatives to faculty governance – served the same function as codetermination (*Mitbestimmung*) in the workplace, merely distracting from the real struggle for a socialist society. Technocratic university reform thus inhibited the development of revolutionary consciousness.[98] The leaflet also stated that the technocratic reforms

95 Ibid., 237–8.

96 Ibid., 240.

97 "Flugblatt einer Berliner SDS-Gruppe" (January 1969), in *PuH*, 260. See also Antonia Grunenberg and Monika Steffen,"Technokratisches Hochschulreform und organisierter Widerstand," *Neue Kritik* (April 1969); reprinted in Kraushaarr, *Frankfurter Schule* 2:311.

98 "Flugblatt," in *PuH*, 264–5.

stood in an old Prussian tradition that dated back to Bismarck, aimed to secure the interests of West German monopoly capitalism, and were "... comparable to the 'concerted action' of Economics Minister Schiller."[99]

Although Habermas contrasted "technocracy" with "democracy" as the students did, their common language did not blind him to the weaknesses of the student case for democratization. The fact that Habermas put "democratization" in quotes and referred to the "so-called progressives" is evidence that he was not entirely convinced by the demands for the democratization of the university. In an article cowritten with philosopher Albrecht Wellmer in 1968, Habermas argued that the problem of democratization of the university required a more subtle approach to the question of the politicization of science than the SDS advocated. While the SDS argued that the university become a site for the schooling of socialist revolutionaries, Habermas and Wellmer argued that democratization would come from prior recognition of the relationship of the sciences to politics.[100] An abstract model of democracy could not be carried over to the university, they asserted; rather, democratization would come from a reorganization of the conduct of science (*Wissenschaftsbetrieb*) in conformity with the intention to spread "critical rationality." Democratization meant that the decisions of the university must be submitted to a rational test of their "legitimacy."[101]

HABERMAS AND THE STUDENT MOVEMENT, PHASE TWO: THE CRITIQUE OF "ACTIONISM"

From June 1967 to February 1969, Habermas's critique of student "actionism" unfolded in different contexts, but the underlying argument remained the same. Habermas's most substantial critiques of the students were written in the immediate wake of the dramatic takeover and renaming of the University of Frankfurt as

[99] Ibid.
[100] Albrecht Wellmer, "Unpolitische Universität und Politisierung der Wissenschaft," *Versuch einer Politischen Universität in Frankfurt* [June 1968], *PuH*, 249; orig. in *Universität und Widerstand*, eds. D. Clausen and R. Vermitzel (Frankfurt/Main: Europäische Verlagsanstat, 1968).
[101] Ibid., 258.

Karl Marx University from May 28–30, 1968. On June 2, Habermas took his case directly to an SDS-convened student congress in the university cafeteria with a talk entitled, "The Phantom Revolution and Its Children." Habermas wrote the long essay introducing *Protestbewegung und Hochschulreform* (protest movement and university reform) immediately after the Frankfurt student strike of December 8–18, 1968, and the occupation of rooms in the Sociology Department and Institute for Social Research of January 24–31, 1969.

Habermas's critique in the 1967–9 texts can be encapsulated as follows: An "actionist" is one who engages in "… [protest] action for action's sake." The actionist's goals are nonspecific; the overriding objective is mobilization for its own sake. The indiscriminateness of the protest is encapsulated in the slogan, the "Great Refusal"(*grössen Weigerung*). Targets are selected randomly. "The new techniques of protest are directed at any phenomenon at random because any one is appropriate for expressing rejection" of the whole.[102] Further, "[e]very calculated realization of interests, whether of preserving or changing the system, is ridiculed."[103] Therefore, the actionist forgoes the concrete goal of institutional reform. Student protest could have repercussions "… precisely where the actionists neither expect nor want them: in political parties, unions, mass organizations."[104] Because the actionist views parliamentary opposition as bankrupt and "social institutions as relatively closed, conflict-free and self-regulating, violent apparatuses," he or she aims to make "manifest the violence of institutions."[105] This leads to the use of "provocationist tactics," that is, those which "intentionally violate liberal rules."[106] Habermas claimed that actionists mistake a nonrevolutionary situation for a revolutionary one and thus miss the only way to bring about "… conscious structural change."[107] Actionism thus represents a failed mediation of theory and praxis because it "… generates the illusion that the situation is so ambiguous that only tactical questions remain," but the truth is that "… the prior theoretical problems" have neither been resolved nor adequately

[102] Habermas, "Einleitung," in *PuH*, 14.
[103] Ibid., 15.
[104] Ibid., 29.
[105] Habermas, "Studentenprotest," in *PuH*, 171.
[106] Ibid., 174.
[107] Habermas, "Einleitung," in *PuH*, 49.

stated.[108] The actionists "... fancy themselves revolutionary fighters against fascism while they are actually doing nothing but exploiting the unexpected latitude granted them by liberal institutions."[109] In intellectual-historical terms, they have a "neoanarchist worldview" that reminded Habermas of Sorel's political doctrines.[110] What Marx called "critical-revolutionary activity" must take the path of "radical reformism."[111]

Most interesting from the perspective of Habermas's later development is the way his encounter with "actionism" helped to solidify his understanding of a nonviolent, but still radical, reform project. The most damaging consequence of the actionist deviation from radical reformist praxis was that it sabotaged the practical reform of the university. Habermas observed: "Students are not a class, they are not even the avant-garde of a class, and they are certainly not leading a revolutionary struggle. *In view of the results* of actionism, I consider this self-delusion in the grand style pernicious."[112] A "fatal division of labor" had grown up between the protest movement and pragmatic university reform. While Habermas credited the SDS for being the "motor" of a movement that opened unexpected possibilities for radical reform, elements of the SDS were now threatening this progress: "In Berlin and Frankfurt the goal of the actionist groups is the hindering of reforms. The hitherto energetically demanded *Drittelparität*[113] has been reinterpreted as the distinctive emblem of technocratic university reform."[114] In 1969, Habermas was losing whatever control of the discourse on technocracy he may have had earlier. He fought back, arguing that the antireform radicals only played into the hands of the reactionaries:

> While the government and political parties put forward hesitant, mainly technocratic reform policies and call for law and order, the population's sentiments against students are growing. *Thus the definitions of revolution upheld by left and right, while equally fictions, can*

[108] Ibid., 44.
[109] Ibid., 29.
[110] Habermas, "Studentenprotest," in *PuH*, 171.
[111] Ibid., 49.
[112] Habermas, "Einleitung," in *PuH*, 48 (emphasis added).
[113] *Drittelparität* is the system of academic codetermination in which all three "estates" – students, university staff, and professors – would share in university governance.
[114] Ibid., 11.

> *mutually confirm one another.* [The two perspectives] ... could mesh, bringing about through the method of self-fulfilling prophecy what has always been evoked: the application of naked repression.... [Thus] the protest movement must not let itself be drawn into the foreseeable defeat of its actionistic blunders.[115]

In order to avoid these outcomes, "a sober analysis is needed" of what the protest movement is and can do. Habermas described technocratic reformers and actionist revolutionaries as opposed fronts. But both, he asserted, misperceived the situation as a revolutionary one. Actionists were playing into the hands of technocrats who would cut the prospects of radical reform out from under them. The passage from the February 1969 introduction is a crucial one. In it, Habermas unwittingly drew a striking parallel between the technocratic view of institutions and the actionist one. Not only were the actionists enabling the very technocratic politics they sought to resist, but their worldview also even came to resemble that of their opponent. By describing the student worldview as one in which institutions are "closed, self-regulating systems," Habermas collapsed his two opponents into one, conflating the worldview of the technocratic conservatives with that of the radical students. Indeed, at one point he slipped, directly naming the student activists "technocrats" (*die Technokraten*).[116]

Finally, Habermas criticized the actionists for an alleged obsession with the impregnable power of institutions that led the students to fetishize violence. The episode in June 1967 when Habermas notoriously charged SDS leader Rudi Dutschke with "leftist fascism" is the paradigmatic example of his critique of actionism.

When Dutschke called for the establishment of "action centers" throughout the Federal Republic that could permit coordinated mobilization, Habermas heard in these remarks the intention to ask students "armed only with tomatoes in their hands" to risk injury or death. The only purpose he could see in provoking the state was to make "... manifest the sublime violence that is necessarily implicit in institutions."[117] This attitude toward revolutionary violence in a

115 Ibid., 13 (emphasis added).

116 Ibid., 37. Habermas's translator, Jeremy Shapiro, translates the passage as "The technocrats of protest in itself." See Habermas, *Towards a Rational Society: Student Protest, Science and Politics* (Boston: Beacon Press, 1970), 46.

117 Habermas, "Reaktion auf das referat Rudi Dutschkes."

nonrevolutionary situation, Habermas considered voluntaristic and thus dangerously close to the spiritual territory of fascism:

> I ask myself why Dutschke needs three-quarters of an hour to develop a voluntaristic ideology here, which in the year 1848 was called utopian socialism, and which he, under today's conditions – in any case, I believe there are grounds for suggesting this terminology – must be named leftist fascism.[118]

This "game-playing with terror," he charged, had "fascist implications."[119] As Habermas began to lose popularity, the left found a less critical mentor in Marcuse.

Habermas's concern with the problem of violence is one of the main themes of a dialogue he conducted with Marcuse in 1968–9. Marcuse's lecture, "The Problem of Violence in the Opposition," was delivered to an audience of more than 2,000 during a conference of the SDS in Berlin on July 10–13, 1967. In July 1968, Habermas asked Marcuse to clarify a section of the essay entitled, "Repressive Tolerance," in which Marcuse spoke of a "… natural right (*Naturrecht*) to resistance for repressed and overpowered minorities."[120] Noting that Marcuse's essay was written in 1965 in the context of the U.S. civil rights movement, Habermas suggested that the level of repression in Germany was not comparable:

> Violence can be legitimately volitional and can promote emancipation only when it is enforced by the oppressive sway of a situation that enters consciousness as something totally unbearable. Only this kind of violence is revolutionary; those who ignore this fact wrongfully carry the nimbus of Rosa Luxemburg aloft.[121]

Although Habermas went to great lengths to maintain the intellectual friendship and dialogue between them, he professed himself "astonished" by Marcuse's embrace of violence in his *Essay on Liberation*.[122]

118 Ibid.

119 Habermas, "Diskussionsbeitrag auf dem Kongress 'Bedingungen und Organisation des Widerstandes" (June 9, 1967), Krausharr, *Frankfurter Schule* 2:128, 250.

120 Habermas, "Zum Geleit" (July 1968) [orig. Habermas, ed., *Antworten auf Herbert Marcuse* (Frankfurt/Main: Suhrkamp, 1968); reprinted in Krausharr, *Frankfurter Schule* 2:227, 444.

121 Ibid. Rosa Luxemburg (1871–1919) was the cofounder of the Spartacus League, which in 1919 became the German Communist Party (KPD).

122 Habermas, "Letter to Marcuse" (May 5, 1969), in Krausharr, *Frankfurter Schule* 2:323, 625.

While some scholars have pointed to a reflexive fear of violence as the explanation for his dramatic outburst, Habermas actually did not disavow all violence in principle. "There is a progressive role for violence, and the analytical distinction between progressive and reactionary violence has a real sense."[123] The distinction between violence and nonviolence therefore was secondary to his distinction between reform and revolution. What made the students' actions flawed was not the turn to violence per se, but rather the fact that students were neither a class nor the avant-garde of a revolution.[124] "The only way I see to bring about conscious structural reform in a social system organized in an authoritarian welfare state is *radical reformism*," he declared.[125] Under contemporary conditions, the categories of reform and revolution were not sharp antinomies. Reformism could and should be radical.[126]

Revolutionary student protestors often disregarded liberal rules and engaged in violence. Their departure from legality put Habermas in a double bind: Affirm the legality of the bourgeois constitution and sacrifice what he saw as democracy's best hope for the future, or affirm the legitimacy of the revolution and forfeit democracy's best achievement to date – the rule of law. Habermas's critique of actionism thus can be read as an immanent critique of the student movement: He envisioned a radical reformism that could combine the legitimacy of revolutionary élan with the legality of the constitution.

TECHNOCRACY, TECHNOLOGICAL UTOPIANISM, AND THE IDENTIFICATION OF UNIVERSAL HUMAN INTERESTS

Key tensions existed within Habermas's positions on technology, technocracy, and "the technical," however. A statement from his February 1969 essay illustrates the problem. On the one hand,

[123] Habermas, "Reaktion auf das referat Rudi Dutschkes" (June 9, 1967), Krausharr, *Frankfurter Schule* 2:130, 254.

[124] Habermas "Über einige Bedingungen der Revolutionierung spätkapitalischer Gesellschaften 1968," in idem, *Kultur und Kritik: Verstreute Aufsätze* (Frankfurt/Main: Suhrkamp, 1973), 70–86. Originally based on a lecture at the Korcula Summer School in August 1968 and published in *Praxis* (Zagreb) 5 (1–2), 212–23.

[125] Habermas, "Einleitung," in *PuH*, 49 (emphasis added).

[126] Ibid.

Habermas credited the student protesters with insight: "[P]rotest has brought to consciousness the distinction between technical and practical problems." But, on the other hand, he is critical of their blind spots: "Mistrust of technocratic developments [at the university] is warranted. But it gets mixed with exaggerated generalizations that can turn into sentiment directed against science and technology as such."[127] In this manner, Habermas distinguished between a valid critique of "the technical" (and its corollary, technocracy) and a critique of science and technology *tout court*, which he considered invalid. Because both technocracy and the technological utopianism of the left seemed to erase the sphere of political action, Habermas shifted into the role of supportive critic of the student movement. The obverse of his critical scolding of the actionist descent into illegality, however, was his almost florid praise for the "New Sensibility" of the student generation – "its special sensitivity to the untruth of prevailing legitimations" of the social order.[128] The students were the first to question the values of possessive individualism, competition, status-seeking, and an orientation toward achievement.[129] Habermas found in their sympathy for these values an affinity with what classical Western philosophers called the quest for the good life.[130] Their "New Sensibility"[131] (*Neuen Sensibilität*) was a product of a generational experience of scientific-technical progress and material abundance that enabled them to ask the right questions. "Why," they asked, "despite the advanced stage of technological development is the life of the individual still determined by the dictates of professional careers, the ethics of status competition, and by values of possessive individualism?"[132]

Their goals represented a laudable break with the historical objectives of German social democracy and the post–World War II European welfare state: "Not for a higher portion of social compensations – income, free time – do they struggle, but against these categories of 'compensation' themselves.... It is ever more difficult to make status assignment on the basis of individual achievement appear even subjectively convincing [to them]."[133] Habermas discerned

[127] Ibid., 16.
[128] Habermas, "Studentenprotest," in *PuH*, 170.
[129] Ibid.
[130] Ibid.
[131] Habermas, "Einleitung," in *PuH*, 36.
[132] Habermas, "Technik und Wissenschaft als 'Ideologie,'" in *TWI*, 103.
[133] Ibid., 85.

a contradiction between the requirements of system-reproduction and a "… crumbling achievement ideology."[134] But "… who will activate this conflict-zone is hard to predict."[135] A society-wide legitimation crisis could be a harbinger of a progressive movement.

Habermas went on to hypothesize that students active in protest tend to come from the humanities and social sciences, where they developed a healthy "immunity" to the technocratic consciousness.[136] He described hippie subcultures with sympathy but detachment: They were "experiments" with forms of "'… un-alienated' group life … [that create] … sensitivity to atrophied modes of experiencing interaction." They aimed to overcome their atomized state of "private learning" through new experiences of "group solidarity."[137]

But Habermas's sympathy for the "New Sensibility" dried up where the protest subcultures ran afoul of the Weberian distinction between the purposive-rational and the aesthetic-expressive. A slogan in vogue among these subcultures – the "New Immediacy" (*der Neuen Unmittelbarkeit*) – became a cue for Habermas's interpretation of the movement. The way he interpreted the hippie subcultures echoes Max Weber's admonition to the German students he believed were immaturely "chasing after experience" in 1917: "What is hard for modern man, and especially for the younger generation, is to measure up to an everyday life of this kind. All that chasing after 'experience' stems from this weakness; for it is a weakness not to be able to view face to face the grave countenance of our times."[138] Habermas framed the problem of the "New Immediacy" in a manner suggestive of the future contours of his theory of communicative action:

> The slogan of the New Immediacy designates an attitude [that] radically rejects adaptation to self-regulating systems in favour of immediate gratification. [Frustrated with] … complex detours through systems of purposive-rational action [that] continually postpone goals … [many students react with] … the insistence that

[134] Ibid., 103.
[135] Ibid., 100.
[136] Ibid., 101.
[137] Habermas, "Einleitung," in *PuH*, 17.
[138] Max Weber, "Science as a Vocation," in Hans Gerth and C.Wright Mills, eds., *From Max Weber*, 418–9.

aesthetic experience, instinctual gratification and expression be realized here and now.[139]

In other words, the students' critique of purposive-rational action had gone too far. The hippies "... convert protest into a way of life that absolves those who lead it from having to ascertain the effectiveness of protest."[140] Recall the similarity with Habermas's critique of the actionist: his rejection of action oriented toward concrete goals crippled the cause of pragmatic reform.

The sensibilities Habermas described proved congenial for the reception of Marcuse's works *Eros and Civilization* (1955), *One-Dimensional Man* (1965), and the essay "Repressive Tolerance" (1965). In 1968, Habermas observed that "Marcuse [has] rightly become the philosopher of the youth revolt."[141] Marcuse's stature as the major intellectual inspiration of the movement encouraged Habermas to engage seriously with his arguments. The most important of these engagements was "Technology and Science as an 'Ideology,'" dedicated to Marcuse – whom he considered a friend – on his seventieth birthday, July 19, 1968.[142] As Habermas worked through Marcuse's work, he seemed torn between the Weberian refusal of the "reenchantment of the world" and Marcuse's affirmation of it. Habermas agreed with Marcuse on a major point: Scientific-technical progress served as a legitimating ideology for contemporary capitalism precisely at the moment when technology had created the potential for major changes in the social order. However, they disagreed as to whether "technical reason" could be rejected as domination *tout court*. Because Marcuse's arguments were so closely linked in his mind with the student movement – its strengths and weaknesses – Habermas's debate with Marcuse was the most productive theater in which Habermas worked out his differences with the student movement in Germany.

In Marcuse, Habermas found a framework that corroborated his own view of the depoliticizing effects of science and technology. "I believe that Marcuse's basic thesis, according to which technology

[139] Habermas, "Einleitung," in *PuH*, 15; *TRS*, 33.
[140] Ibid.
[141] Habermas, "Zum Geleit," 443.
[142] It was published in three different places in 1968: first in *Merkur* (July-August 1968), then in Habermas, ed., *Antworten auf Marcuse* (July 1968), and finally in *TWI* (Frankfurt/Main: Suhrkamp, 1968).

and science today also take on the function of legitimating political power, is the key to analyzing the changed constellation."[143] The problem, they agreed, was the opacity of the "technocratic consciousness" that legitimated excluding practical questions from public deliberation. Habermas also agreed with Marcuse that scientific-technical progress blurred the boundary between technical power and institutional framework, or technology and political decision. The "technocracy thesis [serves as] an ideology for the new politics" and as "… a background ideology that penetrates into the consciousness of the depoliticized mass of the population."[144] While Habermas was convinced by Marcuse's argument that technology was an effective ideology of advanced capitalism, he dissented from Marcuse on two major points, and these dissents helped to sharpen Habermas's own evolving positions.

First, Marcuse proposed that science could be something other than an expression of "instrumental reason." He envisioned a mode of scientific mastery that was liberating rather than repressive: "The viewpoint of possible technical control would be replaced by one of preserving, fostering and releasing the potentialities of nature."[145] Habermas asserted that "Marcuse is tempted to pursue this idea of a New Science … [that] … today constitutes the central thought of [Ernst] Bloch's philosophy, and in reflected forms, directs the more secret hopes of Walter Benjamin, Max Horkheimer and Theodor Adorno."[146] However, since modern science is *inherently* oriented to technical control, this "fraternal" view of nature, Habermas explained, has no place within it: "For scientific-technical progress in general, there is no more 'humane' substitute." Technology is not a "historically surpassable project," as Marcuse had argued, but "a 'project' of the human species *as a whole*."[147] In other words, nature would remain disenchanted, science would remain rational, and technology would remain an inescapable part of the human condition.

By refusing to be compensated for work with money and leisure or to be assigned status on the basis of achievement, wrote Habermas, the students were the first generation that

143 Habermas, "Technik und Wissenschaft," 100–1.
144 Ibid.,105.
145 Ibid., 54.
146 Ibid.
147 Ibid., 86–8.

> no longer understands why ... the institutionalized struggle for existence, the discipline of alienated labor, or the eradication of sensuality and aesthetic gratification should be perpetuated – why in short, the mode of life of an economy of poverty is preserved under conditions of a possible economy of abundance.[148]

Thus Habermas came to his second conclusion: While Marcuse and the students inclined toward this vision of a technologically realized plenitude, Habermas reasserted the primacy of the institutional framework of decision, choice, and practical deliberation. Although he did not explicitly frame his interventions this way, it appears that Habermas found his way theoretically by identifying a middle path between the technocratic right and the Marxist left: "Today, better utilization of an unrealized potential leads to improvement of the economic-industrial apparatus, but no longer *eo ipso* to a transformation of the institutional framework with emancipatory consequences."[149] In other words, the mere fact of a technological surplus did not prescribe the conditions for its use. Where Marcuse seemed to Habermas to have envisioned an automatic translation from a change in the mode of production to a change in social relations, Habermas considered this a mechanistic reading of Marx that formed a disturbing echo to the technocratic erasure of the practical-political sphere. In a footnote to another essay from *Technology and Science as an Ideology*, Habermas went still further in linking technocratic right and Marxist left: "Marcuse analysed the dangers of a reduction of reason to technical rationality and a reduction of society to the dimension of technical execution in his book, *One-Dimensional Man*. In another context, Helmut Schelsky put forward the same diagnosis."[150] That Habermas could equate Marcuse's revolutionary stance with Schelsky's technocratic conservatism is remarkable for two reasons: First, it shows how saturated Habermas's thinking was in the middle to late 1960s by the discourse on technology and technocracy. Second, his discovery of a hidden affinity of Marcuse to Schelsky seems to have spurred him to work out a theory of rationality beyond technical rationality. This was the founding gesture of Habermas's reconstruction of historical materialism via Weber and Western Marxism – his major project of the 1970s.

---

148 "Flugblatt der Berliner SDS-Gruppe," 264–5.
149 Habermas, "Technik und Wissenschaft," in *TWI*, 99.
150 Habermas, "Erkenntnis und Interesse"[1965], in *TWI*, 167.

From mid-1967 to 1969, Habermas's role vis-à-vis the student movement changed dramatically. More and more he felt it necessary to assert the role of the sober and mature analyst who could save the movement. This position of course estranged him from the students who, by his own account, were the only segment of the population that remained sensitive to society's deficiencies. By taking this stance, Habermas unconsciously replicated the role Max Weber had played in the revolutionary situation of Germany in 1918–19. Weber had counseled the students that revolution would not lead to the end of bureaucracy and domination. The state would not wither away and usher in utopia. Politics was the "boring of hard boards." For those who could not "measure up to" the requirements of mature manhood and face the reality of the iron cage of modern life, "the doors of the old churches were still open."[151] Habermas identified Weber's decisionism as a key component of the technocratic conservatism that he considered the most dangerous obstacle in contemporary German politics. Caught off guard by the students' unfamiliar modes of protest, though, Habermas fell back on Weber's distinction between aesthetic-expressive and purposive-rational action, arguing that student tactics blurred this essential difference to disastrous effect. He viewed Marcuse's technological utopianism, increasingly popular with the students, through a similar Weberian lens: Neither nature nor science could be reenchanted. Striking, however, is the equal attention Habermas paid to the weaknesses of the Weberian theory of modernity as rationalization. This was embodied in his repeated recognition that the students' "sensitivity" toward and alienation from the work ethic were both emotionally legitimate and politically promising.

But this movement to and fro – pro and contra Weber – could not have been satisfactory to Habermas for long. The fact that the theory of communicative action contains a major *Auseinandersetzung* (coming to terms with) Max Weber's legacy for Western Marxism lends weight to this supposition. Habermas's intellectual project in the 1970s can be described as the effort to rethink historical materialism through a critique of Weber's theory of rationalization. This project was already announced in the 1968 critique of Marcuse. The theory of communicative action marks no retreat from 1968 but was in fact born that very year.

[151] Max Weber, "Science as a Vocation," in Gerth and Mills, *From Max Weber.*

Habermas's dissatisfaction with his failure to transcend the antinomies of Max Weber encoded his frustrations with the politics of the discourse on technology in the 1960s. Indeed, after the severity of his critique of the students' "actionism" and the acerbity of their response, the theory may be read as a gesture in the spirit of remorse. Far from encoding a defiant critique of the excess of the 1960s, the theory represented a renewed effort to work out the dilemma of combining legality and legitimacy – a combination Habermas wanted to communicate that neither he, nor the actionists, nor the technocrats, had yet resolved satisfactorily.

LANGUAGE, LEGALITY, AND LEGITIMACY IN THE THEORY OF COMMUNICATIVE ACTION

The broader links between the technocratic discourse and its critics in the 1960s and the Habermas of the *TCA* are evident in the fact that most of the essays compiled in *Technik und Wissenschaft als "Ideologie"* (*Technology and Science as "Ideology,"* 1968, *TWI* hereafter) anticipate major features of the theory of communicative action. In the 1968 title essay, for which the rest of the volume is named, Habermas wrote that the "basic assumptions of historical materialism require a new formulation" to represent contemporary capitalism adequately.[152] Habermas thereby invented the categories "work" and "interaction" to solve a problem that arose from the structure of the discourse on technology. "To reformulate what Weber called rationalization," he announced, "I shall take as my starting point the fundamental distinction between work and interaction."[153] The distinction between these two concepts, "work" and "interaction," enabled him to solve a conceptual problem that he thought impaired the left: namely, the belief that a change in the mode of production would automatically result in desirable changes in the relations of production. He seems to have concluded that the technocratic approach of the right and the technological utopianism of the left had converged on a shared premise: Politics no longer required legitimation. The progress of science and technology would lead either to the "formed society," as the right imagined, or

[152] Habermas, "Technik und Wissenschaft," in *TWI*, 92.
[153] Ibid., 60.

to a material surplus so abundant that politics would become irrelevant, as some elements of the left hoped. Habermas's conceptual shift – from "science-politics" to "work-interaction" – is the culmination of his five year-long effort at engagement in the decade's signature debate: the noisy clash of technocratic hubris with the students' "Great Refusal."

In the final pages of *TWI*, we observe Habermas experimenting with his new categories of work and interaction. Habermas rewrote the narrative of scientific-technical progress of his early 1960s writings anew in the terms of work, interaction, and "communicative action."

> I suspect that the general relation of institutional framework (interaction) and subsystems of purposive-rational action ("work" in the broad sense of instrumental and strategic action) is more suited [than historical materialism] to reconstructing the sociocultural phases of the history of mankind.[154]

The purpose of this theoretical reformulation was to help him solve a political problem. By splitting the concept of rationalization into two, Habermas cut the knot represented by the convergence of Marxist left and technocratic right: "It becomes clear that *two concepts of rationalization* must be distinguished.... Rationalization at the level of the institutional framework can occur only in the medium of interaction itself, that is, by removing restrictions on communication."[155] Defining rationalization in terms of two modes – an "instrumental" one and a "communicative" one – was the first stage of his reconstruction of Western Marxism's distinction of instrumental from substantive reason.

The concept of communicative action also served Habermas by consolidating the praise he had offered the youth subcultures. It raised to social-theoretical significance the students' sensitivity to the "atrophy" of the sphere of "interaction": "By communicative action, I understand symbolically mediated *interaction*. It is governed by binding consensual norms, which define reciprocal expectations about behavior and which must be understood and recognized by at

154 Ibid., 92: "Verhaltnis von institutionellen Rahmen (Interaktion) und Sub-Systemen zweckrationalen Handelns ('Arbeit' im weiteren Sinne instrumentalen und strategischen Handelns)."

155 Ibid., 98.

least two acting subjects."[156] Social systems could be distinguished by whether they were dominated by the principle of work or interaction.[157] But scientific-technical progress blurred the line between technical power and institutional framework. The result was that "... men lose consciousness of the dualism of work and interaction."[158] What so impressed Habermas about the technocratic ideology and consciousness was the way it rendered this fundamental dichotomy invisible[159]: "It is a singular achievement of this ideology to detach society's self-understanding from the frame of reference of communicative action and ... the concepts of symbolic interaction and replace it with a scientific model."[160] Habermas's point was that the technical and practical levels could and should be distinguished analytically: The institutional organization of society "... continues to be a problem of practice related to communication, not one of technology, no matter how scientifically guided."[161] The problems of technology thus pointed beyond the particularism of class-based politics to the politics of a universal class.

By "veiling" practical problems, technocratic consciousness "... not only justifies a particular class's interest in domination, and represses another class's partial need for emancipation, but affects the human race's emancipatory interest as such."[162] By making the practical interest "disappear behind" the technical interest in control,

> ... the new ideology ... violates an interest grounded in one of the two fundamental conditions of our cultural existence: in language ... Or more precisely, in the form of individualization and socialization determined by communication in ordinary language. This interest extends to the maintenance of intersubjectivity of mutual understanding as well as to the creation of communication without domination.[163]

In these formulations, we have already arrived at Habermas's search for the anthropologically universal features of communication,

156 Ibid., 62.
157 Ibid., 93.
158 Ibid., 80.
159 Ibid., 84.
160 Ibid., 81.
161 Ibid., 78–9.
162 Ibid., 89.
163 Ibid., 91.

a search that would occupy him with the formal properties of language throughout the 1970s.[164] Thus, in a work published *before* the denouement of the student movement, themes central to his 1981 theory of communicative action are clearly present: among them, the notion of domination-free communication as the normative foundation for critical social theory. The "universal pragmatics" of language he outlined in the 1971 Gauss lectures are a foundation stone for the edifice of the *TCA*. In *TCA*, ideology is understood as "… systematically distorted communication."[165] To understand this concept entails understanding its opposite: "rational" or "non-distorted" communication. As two scholars explained in 1980,

> That we have some such idea is precisely what the programmme of "universal pragmatics" seeks to show. By reconstructing the conditions of possible communication, Habermas [hoped] … to identify the elements necessarily presupposed in the successful exchange of speech-acts and thereby to uncover "the universal validity basis of speech."[166]

Elaborated over the course of the decade, the fundamental insights of "universal pragmatics" culminated in a theory of justice as fairness of communication.[167] Habermas's appropriation of John Austin's theory of "speech-acts" for his universal pragmatics is summarized as follows:

> [Habermas argues that] … in uttering a speech act, the speaker unavoidably raises "validity claims" which can only be "redeemed" in a discourse having the structure of an "ideal speech situation." However distorted the actual conditions of communication may be, every competent speaker possesses the means for the construction

---

164 See Habermas, *Vorstudien und Ergänzungen zur Theorie des kommunikativen Handelns* (Frankfurt/Main: Suhrkamp, 1984).

165 David Held and John B. Thompson, eds., *Habermas: Critical Debates* (Cambridge, MA: MIT Press, 1982), 8. There is a continuity here with Habermas's *Knowledge and Human Interests* (1968).

166 Ibid.

167 For the elaborations, see *Vorstudien und Ergänzungen zur Theorie des kommunikativen Handelns* (Frankfurt/Main: Suhrkamp, 1984) and a partial translation of it in Habermas, *On the Pragmatics of Social Interaction: Preliminary Studies in the Theory of Communicative Action*, trans. Barbara Fultner (Cambridge, MA: MIT Press, 2001). "Was heisst universal Pragmatik?"[1976] is translated in Habermas, *Communication and the Evolution of Society*.

> of a speech situation which would be free from domination and in which disputes concerning the truth of statements, or the correctness of norms could be rationally resolved. Since moreover this situation is necessarily anticipated in every act of speech it attests to the reality and universality of the interest in emancipation.[168]

Remarkably, the core of this vision predates what is described as Habermas's linguistic turn. In a 1971 essay, he notes that already in his 1965 inaugural lecture at Frankfurt he had reached similar conclusions:

> ...[I]n every speech act the *telos* of reaching an understanding [*Verständigung*] is already inherent. "With the very first sentence [we utter] the intention of a general and voluntary consensus is unmistakably enunciated." Wittgenstein has remarked that the concept of reaching an understanding lies in the concept of language.... Every one who speaks a natural language has intuitive knowledge of it and therefore is confident of being able, in principle, to distinguish a true consensus from a false one. In the educated language of philosophical culture, we call this knowledge *a priori* or innate.[169]

The turn to innate anthropological universals thus predates his systematic immersion in the linguistic theories of Wittgenstein, Sellars, Austin, and Searle by at least a half decade, locating the key motive forces behind the *TCA* well before the dramatic West German events of 1967–9. The linguistic turn is thus perhaps better understood as an anthropological turn.

But there also were more immediate stimuli from the West German political context in the 1970s as well. He defended the tradition of Critical Theory associated with the Frankfurt Institute for Social Research against allegations by CDU officials that it had inspired a generation of left-wing terrorists and challenged the laws proscribing "radicals" from employment in the civil service, which were instituted by both Willy Brandt (1969–74) and Helmut Schmidt (1974–81). Habermas frequently worried that he would awake one morning to find a newspaper report of a left-wing terrorist who had attended some lectures on Critical Theory in Frankfurt.[170] As

---

168 Held and Thompson, *Critical Debates*, 8–9.

169 Habermas, "Some Difficulties in the Attempt to Link Theory and Praxis" [1971], in *Theory and Practice*, 17; for the section of his 1965 lecture quoted, see Habermas, "Erkenntnis und Interesse," 163.

170 Conversation with Habermas, July 2004, Flensburg.

left-wing terrorism came to dominate headlines in the 1970s, and even Brandt's government instituted a "ban on radicals" in the civil service that created a climate of persecution and fear, the tradition of Critical Theory was closely scrutinized. Habermas's loyalty to the constitution was often impugned by CDU politicians in the 1970s.[171]

In a 1981 interview, Habermas explained the "psychological" impulses behind his *TCA*. In 1977, a "pogrom-like atmosphere" had developed around the kidnapping and murder of Martin Schleyer, a Cologne industrialist by the Red Army Faction (RAF), on September 5. The Schmidt government had responded to the abduction and a subsequent airline highjacking with repressive measures that Habermas saw as unnecessary, even hysterical:

> It was then [in 1977] that I first took seriously the neoconservatives who had emerged in 1973.... I wanted to clarify for myself the implicit concept of the modern and their departure from it.... That was the one side. The other side was to [understand] the significance of the new protest potentials, new social movements, with which I had never had a relationship, in order to understand them better.... What interested me directly was that both had turned against what Weber called the legacy of occidental rationalism.[172]

Habermas saw himself fighting a two-front battle against different rejections of modernity, both of which threatened to "de-differentiate" the structure of modernity. It was a modernity he understood in Weber's neo-Kantian terms – differentiated into spheres of rationality, each with their own inner logic, that Habermas named the cognitive-instrumental, the moral-practical, and the aesthetic-expressive. The neoconservatives, he wrote in 1978, unbalanced this structure: "Whoever is willing to sacrifice this autonomy [of the spheres] to a combination of a one-sided rationality and a vapid traditionalism, risks costly regressions: on German (blood and) soil we have already conducted the experiment of a modernization restricted to economic growth."[173] For their part, the critics of economic growth among the new social

---

[171] See Wiggershaus, "Afterword," in *The Frankfurt School* and *idem*, *Jürgen Habermas* (Reinbeck bei Hamburg: Rowohlt, 2004), 98–109.

[172] Honneth et al., "Dialektik," in *DNU*, 181–2.

[173] Habermas, "Introduction," *Observations on the 'Spiritual Situation of the Age': Contemporary German Perspectives*, trans. Andrew Buchwalter [1979] (Cambridge, MA: MIT Press, 1985), 15.

movements (peace, environmental, and local autonomy) had lost sight of the fact that "... restricting the growth of monetary-administrative complexity is by no means synonymous with surrendering modern forms of life.... When this opposition sharpens into a demand for de-differentiation at any price, an important distinction is lost."[174] Habermas explained that some representatives of the new social movements of the 1970s and the neoconservatives were both discontented with the workings of the welfare state. Habermas had fought alongside Abendroth for an expansive interpretation of the constitution's *Sozialstaat* clauses. In the late 1970s, after a decade of Social-Liberal rule, a new problem had manifested itself: the problem of excessive "juridification." The coalition government had boosted wages and social spending to historic highs, at least before the recession of 1975.[175] Social spending increased from 24.6 to 32 percent of gross domestic product (GDP) between 1965 and 1975, much of it on welfare provision. Habermas argued in *TCA* that the welfare state had generated its own "pathological side effects":

> As the social welfare state spreads the net of client relationships over private spheres of life, it increasingly produces the pathological side effects of a juridification that is simultaneously a bureaucratization and monetarization of core domains of the lifeworld.... Social welfare guarantees [inadvertently] foster the disintegration of those life contexts.[176]

Significantly, juridification [*Verrechtlichung*], or legal regulation, is the primary empirical example Habermas chose to describe the way the economic and political "system" penetrates or colonizes the "lifeworld."[177] "System" and "lifeworld," the terms of art Habermas used in *TCA*, were the descendants of "work" and "interaction," respectively. But new conflicts in advanced Western societies had developed in the last "ten to twenty years" that transcended the class struggle over resources:

> They do not flare up in areas of material reproduction, they are not channeled through parties and associations and they are not

[174] Thomas McCarthy, "Translator's Preface," in *Theory of Communicative Action*, Vol. I, xliv.
[175] Thornhill, *Political Theory*, 160.
[176] Habermas, *Theory of Communicative Action*, Vol. II, 532–4.
[177] Rüdiger Voigt, ed., *Verrechtlichung: Analysen zu Funktion und Wirkung von Parlamentarisierung, Bürokratisierung und Justizialisierung sozialer, politischer und ökonomischer Prozesse* (Königstein: Athenäum, 1980).

> allayed by compensations that conform to the system. Rather these new conflicts [concern] protecting and restoring endangered ways of life or of establishing reformed ways of life. In short, these new conflicts do not flare up around problems of distribution but around questions concerning the grammar of forms of life.[178]

In focusing his critical attention on the "seams between system and lifeworld" Habermas returned in spirit to the student movement's "New Sensibility," the "postmaterial values" it espoused, and the corresponding legitimacy deficit faced by the Bonn Republic. Combining the commitment to legality he had found in the extra-parliamentary opposition's campaign against the emergency laws with the legitimacy demanded by the students had proved a difficult puzzle. Now – in the 1970s – he returned to the tradition of Western Marxism in which he had always felt most at home, this time trying to rewrite Adorno and Horkheimer's *Dialectic of Enlightenment* but with a determination to shake off the weight of Weber's one-sided account of modern society as an "iron cage." This is where Weber had led Adorno and Horkheimer astray, he concluded.[179] Habermas's reconstruction of Western Marxism thus would involve a sustained *Auseinandersetzung* with Weber.

He began an in-depth study of Weber in 1971, although, as we have seen, he had written on Weber in the early 1960s too.[180] According to the translator of *TCA*, Habermas sometimes described his theory of modernity as a "... second attempt to appropriate Weber in the spirit of Western Marxism."[181] What made this enterprise particularly burdensome was the way in which Weber's representation of law overstated its system-supporting characteristics and downplayed its rootedness in the lifeworld. Put another way, Weber characterized law as a mode of domination, useful to both capitalism and the state, but independent of morality.

In a section of *TCA* entitled, "The Rationalization of Law: Weber's Diagnosis of the Times," Habermas wrote, "In Weber's theory of rationalization the development of law occupies a place as prominent as it is ambiguous."[182] Weber dramatized

[178] Ibid., 576.
[179] For a discussion of the "dead end" of Critical Theory, see McCarthy, "Translator's Preface," xviii-xxi.
[180] Honneth et al.,"Dialektik," 216.
[181] McCarthy, "Translator's Preface," xxxiv.
[182] Habermas, *Theory of Communicative Action*, Vol. I, 243.

"... his vision of an iron cage [of modernity] whose moral-practical substance has dried up [by assigning] morality and law to different complexes of rationality."[183] By doing so, he "... [played] down the structural analogies that obtain between moral development and the rationalization of the law."[184] The result was a vision of law and legal domination that emphasizes the

> ... formalism of a law that is systematized by specialists and with the positivity of norms that are enacted.... But he neglects the moment of a need for rational justification.... [He] detaches the rationalization of law from the moral-practical complex of rationality and reduces it to a rationalization of means-ends relations.[185]

This approach is illustrated by Weber's "positivistic equation of legality and legitimacy" that, Habermas claims, "lands him in an embarrassing situation":

> Assuming that legitimacy is a necessary condition for the continued existence of every type of political domination, how can a legal domination whose legality is based on a law that is viewed purely in decisionistic terms (that is, a law that devalues all grounding in principle) be legitimated at all? Weber's answer, which has found adherents from Carl Schmitt to Niklas Luhmann, runs as follows: through procedure.[186]

However, this results in a vicious circle:

> It remains unclear how the belief in legality is supposed to summon up the force of legitimation if legality means only conformity with an actually existing legal order, and if this order, as arbitrarily enacted law, is not in turn open to practical-moral justification. The belief in legality can produce legitimacy only if we already presuppose the legitimacy of the legal order that lays down what is legal. There is no way out of this circle.[187]

In the same decade that Habermas was working through Anglo-American theories of language, he also was engaged in an equally

[183] Ibid., 251
[184] Ibid.
[185] Ibid., 262
[186] Ibid., 265. This is the opposite of what Habermas means by "procedure"; his is closer to that of Robert Alexy (1978) and Ralf Dreier (1981). For an elaboration of Habermas's "procedural turn," see Chapter 5.
[187] Ibid.

important critical reception of the systems theory of his fellow sociologist and '58er, Niklas Luhmann. The *Auseinandersetzung* with Luhmann is beyond the scope of this study, but a few remarks can be made. Already in his 1973 *Legitimation Crisis*, Habermas professed to consider Luhmann's systems theory dangerous: "[In Luhmann] the belief in legitimacy thus shrinks to a belief in legality: the appeal to the legal manner in which a decision comes about suffices."[188] According to Habermas, Luhmann "… is here following the decisionistic legal theory founded by Carl Schmitt."[189] Revisiting Luhmann in his major 1992 work, which is the subject of Chapter 5, Habermas wrote similarly about the systems theory viewpoint: In it, law is detached from all "internal relations" to morality and politics, "… reduced to the … administration of law," and one misses the "… internal connection … to the constitutional organization of … political power."[190] Luhmann's sociology of law is interesting, writes Habermas, "… merely as the most rigorous version of a theory that assigns law a marginal position (as compared with its place in classical social theories) and neutralizes the phenomenon of legal validity by describing things objectivistically."[191] The threat of a decisionistic politics set free from questions of the good life was the subject of his inaugural lecture at Marburg in 1961. For all the changes of method and form in the interim, his magnum opus of 1981 was written very in much the same spirit.

---

[188] Habermas, *Legitimation Crisis*, 98.
[189] Ibid.
[190] Habermas, *Between Facts and Norms*, 50.
[191] Ibid., 48.

4 Civil Disobedience, Constitutional Patriotism, and Modernity: Rethinking Germany's link to "the West" (*Westbindung*), 1978–1987

In the early 1980s, a reheating of the Cold War between the superpowers had far-reaching consequences for West German politics. The four-year-long debate over a North Atlantic Treaty Organization (NATO) decision to station nuclear missiles in West Germany, known as the "Euromissile debate," broke up the Social-Liberal coalition in 1982 that had ruled for thirteen years. Helmut Kohl became chancellor in 1982, a position he would hold for the next sixteen years. This new phase of the Cold War produced *die Wende* (the turn) in German politics. The years surrounding *die Wende* drew Habermas into two major public debates. The first concerned the Euromissiles, the second the *Historikerstreit*, or "historians' controversy." Underlying both, according to Habermas, was the agenda of Helmut Kohl, whom he described as a "neoconservative." In response to this neoconservative challenge in both foreign policy and vis-à-vis the memory of the Nazi past, Habermas formulated three new theoretical positions that have left a lasting imprint on his oeuvre. The first was a theoretical defense of civil disobedience; the second was an articulation of modernity, identified with an Enlightenment notion of public, rational critique, and a "project worth completing"; and the third was an explication of "constitutional patriotism," a source of national pride for Germans centered on the idea of constitutional rights. The connection between the three theoretical positions has been neglected by scholars. Viewed together and in the political context of *die Wende*, the three positions gain a powerful intellectual coherence. Together they offered a solution to the major political-cultural problem West Germany faced in the first half of the 1980s: the problem of Germany's link to or integration with the West (*Westbindung*). The essays Habermas wrote between 1978 and 1987 on the subjects civil disobedience, modernity, neoconservatism, and "constitutional patriotism" each represent a different facet of Habermas's argument for *Westbindung* properly understood. It is during these years that Habermas's status as a Westernizer of German political culture best comes into focus.

The Euromissile debate resulted in a multidimensional political crisis. For intellectuals, it problematized the question of *Westbindung* and raised the specter of German neutralism, that is, withdrawal from NATO and the demilitarization of the two Germanies. Habermas's writings on modernity from 1980–4 and on constitutional patriotism from 1985–7 contain explicit critiques of neutralism in foreign policy and mark his distance from the Green Party. Faced with a discourse on the right that treated protest as disloyalty and that made unwavering adherence to NATO policy the measure of the commitment to the values of democracy, Habermas redefined *Westbindung* as a question of political culture. Membership in the political culture he envisioned required its citizens' loyalty to the constitution but also their capacity for independent moral judgment. In working through this question of the nature of a "mature" democratic polity in his political writings, Habermas arrived at a view of the constitution as something that could and must evolve – an open, fallible learning process – in short, an exemplar of the characteristics he ascribed to the "project of modernity" championed in his philosophical writings.

The dynamics of the debate on the "right of resistance" in the years of the Euromissile debate created a theoretical problem for Habermas. Neither the criminalization of civil disobedience by the conservative majority of the constitutional law profession nor the arguments for its legalization by the minority of the profession was convincing to him. Both missed what Habermas considered the correct relationship of legality to legitimacy in a democracy. Habermas solved his problem by introducing a concept of a *Rechtsstaat* that was "nonidentical" with itself. What this meant was that the constitutional framework of the *Rechtsstaat* needed to be supplemented by what Habermas called the "non-institutionalizable" mistrust of the state by its citizens. Toleration for civil disobedience was the "test case" of a "mature" democratic political culture, to use Habermas's language, because it shifted the burden from institutional design to the consciousness of the citizen.

THE EUROMISSILE DEBATE AND THE PARTY-POLITICAL REALIGNMENT OF 1982 AS CONTEXT FOR THE DEFENSE OF "MODERNITY"

On December 12, 1979, NATO foreign and defense ministers decided to deploy over 500 intermediate-range nuclear missiles (Pershing II and cruise) in Western Europe, partly in West Germany. Helmut Schmidt had begun his career in national government as the Defense Minister to Willy Brandt; he had been chancellor since 1974. Schmidt supported the missiles on the grounds that the deployment of comparable missiles (SS-20s) in Eastern Europe by Soviet Premier Leonid Breszhnev constituted a breach of a May 1978 agreement to maintain nuclear parity with the West. The decision sparked a divisive four-year-long debate over German foreign policy, exacerbating tensions within the Social Democratic Party (SPD) between its left and right wings that contributed to the unraveling of the Social-Liberal coalition.

The December 1979 decision of SPD Chancellor Helmut Schmidt to press forward with the deployments produced huge opposition, creating the largest political demonstrations in the history of the Bonn Republic and adding strength to the newly established Green Party. From 1979 until the end of his government in October 1982, Chancellor Schmidt was under pressure from intellectuals and activists of the peace movement to revise his decision on the missiles. Although Schmidt insisted that Soviet advantages in conventional and nuclear forces required a response, the large majority of his own party disagreed with him. This exacerbated a trend visible from the mid-1970s – the SPD was losing support on its left flank. Heterogeneous groupings representing broadly pacifist, environmentalist, and feminist positions developed in some *Länder*. In March 1979, the "Other Political Association"(SPV) was founded with the support of Nobel Prize–winning author Heinrich Böll and German Socialist Students' League (SDS) veteran Rudi Dutschke. Petra Kelly was its most charismatic leader. In October, a Green Party list got into the Bremen Land Parliament with just over 5 percent of the vote, and the Greens became a nationwide political party on January 13, 1980. Although the Greens did not reach the minimum 5 percent threshold for parliamentary representation in the November 1980 federal elections, their growing popularity underlined the disagreement over the direction of the

SPD. The conservative policies of Free Democratic Party (FDP) Economics Minister Lambsdorff had strained the alliance with traditional Social Democrats, but the FDP made significant parliamentary gains in 1980.[1] A rift developed within the SPD over strategy for the future. Brandt thought the party should move to the left to outflank the Greens, whereas Schmidt pressed forward with the nuclear missile decision.

A month after the election, Petra Kelly joined with aged Protestant Pastor Martin Niemöller (1892–1984) and others in formulating the Kreffeld Appeal rejecting the missiles. On November 15–16, a thousand participants attended the first Kreffeld Appeal forum. By mid-1983, 4 million signatures had been obtained. After threatening to resign in May 1981, Schmidt ultimately secured the *Bundestag*'s support for the missile decision by a narrow margin: 254 to 234.[2] The SPD now faced a dynamic similar to that which it had faced in 1967, when those who had felt betrayed by the Great Coalition's support for the Vietnam War had joined the extraparliamentary opposition (*Äusserparlamentarische Opposition*, or APO). Schmidt's narrow victory similarly was felt as a betrayal that generated mass protest – ultimately in the hundreds of thousands.

In August, a beleaguered Schmidt retreated to an academic congress on "Kant in Our Time" to deliver a speech in which his decision was stylized as an example of what Max Weber famously had described as the "ethic of responsibility"; the peace protestors were framed as the politically irresponsible *Gesinnungsethiker*.[3] Schmidt's opponents in turn derided him as a technocrat and the SPD, in the words of Green Rudolf Bahro, as "the party of moderate exterminism."[4] On September 13, the visit by U.S. Secretary of State Alexander Haig to West Berlin was greeted by 30,000 to 40,000 protestors. Violence ensued, with several hundred injured (including fifty policemen) in battles with police. Protests ranging from 50,000 to 300,000 occurred in other major European cities.[5]

[1] See Anthony Nicholls, *The Bonn Republic: West German Democracy, 1945–90* (New York: Longman, 1997), 273.

[2] Jeffrey Herf, *War by Other Means: Soviet Power, West German Resistance, and the Battle of the Euromissiles* (New York: The Free Press, 1984), 126.

[3] *Gesinnungsethiker* can be translated as "those who adhere to a morally pure 'ethic of conviction.'" Herf, *War by Other Means*, 131.

[4] Herf, *War by Other Means*, 151.

[5] Ibid., 135–7.

The demonstration in Bonn on October 10, 1981, was attended by 250,000 people – the largest in the history of the republic. Schmidt soon was marginalized with the tiny fraction of his party against the majority who passionately opposed the deployments.

By June 1982, Foreign Minister Hans-Dietrich Genscher had begun to contemplate taking the FDP out of the coalition with the weakened SPD. In late August, Genscher was concerned about the rise of neutralist sentiment in the SPD.[6] Genscher's FDP instead chose to seek a coalition with the Christian Democratic Union (CDU) and its leader Helmut Kohl.[7] In September's parliamentary debates, the majority of Social Democrats argued that acceptance of the missiles was not in the German national interest. As the leader of a party long restive in its coalition with the SPD, Genscher resigned as foreign minister. By an unprecedented use of the parliamentary constructive vote of no confidence on October 1, 1982, the thirteen-year rule of the Social-Liberal coalition had reached its end.

In the March 1983 elections called to replace Schmidt's government, the SPD put forward a former justice minister and mayor of Munich, Hans-Jochen Vogel, and proceeded to suffer its worst defeat since 1961. The Green Party broke the 5 percent mark for the first time, becoming the first new party to enter Parliament since 1953.[8] *Die Wende* signified by Chancellor Kohl's election had begun. The *Bundestag* voted for the missiles 286 to 226. Five days later, the missiles arrived in West Germany.

HABERMAS AND *DIE WENDE*: "MODERNITY" AND VARIETIES OF CONSERVATIVE CHALLENGE

The four years of the Euromissile debate, between the December 1979 NATO decision and the stationing of the missiles in November 1983, reoriented the Federal Republic politically. We shall turn to Habermas's view of the protestors in a section devoted to his legal theory below. Here, we examine Habermas's view of the ideological significance of *die Wende* as it was reflected in both his philosophical writings on "modernity" and his political writings on the growth of

[6] Ibid., 158.

[7] Ibid., 159.

[8] The results of the election were CDU 45.8 percent, FDP 6.9 percent, SPD 38.2 percent, and Greens 5.6 percent.

"neoconservatism"; the two were interrelated in complex ways for Habermas.

In 1981, Habermas left the Max Planck Institute in Starnberg, which he had directed for ten years, and spent the next two years between academic positions. The change in his professional surroundings thus coincided with the breakup of the Social-Liberal coalition in 1982. When he returned to a position at the University of Frankfurt in April 1983, Kohl had just won the election. The first series of lectures Habermas gave in this new professional and political situation was on the subject of modernity. The lectures therefore were composed in the wake of the Euromissile crisis, an intensely political moment in the Bonn Republic's history with which Habermas was seriously intellectually engaged.

In September 1980, Habermas received the Adorno Prize of the city of Frankfurt. His prize lecture, "Modernity and Postmodernity," can be read as the opening salvo in a battle with French poststructuralist philosophers, whom he critiqued at greater length in *The Philosophical Discourse of Modernity*, a series of twelve lectures composed in 1983–4.[9] But his lecture on "Modernity and Postmodernity" faces backward to the battles of the 1970s as much as it anticipates the conflicts of the mid-1980s: "An emotional current of our times which has penetrated all aspects of intellectual life has placed on the agenda theories of post-enlightenment, postmodernity, even of posthistory," his lecture began.[10] "What I call 'the project of modernity' comes only into focus when we dispense with the usual concentration upon art."[11] His thesis was "I think that instead of giving up modernity and its project as a lost cause, we should learn from the mistakes of those extravagant programs which have tried to negate modernity."[12] Among these mistaken programs he distinguished three: the *antimodernism* of the young conservatives, the *premodernism* of the old conservatives, and the *postmodernism* of the

[9] The first four lectures were held at the Collège de France in March of 1984. Cited in *The Philosophical Discourse of Modernity: Twelve Lectures* (*PDM* hereafter), trans. Frederick Lawrence (Cambridge, MA: MIT Press, 1987), Preface, ixx.

[10] Habermas, "Modernity and Postmodernity," *New German Critique* 22 (Winter 1981), 3.

[11] Ibid., 8.

[12] Ibid., 11.

neoconservatives.[13] We must pause for a moment to identify what Habermas meant by these terms of art.

With "young conservatives," Habermas provocatively labeled the poststructuralism gaining adherents in France – "this line leads from Bataille via Foucault to Derrida" – and linked it to interwar German conservative intellectuals who had rejected the Weimar Republic and modernity more broadly; Habermas elsewhere also names Gottfried Benn and Ernst Jünger "young conservatives." By the old conservatives' "premodernism," he refers to the neo-Aristotelianism inaugurated by Leo Strauss – a position anterior to modernity and associated with natural law; in West Germany, '58er Robert Spaemann is an example. With the "neoconservatives," he refers to a trans-Atlantic network of intellectuals, many of whom, like the sociologists Daniel Bell and Irving Horowitz, connected with *Commentary*, embraced the term. Their "postmodernism" consisted in their asymmetrical yes and no to modernity; that is, they embraced modern science insofar as it promoted economic growth and new technologies but rejected the "explosive contents of cultural modernity."[14] They thus blamed cultural modernity for the pathologies of social rationalization – confusing cause and effect:

> Neoconservatism shifts onto cultural modernism the uncomfortable burdens of a more or less successful capitalist modernization.... The neoconservative does not uncover the economic and social causes for the altered attitudes towards work, consumption and leisure. Consequently he attributes [behaviors such as] ... hedonism, the lack of social identification, the lack of obedience, narcissism, the withdrawal from status and achievement competition – to the domain of "culture."[15]

In a 2005 interview, Habermas reiterated this definition: "What the early 'neoconservatism' in the USA and in Germany designated was what we in Bayern call '*lederhosen* and high-tech': antimodernism in culture ... and conservative progressivism (earlier in a bureaucratic or technocratic version than in the market-liberal version, imported from the USA, we have today)."[16]

[13] Ibid., 13.
[14] Ibid.
[15] Ibid., 7.
[16] Author's private correspondence with Habermas, June 7, 2005.

Habermas concluded his Adorno Prize lecture on a cryptic note that seems to refer to the political constellation of political parties two years before *die Wende*. He spoke of an "alliance of postmodernists with premodernists," conceding that these were rough ideal-types:

> I fear that the ideas of antimodernity, together with an additional touch of premodernity, are becoming popular in the circles of alternative culture. When one observes the transformations of consciousness within political parties in Germany, a new ideological shift becomes visible. And this is the alliance of postmodernists with premodernists.[17]

To what political trends did this coded speech refer? As we have seen, 1980 was the year the Greens first emerged on the national stage. The first statement about "antimodern" sentiments gaining in the alternative scene appears to refer to the antigrowth politics of the new Green Party, the founding of which Habermas had opposed on the grounds that they would not weather well the transition from social movement to political party.[18] By the coming alliance of "postmodernists with premodernists" in the sphere of party politics, he appears to anticipate the coming alliance of the FDP ("postmodernists" because of their economic liberalism) and the CDU ("premodernists" because of their cultural traditionalism about moral values). Although Habermas has rejected this interpretation – "No, I consider it impossible to map [*unmittelbar abzubilden*] theoretical positions directly onto party-political ones"[19] – in the absence of an alternative account, this one seems to do it justice.

Moreover, a lengthy interview Habermas gave to Axel Honneth in the summer of 1981 reinforces this interpretation, enhancing the impression we have of the fundamental interconnectedness of his philosophical work on the modernity concept (and the closely linked social-theoretical concept of rationalization in Max Weber's sense) with his political concerns about the rise of intellectual neoconservatism. In the 1981 interview he indicated that his interest in working on the concept of modernity stemmed from the growing impact of "neoconservatives" on German public debate since

[17] John Torpey, "Introduction: Habermas and the Historians," in *New German Critique* 44 (Spring-Summer 1988), 14.

[18] Honneth et al.,"Dialektik," in *Die Neue Unübersichtlichkeit* (Frankfurt/Main: Suhrkamp, 1985; *DNU* hereafter), 250.

[19] Author's private correspondence with Habermas, June 7, 2005.

1973: "I wanted to make clear to myself the concept of modernity implicit in those [neoconservative] interpretations and a departure from the ideas that had supported the *Bundesrepublik*, modernity, radical democracy and enlightenment."[20] He reiterated the notion that the project of modernity was threatened by neoconservatives and elements of the alternative culture – although he did not expressly name the Greens. Since about 1975, Habermas believed, neoconservatives and "critics of growth" appear to have converged. He described both as "syndromes": "I fear that between these two syndromes … the valuable substance of genuine Western traditions and inspirations will get left aside."[21] Beginning in the summer of 1983, Habermas took part in monthly discussions with Green Party member Joschka Fischer, but he was never a member of the Greens.[22] In a lecture to the Spanish Parliament in 1984, he referred to "dissidents of industrial society" who "fall behind the insights" represented by the postwar welfare state compromise.[23] In a 1981 interview, Habermas was asked what "mountain" he would climb next; he had just completed the two-volume *Theory of Communicative Action* (*TCA* hereafter). His answer: "Hills, only small hills. I will probably go to the University of Frankfurt. I plan a series of lectures on theories of the modern. That will surely make me happy."[24]

When interviewed about the political context of his modernity lectures in 2005, Habermas demurred, asserting that they responded exclusively to the promptings of the philosophical context.[25] He presented the same argument in the published Preface: "The challenge from the neostructuralist critique of reason defines the perspective from which I seek to reconstruct here, step by step, the philosophical discourse of modernity."[26] It was his attempt to meet the "challenge" represented by French poststructuralism, an effort he felt was overdue, he confessed in an interview[27]; it was a "mistake" not

[20] Honneth et al., "Dialektik," in *DNU*, 181.
[21] Ibid., 183.
[22] Wiggershaus, *Jürgen Habermas*, 121.
[23] Habermas, "Krise der Wohlfahrtsstaat und die Erschöpfung utopischer Energien," in *DNU*, 155–6.
[24] Honneth et al., "Dialektik," in *DNU*, 208.
[25] He describes it as a separate sphere of "academic work." Author's private correspondence with Habermas, June 7, 2005.
[26] Habermas, "Preface," in *PDM*, xix.
[27] Habermas, "Konservative Politik, Arbeit, Sozialismus und Utopie heute," an interview with Hans-Ulrich Reck (April 2, 1983), in *DNU*, 60–2.

to have engaged the work of the French poststructuralist philosophers earlier and more seriously.[28] Later, though, he acknowledged the promptings of the external context:

> Since the middle of the 1970s I have felt the pressure of the neoconservative and poststructuralist critiques of reason, to which I responded with the concept of communicative rationality. This constellation remained unchanged in the 1980s and it was for this reason that I continued to work on a critique of the philosophy of consciousness.... In *The Philosophical Discourse of Modernity* I tried to show that "representational thinking" can be replaced with something other than the defeatism of the deconstructionists or the contextualism of the neo-Aristotelians.[29]

The discourse of philosophy enjoys some relative autonomy from the intellectual field as a whole, but this easily can be overstated in Habermas's case:

> The concept of a communicative concept of reason ... is intended to lead away from the paradoxes and levelings of a self-referential critique of reason. On another front, it has to be upheld against the competing approach of a systems theory that utterly shoves the problematic of rationality aside.... This double battlefront makes the rehabilitation of the concept of reason a risky business.[30]

Given the persistent interrelation of theory and praxis in his intellectual career, Habermas's choice of language – "defeatism" and of a double "battlefront" – is revealing.

After resigning his directorship at Starnberg in 1981, Habermas considered professorships in Berkeley and Bielefeld before accepting a chair in philosophy at the University of Frankfurt in the summer of 1983, a position he would hold until his *emeritierung* there in 1994.[31] From 1982 to 1987, Habermas engaged in battle with various manifestations of the intellectual neoconservatism that he believed Kohl and his advisors embodied, from the Euromissile debate to a national debate on the meaning of the Nazi past. In October 1982, Habermas delivered a lecture to the Friedrich Ebert Foundation, the intellectual affiliate of the SPD, that bore the title, "Neoconservatism

[28] Ibid.
[29] Habermas, "Interview with T. H. Nielsen," *Nachholende Revolution*, 116.
[30] Habermas, "The Normative Content of Modernity," in *PDM*, 341.
[31] Wiggershaus, *Jürgen Habermas*, 112.

in the U.S. and the Federal Republic."[32] Writing after Genscher's resignation but before the dissolution of the Social-Liberal coalition, Habermas claimed that the ideological shape of the coming coalition was already visible. He quoted from a parliamentary speech Helmut Kohl had given the previous month in which he had spoken of a "spiritual-moral crisis" in West Germany.[33]

Neoconservatism was, Habermas believed, a symptom of a deep-rooted weakness of liberalism in Germany dating back to Bismarck. The National Liberals had had their "back" broken by Bismarck; today, Habermas declared, "That the National-Liberal wing of the FDP caused the domestic turn to neoconservatism is no historical accident."[34] Habermas surveyed both the domestic and foreign policy dimensions of neoconservatism. On the domestic side, technocratic leadership still threatened democracy:

> [Other neoconservatives] ... assume, in the frame of the technocratic thesis, that the intervention of the state should primarily be restricted to the role of a referee, simply to supervise the distribution of relevant competencies so that the legality of the functionally specific subdomains "independent of the general political decision-making process" can be applied.[35]

The force of the Euromissile debate seems particularly clear in his references to Carl Schmitt: Habermas argued that the neoconservatives used threats to internal and external security to legitimate their opposition to university reforms and curtailment of civil liberties (for example, restrictions on the right of demonstration).[36]

> [Following] ... Hobbes and Schmitt, [the neoconservatives] ... proceed from the claim that the state must legitimize itself by defending itself against foreign and domestic enemies. This perspective explains the priority of the problem of inner security, above all the stylization of a competition between *Rechtsstaat* and democracy.[37]

What accounts for the dire tone of this portrayal? Perhaps the arms race and its domestic implications had rattled Habermas. He

---

[32] Habermas, "Die Kulturkritik der Neokonservativen in den USA und in der Bundesrepublik," in *DNU*, 30–58.
[33] Ibid., 45.
[34] Habermas,"Neokonservativen," 54.
[35] Ibid., 51.
[36] Ibid., 65.
[37] Habermas, "Neokonservativen," 50.

spoke of the dangers posed by the rearmament "insanity."[38] By the late summer of 1982, Genscher was still trying to underscore the importance of the missiles for Germany's *Westbindung*, but in so doing he revived a language of friend and enemy that was foreign to the *Ostpolitik* that he had long represented.[39] This could have been the trigger for Habermas's remarks on the new Schmittianism. Since 1969, Willy Brandt had conducted a new version of *Ostpolitik* – initiatives with the USSR and Eastern Bloc countries aimed at reducing the danger of war and nurturing liberalization in the East through gestures of reconciliation. In 1972, West Germany signed the Basic Treaty with East Germany, thereby establishing formal diplomatic recognition between the two states for the first time.

The stationing of the Euromissiles was a watershed moment in postwar German political culture because it lifted the taboo on the discussion of German reunification. Helmut Kohl recommitted West Germany publicly to the cause of German reunification and believed in the value of a more confrontational politics with the USSR. The heightening of Cold War tensions during the Euromissile debate created an atmosphere reminiscent to Habermas of the conservative 1950s. Kohl's anticommunism reminded him of Adenauer's. But the political utility of rhetorical anticommunism was one thing, policy another. Kohl retained Genscher as foreign minister, thereby confirming his support for détente and maintenance of the treaties with Moscow and the German Democratic Republic (GDR). *Ostpolitik* was not dead, but the tone had changed.

When Kohl became CDU chairman in 1973, he argued that the party should emphasize the "value order"(*Wertordnung*) and "value-premises" of German democracy that bound it to NATO and the West.[40] This was the language of militant democracy employed during the 1950s by the Federal Constitutional Court that Habermas had contested. Now, as the Cold War reheated, the old language was revived. At a party conference in May 1980, Kohl charged that the SPD was "no longer speaking the same language" as it had when its post-1945 leaders, Kurt Schumacher, Ernst Reuter, and Carlo Schmid, had held power.[41] Kohl critiqued the SPD for

---

38 Honneth et al., "Dialektik," in DNU, 183.

39 Habermas, "Neokonservativen," 158: "We will not forget who our friend and ally is, and who is not our friend and ally … like the U.S.A., we are part of the West."

40 Herf, *War by Other Means*, 99.

41 Ibid., 110–11. Kohl's speech to annual party conference of CDU in May 1980

leading Germany down the path of "neutralization," conjuring the image of a gloomy anti-Americanism reminiscent of the SPD before it committed to NATO at the Bad Godesburg Conference in 1959. As Kohl said of the demonstrators who had massed in Bonn to protest the missiles: "The real problem in Bonn is that the contours between democrats and the enemies of democracy are blurring."[42] Like the protestors, Habermas rejected Kohl's claim that the peace movement blurred the boundary between the friends and enemies of democracy. Did this make Habermas a "neutralist" or "soft on communism"? Where did Habermas fit in this constellation of political language, and how much influence did he exert on the protest movement?

Habermas agreed with key premises shared by the leading intellectuals of the SPD's left wing – Willy Brandt, Egon Bahr, Oskar Lafontaine, and Erhard Eppler: The missiles were not necessary for West Germany's defense and endangered Europe as a whole. While he was not aligned with all the peace movement's positions, he stood close to Lafontaine and Joschka Fischer at this time.[43] Habermas asserted no moral equivalence between the superpowers. He had expressed no interest in German reunification since the early 1950s. In 1984, he stated: "... the German question is no longer open. The talk about a new German nationalism I consider meaningless."[44] Habermas did not believe West Germany should withdraw from NATO or cultivate a broader Gaullism of the left.[45]

One comprehensive study of the Euromissile crisis and its broad ideological repercussions argues that leading partisans of German withdrawal from NATO, such as Erhard Eppler, were influenced by the Frankfurt School critique of instrumental reason in general and Habermas's critique of technocracy in particular.[46] Eppler, the author of two of the most widely read critiques of the Euromissiles, was a Protestant member of the SPD Executive Committee and considered by Habermas a serious and thoughtful intellectual.[47]

[42] Ibid., 137.

[43] Author's private correspondence with Habermas, June 7, 2005.

[44] The context was a recent speech delivered by Willy Brandt in Munich. "The West German left has not the slightest reason to repeat this error." In Habermas, "Interview with the *New Left Review*," 251.

[45] See Herf, *War by Other Means*, 139, 149.

[46] Ibid., 124.

[47] Habermas, "Testfall," 45; Erhard Eppler, *Weg aus der Gefahr* (Reibek bei Hamburg: Rowohlt, 1981); *Die tödliche Utopie der Sicherheit* (Reinbek bei Hamburg: Rowohlt, 1983).

But Habermas did not stand near the center of an "internationalist mood."[48] This argument misses Habermas's clear endorsement of *Westbindung*. Habermas's positions from this period do represent a break with the political language of Adenauer and Schumacher's early Cold War antitotalitarian consensus. But, rather than signifying the erosion of moral standards or boundaries, it shows that Habermas reaffirmed *Westbindung* on his own terms. Where Kohl, Genscher, and CDU General Secretary Roland Geissler linked the commitment to the "intellectual and spiritual foundations of democracy" with unwavering allegiance to NATO, Habermas delinked the two issues.[49] This was not tantamount to delinking West Germany from the West, however. Through a sophisticated interpretation of civil disobedience, as we shall see in the concluding section of this chapter, Habermas redefined the "moral substance of democracy" of which Kohl and Geissler spoke.

Habermas concluded his 1982 lecture on the neoconservative cultural-political project by claiming that it represented a historic break with the "political culture of the *Bundesrepublik*" that had taken root after 1945:

> The Federal Republic opened itself to the West without reserve for the first time; we took up the political theory of the Enlightenment ... learned of religious pluralism, of the radical-democratic spirit of Pierce, Mead and Dewey. The neoconservatives turn away from these traditions.[50]

Habermas thus framed the coming CDU-FDP coalition as an expression of a German neoconservatism that was incompatible with the "political culture of the West." In the political context, this was a clever reformulation of the debate. Kohl saw himself as an *Adenauerianer* and consciously modeled his politics on the chancellor who had been the primary architect of West Germany's *Westbindung*. Meanwhile, in the 1980s, the SPD left and the Greens were still arguing that Adenauer had foreclosed the route to a united, demilitarized Germany. By describing the security thinking of the neoconservatives as an expression of traditional German statism, Habermas articulated a different vision of what linked Germany

[48] Herf, *War by Other Means*, 266.
[49] Ibid., 186.
[50] Habermas, "Die Neokonservativen," in *DNU*, 54.

to the West, which could counter the visions of both the neoconservatives and the neutralist left. In sum, Habermas tried to reinvent the Social Democratic language of *Westbindung* in a way that transcended the formulations of Adenauer, Schumacher, and Kohl alike.

"CONSTITUTIONAL PATRIOTISM" AS REBUKE TO BOTH THE NEOCONSERVATIVE RIGHT AND THE NEUTRALIST LEFT

Within two years of *die Wende*, Habermas was at the center of a different, acrimonious public debate. Kohl's commemorations of the fortieth anniversary of the Allied victory over Germany prompted a firestorm of controversy about how the Federal Republic should remember Nazism and the Holocaust. On May 8, 1985, President Reagan joined Kohl in a memorial service held at the Bitburg Cemetery, which housed the graves of former SS officers. The scandal of Bitburg gave new impetus to an existing debate over public memory and West German national identity. Kohl's push to establish museums of German history in Bonn and Berlin indicated that a struggle was underway concerning the right way to remember the Nazi past.

The *Historikerstreit* that unfolded in the feuilleton pages and in public symposia from 1985–7 centered on whether the Holocaust could be viewed as a singular event given the scale of mass murder that occurred under Soviet Communism. Was not "totalitarianism" the major foe of the twentieth century? Conservative historians Andreas Hillgruber and Ernst Nolte argued that Nazi crimes needed to be viewed in the context of Bolshevist and Stalinist mass murder.[51] As Habermas decoded the Bitburg affair:

> Whoever does Bergen-Belsen in the morning and in the afternoon arranges a meeting of war veterans in Bitburg has a different conception of things ... The juxtaposition ... of SS graves and the mass graves in a concentration camp took away the singularity of

[51] See Hans-Ulrich Wehler, "Den rationalen Argumenten standhalten," *Das Parlament* (May 17–24, 1986); cited in Habermas, "Eine Art Schadensabwicklung," (*EAS hereafter*) *Die Zeit* (July 11, 1986)], 134. Reprinted as "A Kind of Settlement of Damages (Apologetic Tendencies)," *New German Critique* 44 (Spring-Summer 1988), trans. Jeremy Leaman, 25–39.

> Nazi crimes. And finally the handshakes of the veteran generals in the presence of the American President could confirm that we Germans had always been on the right side in the struggle against the Bolshevist enemy.[52]

The impulse to relativize Nazi crimes seriously disturbed Habermas the '58er, eliciting several widely read critical essays between May 1985 and May 1987.[53] The Bitburg affair and the *Historikerstreit* drew Habermas in because they illustrated the threatening neoconservative impulses he had diagnosed in West German domestic and foreign policy since 1980. On the domestic front, Habermas rejected the morally relativizing implications of the comparison, treating it as part of a neoconservative cultural project, the roots of which he traced back to the early 1970s. Habermas's friend, the historian Hans-Ulrich Wehler, wrote that the *Historikerstreit* revealed "… symptoms of a minor 'cultural revolution' from the Right. The *Historikerstreit* doggedly continues the long conceptual and political struggle for hegemony which the neoconservatives have so zealously pursued."[54] The question of the correct historical understanding of the Nazi past was not merely an academic one but one with broad cultural-political stakes. Habermas believed that Kohl's domestic and foreign policy goals were of a piece. If German identity could be "normalized" through revisionist history-writing and museum work, German nationalism would be strengthened; a stronger national identity would enable excessive German assertiveness in *Mitteleuropa*.

Habermas's deployment of the concept of constitutional patriotism (*Verfassungspatriotismus*) was clearly designed as a discursive countermove to the conservative historians around Chancellor Kohl.[55] But less obvious is that his concept of constitutional patriotism also aimed to stem the threat of German neutralism and nationalist tendencies on the German left. Habermas interpreted

[52] Habermas, "Apologetische Tendenzen," in *EAS*, 122–3.

[53] "Entsorgung der Vergangenheit" [orig. *Die Zeit* (May 17, 1985)]; "Keine Normalisierung der Vergangenheit" [orig. "Der Intellektuelle ist mit seinem Gewissen nicht allein," *Süddeutsche Zeitung* (November 18, 1985)]; "Geschichtsbewusstein und posttraditionale Identitat," Sonning Prize Lecture, Copenhagen, May 14, 1987.

[54] Torpey, "Habermas and the Historians," 18. In his reading of the historians, Habermas was influenced by his friend, Hans-Ulrich Wehler, with whom he had attended Gymnasium in Gummersbach.

[55] Ibid.

Kohl's Bitburg visit as a symbolic staging of the Western Alliance for the purpose of defanging the German neutralism that had surfaced during the Euromissile debate:

> The *mise en scène* had the intention that a Federal Republic firmly anchored in the Atlantic community of values should regain national self-confidence through an identification with a past which can be agreed upon, without getting on to the false track of the *neutral nation-state*.[56]

A statement from historian Michael Stürmer, an advisor to Kohl, and Habermas's reaction to it illustrate the subterranean connection between the ostensibly separate *Historikerstreit* and Euromissile debates. Both concerned the problematic of *Westbindung*: "Our European neighbors want to know where are we headed," wrote Stürmer:

> The Federal Republic … is the centerpiece in the European arc of defense in the Atlantic system. However there are signs that every generation living in Germany has … opposing pictures of the past and future … The search for one's lost history is [not abstract] … it is a question of the inner continuity of the Federal Republic and of its foreign policy predictability.[57]

Habermas's response to Stürmer in July 1986 repeats an important figure of speech he had used in 1982: the "unreserved opening to the West"[58]:

> The unreserved opening of the Federal Republic to the political culture of the West is the great intellectual achievement of the postwar period, of which my generation in particular can be proud. The result will not be stabilized by a NATO philosophy colored by German nationalism. That opening has been achieved by overcoming precisely that ideology of the center which our revisionists are warming up to again with their geopolitical palaver of the "old central position of the Germans in Europe" [Stürmer] and "the reconstruction of the destroyed center of Europe" [Hillgruber].[59]

---

[56] Habermas, "Apologetische Tendenzen," 123 (emphasis added).

[57] Michael Stürmer, "Geschichte in geschichtslosem Land," [History in a Land without History], *Frankfurter Allgemeine Zeitung* (April 25, 1986). Cited by Habermas in *EAS*, 133.

[58] The German expression is "*vorbehaltlose Öffnung*."

[59] Habermas, "Apologetische Tendenzen," in *EAS*, 135.

Habermas argued that orientation to the West was not at issue in the *Historikerstreit*. The difference between the two camps was that "… one thinks of this in terms of military alliance and foreign policy, the other in terms of *Aufklärungskultur* [the political culture of the Enlightenment]."[60] Habermas's distinction is not entirely convincing because Geissler, Genscher, and Kohl also tried to defend *Westbindung* on the grounds of shared democratic values. Nonetheless, Habermas insisted that the neoconservatives' version of *Westbindung* would revive German nationalism. Influenced in the 1970s by psychologist Lawrence Kohlberg's writings on postconventional morality, Habermas insisted that a "postconventional identity" was the only appropriate identity for Germany.[61] In response to "the conservatives [who] would like to place a revisionist history" at the service of a "national-historical refurbishment of a conventional identity," Habermas proposed "constitutional patriotism" as the "only reliable basis for our link to the West."[62] Constitutional patriotism emerged therefore as a critique of Kohl's reduction of *Westbindung* to "NATO philosophy colored by German nationalism":

> The only patriotism which does not alienate us from the West is a constitutional patriotism. A commitment to the universalistic constitutional principles which is anchored by conviction has unfortunately only been able to develop in the German *Kulturnation* since – and because of – Auschwitz. Whoever wishes to exorcise the shame surrounding this fact with such phrases as the obsession with guilt [Stürmer and Oppenheimer], whoever wishes to pull Germans back to a conventional form of national identification, is destroying *the only reliable basis for our link to the West.*[63]

The "majority of the historians' guild," wrote Habermas, following Wehler, had "always thought and argued in terms of Reich nationalism, statist consciousness and power politics."[64] Historiography should aim at enlightenment, not social integration. Habermas characterized Stürmer's vision of historiography in terms

---

60 Habermas, "Westorientierung der Bundesrepublik," in *EAS*, 162.
61 See, for example, Lawrence Kohlberg, *Essays on Moral Development* (San Francisco: Harper and Row, 1981).
62 Habermas, "Apologetische Tendenzen," in *EAS*, 133.
63 Ibid., 135 (emphasis added).
64 Ibid.

that recall his critique of both technocracy and the paternalistic welfare state: A citizen could never be autonomous if meaning and identity are provided for him[65]: "Whomever allows himself to be guided by functional imperatives of calculability, consensus formation and social integration by means of the provision of meaning, must shun the enlightening effect of historiography."[66] Through a close study of the theory and practice of civil disobedience, Habermas arrived at the conclusion that the task of *Westbindung* was too important to be left to the historians or to NATO's security planners.

DYNAMICS OF THE DEBATE ON THE RIGHT OF RESISTANCE: A CHANCE AND TWO DANGERS

The Bonn demonstration against the NATO decision on deployment was the biggest in West German history,[67] but Habermas made no public statement about it. He entered the public debate on the matter for the first time in 1983; by then, the stationing of missiles was essentially a fait accompli. The state's identification of "inner enemies" is what lured him into the debate. In 1983, the *Rechtsstaat* appeared to him threatened by authoritarian legalism in a manner reminiscent of the previous decade: "In the name of militant democracy [*wehrhafte Demokratie*] the patriots of the fall of 1977 emerged, smelling inner enemies and not grasping that the legitimacy of *rechtsstaatlichen* institutions rests in the end on the non-institutionalizable mistrust of the citizens."[68] Once engaged in the debate, Habermas found a discussion of the right of resistance that oscillated between two poles. Each side in the Euromissile debate drew its own lessons from German history, but neither was convincing to him. The left used the terms "nuclear Auschwitz" and "nuclear Holocaust" to legitimate its call for resistance to deployments it saw as suicidal for Germany. The right invoked the failed appeasement policies of the 1930s. Habermas chafed against a debate structured by these antinomies.

---

65 Ibid.
66 Ibid.
67 Herf, *War by Other Means*, 137.
68 Habermas, "Über den doppelten Boden des demokratischen Rechtsstaates" [1985], in *EAS*, 23.

In the parliamentary debate on the missiles in June, Joschka Fischer of the Greens said: "I am not making an analogy with Auschwitz, but I say that Auschwitz warns us to denounce this logic [of preparing means of mass annihilation]." Using the language of the technocracy debate, Fischer stated that the "atomic holocaust" will be the result of "objective-technical necessities [*Sachzwängen*]."[69] In other words, atomic technology would compromise democratic decision-making. Geissler responded with the claim that it was pacifism (the British pacifism of the 1930s) that made Auschwitz possible – an argument that led to a storm of SPD and Green protest and calls for Geissler's dismissal.[70] Kohl defended Geissler, saying that "the so-called peace movement" tries to put the West "on the moral defensive" by "morally equating the policy" of the United States and the USSR. The "Geissler affair" of June 1983 illustrates how the missile debate was acutely intertwined with the politics of memory of the Nazi past.

Habermas was concerned that the peace movement might invoke the right of resistance codified in Article 20 (Section 4) of the Basic Law. It reads: "All Germans shall have the right to resist any person seeking to abolish this constitutional order, if no other remedy is available." On September 26, 1983, Habermas participated in a forum of the SPD devoted to rebuttal of the arguments made that summer in Bad Godesburg at a conference entitled, "The Right to Resistance" (*Recht auf Widerstand*).[71] On the right, civil disobedience was being treated as an ordinary crime, and even peaceful resistance was being interpreted as a violent act. Habermas's contribution to the debate, "Civil Disobedience: Test-Case for the Democratic Constitutional State," is a little-noted but extremely important essay.[72] At that forum, SPD Secretary General Peter Glotz worried that if anybody died in the course of the protests, he or she could become "the Benno Ohnesorg of the eighties."[73] In other words, the

---

[69] Herf, *War by Other Means*, 189–90.

[70] Ibid., 185–92.

[71] Conference of the Cultural Forum of the SPD. Papers collected in Peter Glotz, ed., *Ziviler Ungehorsam im Rechtsstaat* (Frankfurt/Main: Suhrkamp, 1983).

[72] Habermas, "Ziviler Ungehorsam – Testfall für den demokratischen Rechtsstaat. Wider den autoritären Legalismus in der Bundesrepublik," in *DNU*, 79–99.

[73] Peter Glotz, "Nachwort," in *Ziviler Ungehorsam Ziviler Ungehorsam im Rechtsstaat*, ed. Peter Glotz (Frankfurt/Main: Suhrkamp, 1983), 150.

situation could spiral out of control. "Never before in the Federal Republic have so many people taken to the streets for a political goal which many of us consider pressing and rational," wrote Habermas in the immediate wake of the movement's "Week of Action" in late October 1983.[74] The unprecedented scale of mobilization and the widespread practice of civil disobedience by the peace movement in response to the Euromissile debate marked "a turning point in the political culture of the Federal Republic." The practice of "nonviolent resistance" by thousands "… [gave] the public, for the first time, the chance to liberate itself from a paralyzing trauma and look without fear on the previously taboo question of the formation of radical democratic consciousness."[75] Civil disobedience was the major tactic used by the Euromissiles' opponents. Two of Habermas's former research assistants at the Max Planck Institute in Starnberg, Ernst Tugendhat and Claus Offe, were among the members of the so-called Promi-Blockade ("blockade by the prominent") in which protesters formed "human chains" to blockade a U.S. depot of Pershing missiles in Mutlangen from August 30 to September 3. Prominent politicians and intellectuals such as Oskar Lafontaine, Petra Kelly, Erhard Eppler, Heinrich Böll, and Heinrich Göllwitzer also participated.

In the two essays Habermas wrote on the subject of the peace movement and civil disobedience, he took a strong position against the missiles on policy grounds.[76] The installation of "first-strike atomic weapons" caused a "destabilization of the relation between the superpowers," Habermas wrote. His characterization of the Pershing missiles as first-strike weapons clearly identifies him as an anti-Euromissile partisan. But he took pains to be clear that he was neither calling for civil disobedience nor endorsing the position that there should be a formal right to it: "I find myself in the role of a sympathizer who inclines towards an affirmative answer" on whether breeches of the law can be justified as civil disobedience.[77] Habermas implied that individuals who broke the law were patriotic and morally courageous, but they should have to bear the legal consequences of their decision. That emergency measures were being

[74] Habermas, "Recht und Gewalt. Ein Deutsches Trauma," in *DNU*, 100; "Right and Violence: A German Trauma," in *Cultural Critique* 1 (Autumn 1985), 125–39.
[75] Ibid., 101.
[76] Habermas, "Recht und Gewalt," 116.
[77] Ibid., 114.

considered in response to the civil disobedience and criminal penalties were being augmented as he wrote gave Habermas's theoretical considerations practical urgency.[78]

"Those who still follow the ever less accountable U.S. government – if not for military, than for political reasons – will have to try to somehow break out of the fatal logic of the arms race,"[79] he urged. By taking this position in-between, Habermas reenacted the position he occupied in 1967–9 when he sought to carve out a space between the technocratic conservatives and their "actionist" opponents. In both episodes, Habermas positioned himself in the role of friendly critic of the left and determined opponent of the right. As in 1967–9, so too now he saw the potential for a dangerous dialectic of misrecognition: The state would imagine a violent citizenry, and the citizenry would imagine a violent state. Each would confirm the other's projection, he believed, and a self-fulfilling prophecy would result.

The first dangerous scenario Habermas envisioned was that peacefully practiced civil disobedience would degenerate into violent resistance. The second was that the state, having already stiffened criminal penalties for civil disobedience in the CDU-led states, would go further, perhaps declaring a state of emergency.[80] With the stationing of the missiles nearly a foregone conclusion, the situation could deteriorate sharply. The *Rechtsstaat* appeared to Habermas to be threatened from two sides: "instrumentalism," or lawlessness, on the one hand, and an "authoritarian legalism," on the other, that "draws the line" between legality (*Recht*) and violence in the wrong place.[81] Habermas assumed a place in the debate that was again – characteristically for this '58er – "in between."

The protestor must "prove scrupulously" whether the choice of "spectacular means" is appropriate and not a expression of elite conviction or narcissistic desire. The state, meanwhile, must recognize the historical contingency of its laws. Habermas argued that because civil disobedience moves in the "twilight of contemporary history," it is hard to judge it from a present-day perspective. From this sense that historical actors are inevitably morally fallible, he

[78] Habermas, "Testfall," 51. The CDU had recently changed the criminal law on demonstrations.

[79] Habermas, "Recht und Gewalt," 100.

[80] Habermas, "Testfall," 51.

[81] Habermas, "Recht und Gewalt," 104.

urged "restraint on both sides."[82] But the greater weight of his critique was aimed at the right. Habermas ascribed an "intimidating definitional power" to the dominant tradition in German jurisprudence, which he termed the "authoritarian-legalistic." The defining characteristic of, and chief problem with, this "... German line of ... constitutional state-thinking" is that questions of legitimation are subsumed under the problem of the guarantee of their legality, which thereby "permits them to be avoided."[83] Here we see themes percolating in Habermas's thought and rhetoric with a pedigree stretching back to the 1950s debates over German statism. Originating in "that curiously effective Hobbesianism elaborated in German constitutional theory by Carl Schmitt,"[84] its effects are dramatically clear. Habermas accorded the jurists a leading role in the drama that surrounded the citizen mobilization against the Euromissiles: The "tenor of public debate" is chiefly shaped by the "state-supporting dogma" of "the law is the law mentality."[85] Moreover, the political class opposed it as well: "The President of the Federal Constitutional Court, the government, the opinion leaders among politicians and journalists present [the dominant] opinion among German jurists: that illegal protest is not only punishable but also morally reprehensible."[86] Habermas placed the lion's share of responsibility for the weaknesses of German political culture on its jurists.

Habermas's frustration with the politics of law in the Euromissile debate was not simply attributable to his position on the losing side of one battle, however. In essence, Habermas feared that the tradition of authoritarian legalism was responsible for a version of the German *Sonderweg* (special path of development), that is, that the retardation and truncation of German democracy had roots stretching into the nineteenth century. The statist bias of German jurisprudence stemmed from legal relationships that Habermas provocatively labeled "premodern": "These conventional concepts of the state, which stem from premodern legal relationships, truncate the

82 Habermas, "Testfall," 41.

83 Habermas, "Recht und Gewalt," 108.

84 Ibid., 107. Disappointingly, Habermas has not drawn fine enough distinctions between Hobbes and Schmitt to help us categorize the neoconservatives more precisely. See also "Recht und Gewalt," 113; "Neokonservativen," 50.

85 Habermas, "Testfall," 35.

86 Ibid., 101; "Right and Violence," 126.

moral foundations and political culture of a developed democratic community."[87] Given Habermas's contemporaneous call to complete the "project of modernity," the clear implication is that statist German jurisprudence stood in the way of completing Germany's modernity. This conjuncture in German politics was both a crisis and an opportunity for Germany to mature:

> As the comparison with the student movement teaches, the present movement gives us the *first chance*, even in Germany, to grasp civil disobedience as an element of a ripe political culture.[88]
>
> The practice gives the German public, for the first time, the chance to liberate itself from a paralyzing trauma and to look without fear on the previously taboo question of the formation of a radical democratic consciousness. The danger is that *this chance – which other countries with a longer democratic tradition … have integrated productively* – will be passed up.[89]

It was no accident that Habermas invested in the practice of civil disobedience his hope for an epochal maturation of German public life. On January 30, 1983, Germans were confronted with the fiftieth anniversary of Hitler's seizure of power. Anniversaries in the Federal Republic were an important occasion for the construction and reconstruction of public memory. Getting the concept of "resistance" right in 1983 thus meant preventing misuses of the legacy of the resistance shown by the plotters of July 20, 1944, and the members of the White Rose. Understanding what distinguished civil disobedience from resistance meant being able to grasp what distinguished the "halfway functioning constitutional state" in Bonn from Hitler's tyranny.[90] Inflating dissent and symbolic protest into resistance seemed to devalue the wartime acts of resistance and risked incurring disproportionate repression by the state.

Civil disobedience differed from resistance in three ways, Habermas explained: It did not challenge the entire legal order, it appealed to the "legal sensibility" of the majority, and it made this appeal in the name of explicit constitutional values. Habermas

---

87 Habermas, "Testfall," 43.

88 Ibid., 32.

89 Habermas, "Recht und Gewalt," 101; "Right and Violence," 126 (emphasis added).

90 The phrase is Habermas's own. See Habermas, "Introduction," *Spiritual Situation of the Age*, 11 (orig. at *Kleine Politische Schriften* I-IV, 411–41).

evidently was influenced by John Rawls's definition that civil disobedience consists of "public, peaceful, conscience-determined, illegal actions which usually seek a change in the laws. "[91] "Until now," the movement protesting the Euromissiles had "expressed in word and deed" the idea that actions, including calculated breeches of the law, must maintain a "symbolic" character; that is, they may only be carried out with the intention of "... appealing to the understanding and legal sensibility of the majority."[92] By contrast, the student movement of 1967–9 had been inspired by false notions (*Vorbilder*) of revolution and "lacked the identification with the constitutional principles of a democratic republic."[93] The students' failure to identify with the constitution thus "left in suspense" whether their "political resistance" (*Widerstand*) was legal protest or revolutionary action (*Kampfhandlung*).[94] Habermas declared, "It is precisely this lack of clarity which I cannot discern in the peace movement." By this logic, he concluded that the peace movement represented a clear advance over the student movement.

Habermas criticized the jurists for conflating the issues raised by civil disobedience with the question of resistance against an illegal state.[95] "The fact of German Hobbesianism explains why there are so many arguments today that psychiatrists would call tangential responses: answers to questions that were not posed. The issue confronting us is not resistance against an illegal state, but rather civil disobedience within the *Rechtsstaat*."[96] But, in fact, Habermas was concerned that the peace movement's use of the language of resistance was ambiguous and could lead to dangerous misunderstandings: "Certainly, the talk is of peaceful *resistance* [*Widerstand*]," but Habermas noticed that a minority of the protestors continued to invoke their constitutional right of resistance under Article 20, Section 4, and criticized them for it, insisting that they "... should abandon all indirect references to this type of constitutionality."[97] He chided Marburg theologian (and future bishop) Wolfgang

[91] Habermas, "Testfall," 34. For his discussion of Rawls, see "Testfall," 34–8. See also John Rawls, *A Theory of Justice* (1971); first German trans. *Eine Theorie der Gerechtigkeit* (Frankfurt/Main: Suhrkamp, 1975).

[92] Habermas, "Testfall," 32–3.

[93] Ibid, 32.

[94] Ibid, 33.

[95] Habermas, "Recht und Gewalt," 110.

[96] Ibid.

[97] Habermas, "Testfall," 33.

Huber, for example, for "… [taking] cover under the weighty obligation of the church to 'resistance at the right time.'"[98] In context, therefore, Habermas's position represented a clear dissent from the invocation of the right of resistance by many other important figures in the Green Party and the peace movement, raising the question: Why would Habermas distance himself from a right anchored in the constitution itself?

At an SPD-sponsored event in the Frankfurt *Paulskirche* convened on January 30 to mark the fiftieth anniversary of Hitler's seizure of power, novelist Günter Grass drew a direct analogy between the impending danger represented by the missiles and the failure to resist Hitler's assumption of power:

> If against all reason, the middle range rockets come on German soil, resistance is the only recourse.… We are falling under a dictatorship of technocracy and becoming a surveillance state. The two trends reinforce each other. With the stationing of the missiles, the internal security needs of the state increase.[99]

In parliamentary debate in June, Green Party delegate Otto Schilly claimed the German antifascist resistance as "… our historical reference point, to which we have oriented ourselves politically."[100] While another Germany could have arisen from its antifascist resistance, instead, the two states had become vassals of the Cold War. Schilly thus reproduced a long-established narrative about Adenauer's role in foreclosing the option of a neutral, unified, demilitarized Germany. On July 6, the Bremen SPD fraction invoked the constitutional right of resistance, arguing that "… parliamentary majorities do not legitimate NATO governments to raise the danger of a nuclear war which would make their own peoples victims."[101] Grass, Schilly, and the Bremen SPD spoke the language of resistance with pathos.

While Habermas conceded that the notion of resistance was a powerful mobilizing tool, he concluded that by using the language

98 Habermas, "Recht und Gewalt," 106.

99 Günter Grass, "Vom Recht auf Widerstand," Rede bei der Gedenkveranstaltung der SPD zum 50. Jahrestag von Hitlers Machtergreifung am 30. Januar 1983 in Frankfurt, in idem, *Widerstand Lernen. Politische Gegenreden, 1980–83* (Darmstadt and Neuwied: Luchterhand, 1984), 65–6.

100 Herf, *War by Other Means*, 189; Habermas, "Testfall," 51.

101 Herf, *War by Other Means*, 193.

of resistance, however loosely or metaphorically, the movement was playing into the hands of the conservatives.[102] Grass's statements made him an easy target; his speech had been denounced at the conference on the right of resistance as that of a "belated resistance-fighter."[103] As one professor of constitutional law and former judge wrote, "Without the bad German conscience about the state (*Staatsgewissen*), this resistance would not be possible."[104] He complained that the invocation of the right of resistance by "house-occupiers, environmental protectors, anti-nuclear energy fanatics and other 'alternative people' … means a sell-off of the right of resistance at rock-bottom prices."[105] Josef Isensee, another professor of law, captured the essence of the conservative critique with his comment that this resistance "… aims at National Socialist domination but it hits the parliamentary democracy of the Basic Law."[106]

Conservatives at the conference also exploited the semantic ambiguity of the word "resistance"; its blurriness facilitated their attempt to discredit the left's distinction between active (violent) and passive (nonviolent) resistance. "Resistance, be it with violence or without it, destroys our constitutional order," they insisted.[107] This view was widely disseminated by government and media. "For months," noted Habermas in October, "the Justice Minister and Interior Minister of the federal government have been singing the refrain … even 'violence-free resistance is violence.'"[108] Habermas was referring to the fact that protestors who had restricted others' freedom of movement by forming human chains were being construed by the authorities as violent actors. This, in turn, raised the

102 Habermas, "Testfall," 33–4.

103 Josef Isensee, "Ein Grundrecht auf Ungehorsam gegen das demokratische Gesetz? Legitimation und Perversion des Widerstandsrechts," in *Frieden im Lande. Vom Recht auf Widerstand*, ed. Basilius Streithofen (Bergisch-Gladbach: Bastei Lübbe, 1983), 156. Isensee was professor of public law at Bonn.

104 Arthur Kaufmann, "The Small-Coin Right of Resistance: An Admonition to Civil Courage," in *Prescriptive Formality and Normative Rationality in Modern Legal Systems: Festschrift for Robert S. Summers*, eds. Werner Krawietz and Neil MacCormick (Berlin: Duncker & Humblot, 1994), 573–9. Kaufmann, professor of law at the University of Munich and a former judge, also was the editor of Radbruch's twenty-volume *Gesamtausgabe*.

105 Arthur Kaufmann, "Small Coin Right," 573.

106 Isensee, "Grundrecht auf Ungehorsam," 155–6.

107 Streithofen, "Einführung," in *Frieden im Lande*, 11.

108 Habermas, "Testfall," 29.

issue of whether coercion of a psychological character represented "violence." Isensee argued that the juridical concept of nonviolence excluded restrictions on the freedom of movement of a third party; Habermas sided with another law professor, who argued, on the contrary, that the "freedom from violence" did not preclude the application of psychological pressure.[109] With obvious anger, Habermas dismissed the media's distorted picture of these tactics: "[T]hey report about these plans as if about war-preparations of an attacker who threatens national security."[110] "It is only a step from contempt for the moral-political motivating principles of those who breach the law to the disqualification of the protestor as an enemy of the state."[111] Habermas feared that the state was poised to misjudge the severity of threats to the liberal democratic order, much as it had in 1977. Criminalizing protest was wrong.

One strategy that the peace movement used to fight back against its criminalization was to claim that it acted in the name of explicit constitutional rights. Habermas argued that weapons of mass destruction might indeed constitute an injustice (*Unrecht*), but he could find no grounds for describing them as an "obvious infraction of the basic rights."[112] He thus weighed the protestors' arguments on the basis of a constitutional right to life and safety from bodily injury and the fundamental obligation of the state to maintain peace, but ultimately he rejected them on the grounds that these arguments as easily could be invoked by the advocates of nuclear deterrence.[113]

Nor was Habermas convinced by the more innovative constitutional arguments proposed by some of the leading figures in the dissenting or "critical" legal tradition, explaining that "[o]verreactions by the state make it understandable that critical jurists want to legalize [a right to civil disobedience]."[114] He admitted there were "good grounds" for recent efforts to legalize civil disobedience through an expanded interpretation of the rights to demonstration and

109 Ralf Dreier, "Widerstandsrecht und ziviler Ungehorsam im Rechtsstaat," in Glotz, *Ziviler Ungehorsam*, 62. Dreier was professor for general legal theory at the University of Göttingen.
110 Habermas, "Testfall," 31–2.
111 Habermas, "Recht und Gewalt," 102.
112 Habermas, "Testfall," 45.
113 Habermas, "Testfall," 45.
114 Ibid., 42.

assembly.[115] But Habermas did not accept any of these efforts. Why? It seems that neither criminalization nor formal legalization of a right to civil disobedience was compatible with his distinct vision of the democratic idea of law.

According to a Rawlsian definition that Habermas accepted, civil disobedience is a "morally grounded act" that must appeal to publicly recognized principles.[116] In September 1982, an article critical of the protestors appeared in *Die Zeit* under the title, "The Search for Absolutes."[117] In his rebuttal, Habermas argued that Henry Thoreau and Martin Luther King "... did not absolutize their private convictions but rather, appealed to principles in the constitution."[118] The connection between publicness and legitimacy, Habermas explained, follows the Kantian intuition that general principles derive their validity from the fact that they could be freely assented to by all those affected. The "unusually high legitimation claim" of the modern constitutional state (*Verfassungsstaat*) is that it is based on free recognition of its normative qualities. "The state can only expect legal obedience if, and insofar as, it relies on principles worthy of recognition, in whose light then, what is legal can be justified as legitimate."[119] The legitimacy of legality depended indirectly on its quality as a publicly recognizable norm.

Habermas argued that Thoreau and King did not "absolutize" their private convictions but rather claimed valid constitutional principles as the source of the legitimacy of their acts. According to jurist Martin Kriele, Dr. King did not attempt a juristic justification for civil disobedience; he never said that the police should not defend the laws or that the judges should not apply the criminal laws. By accepting the legitimacy of legal sanctions, King highlighted the discrepancy between positive law and moral injustice, but from the perspective of fidelity to a higher law: the morality of natural law. Dr. King's citations from St. Thomas Aquinas in his "Letter from a Birmingham Jail" illustrated this feature of King's

[115] Ibid. Also see Helmut Simon,"Fragen der Verfassungspolitik," in Glotz, *Ziviler Ungehorsam*, 99–107.
[116] Habermas, "Testfall," 35.
[117] Christian von Krockow, "Die Versuchung des Absoluten," *Die Zeit* (September 2, 1983). Cited in Habermas, "Testfall," 44. See Kriele, "Widerstandsrecht in der Demokratie? Über die Legitimität der Staatsgewalt," in *Frieden im Lande*, 43.
[118] Habermas, "Testfall."
[119] Ibid.

thought: " Unjust law is that which has fallen out of harmony with the moral law. An unjust law is a human law that is not rooted in the perpetual and in the natural law."[120] Kriele's argument was one factor driving Habermas to define civil disobedience in terms other than natural law. The rhetorical strategies of the peace movement must have appeared to blur the key boundary between public and private morality: "Any action based on some or other private morality [*Privatmoral*], a special right [*Sonderrecht*] or a privileged access to truth" forfeits its claim to legitimacy, Habermas argued.[121]

One suspects that Habermas's argument was prompted by a strong tendency in the rhetoric of the peace movement to counterpose women's supposedly superior capacity for peace-making to the inherently belligerent propensities of men. As one historian of the movement has written: "This sense of women's special mystical powers, of which however it seems men could sometimes partake – was crucial to the peace coalition that brought millions together."[122] Similarly, militarism was anatomized as a form of "male madness" and counterposed to the higher rationality of women's fear. Women's "… greater emotional capacity and awareness (for many but not all, a function of their ability to bear children)" ostensibly made them better judges of the threat posed by the nuclear arms race. Green Party leader Petra Kelly, for example, "… averred that overweening power of technology could only be counteracted by embrace of nature and God: by 'reconciling with oneself with the cosmos', an act she associated most closely with women."[123] Habermas may well have categorized this argument as a privileged claim to truth.

Alternatively, Habermas may have decided that the political price for purchasing a new constitutional right was too high or the rhetoric too histrionic. Activist Dorothée Sölle equated German "slavery" to U.S. foreign policy with African-American slavery.[124] Helmut Simon similarly had argued at an Evangelical Church conference in Hannover that the moral unacceptability of the use of

[120] Martin Luther King, Jr., "Letter from a Birmingham Jail" and "I Have a Dream." Atlanta: Southern Christian Leadership Conference, 1963.

[121] Habermas, "Testfall," 36–7.

[122] Belinda Davis, "The Gender of War and Peace: Rhetoric in the West German Peace Movement of the Early 1980s," *Mitteilungsblatt des Instituts für Soziale Bewegungen* (Special Issue, "Peace Movements As Social Movements") 32 (Dec. 2004), 103.

[123] Davis,"Gender of War," 126.

[124] Ibid., 129.

weapons of mass extermination was comparable to slavery and from his seat on the Federal Constitutional Court endorsed a constitutional amendment banning nuclear weapons.[125] Habermas may not have wanted to squander moral resources on hyperbolic arguments or risk comparisons with the kind of moral argumentation from "traditional values" for which he faulted German conservatives. To the question, how could basic norms (*Grundnormen*) be justified, Habermas excluded the "… today-popular return to a material value order."[126] In either case, adding new constitutional rights would have added power to the conservative judges whose job it would be to interpret and enforce them. Moral progress was less likely to come by fiat from Karlsruhe than from protest in Bonn, he reasoned. Democracy was not just about the content of decisions but also about how they were produced. Habermas feared the countermajoritarian power of judges and insisted that legislation remain the *via regia* to democratic decision-making.

The argument for civil disobedience most compelling to Habermas was that decisions concerning German security policy possessed a distinct moral gravity that demanded a higher degree of legitimation than a simple majority vote of the *Bundestag*.[127] Habermas proffered the argument that representative democracy must at times be supplemented or superseded by a plebiscitary element. Habermas pointed out that the potential irreversibility of security decisions raised the threshold for legitimating them to this higher democratic level: "In the face of a provocation like the uncontrolled arms race, the citizens must intervene directly in their role as sovereign and give notice that corrections or revisions are overdue."[128] Despite its potential countermajoritarian implications, Habermas justified the "plebiscitary pressure of civil disobedience" on the ground that it might be the "last chance" to correct errors. If the

> … representative constitution fails before demands which concern all, then the people, in the form of its citizens … must be allowed to assume the originary rights of the sovereign. The democratic

[125] Habermas, "Testfall," 48; "Recht und Gewalt ," 114–7. Simon was elected by the SPD and served from 1970–87.
[126] Ibid., 38. See Chapters 1, 2, and 5 for further discussion of value jurisprudence.
[127] Ibid., 48–50.
[128] Habermas, "Recht und Gewalt," 112.

Rechtsstaat is in the last instance directed to this guardian of [its] legitimacy.[129]

With these arguments, Habermas left himself vulnerable to the criticisms of jurists such as Isensee and Kriele, who emphasized the undemocratic implications of his argument: "The democratic constitution gives neither individuals nor groups the right … against the will of the population and against its democratic representatives, to raise itself up to the guardian of the constitution. The right of resistance is not a substitute for the general democratic discourse and cannot be its legitimate conclusion."[130] Kriele further noted that intellectual appeals to a moral majority were undemocratic, sarcastically stating that "[w]e the majority of the democratic citizens are intellectually dull and morally deaf.… If we are corrected by the enlightened and sensible elite, this is only for our own good."[131] On the Social Democratic left, too, Peter Glotz expressed the concern that right-wing groups could take advantage of the identical plebiscitary argument for their own issues.[132]

There were other ironies and tensions in Habermas's argument. Habermas's claim that civil disobedience represented an opportunity for Germany to become "mature" was contradicted by his concession that the practice of civil disobedience requires a political culture tolerant of it in the first place. His claim that civil disobedience could be justified only under conditions of a "fully intact *Rechtsstaat*" was in tension with his description of it as the appropriate response to a threat of a severe or imminent "breakdown" of the *Rechtsstaat*. On the other hand, Habermas described civil disobedience as a mode of experimentation that functioned as the "moral pacesetter" for both societal evolution and constitutional "innovation."[133] "In these cases," he explained, "infractions of civil law are morally grounded experiments without which a vital republic can preserve neither its capacity for innovation nor the faith of its citizens."[134] In Habermas's hands, civil disobedience had both conservative and

129 Habermas, "Testfall," 88; see also "Recht und Gewalt," 112–3.
130 Isensee, "Ein Grundrecht auf Ungehorsam," in Streithofen, *Frieden im Lande*, 165.
131 Kriele, "Widerstandsrecht in der Demokratie?" 150.
132 Glotz, "Nachwort," 148–9.
133 Habermas, "Testfall," 41.
134 Ibid., 40–1. Habermas cites Dworkin, "Civil Disobedience," in *Taking Rights Seriously* (Cambridge, MA: Harvard UP, 1977).

progressive functions: It could function conservatively as the measure of last resort for averting a great threat, or promote social progress. In his struggle with German statism, explicating the qualities of civil disobedience helped Habermas to work out a new framework for combining legality and legitimacy.

THE "NONIDENTICAL" *RECHTSSTAAT* AS SYNTHESIS

To escape the antinomies of the debate on the right of resistance, Habermas had to craft a new account of the democratic *Rechtsstaat*. Neither the "authoritarian-legalist" nor the moral resistance fighter fully grasped democratic citizenship, he explained. The authoritarian legalist downplayed the question of legitimacy or argued that representative institutions secured sufficient legitimacy for any decision of the majority. The critical jurist or moral resistance fighter who sought to legalize his resistance diluted and devalued legal order and moral protest equally. Both the criminalization of civil disobedience and its legalization drained the reservoir of legitimacy on which democratic legality drew.[135] Habermas proffered an illuminating metaphor: Civil disobedience must remain *suspended between* legality and legitimacy; only then could it signal that the democratic *Rechtsstaat* "points beyond" its legitimating constitutional principles.[136] Habermas's introduction of the concept of "remaining in suspense" (*in der Schwebe bleiben*) was the critical move. There is a "relationship of tension" between legality and legitimacy that must be maintained if democracy is to retain its open, evolving character: in short, its "modern" sense of time.[137]

The repression of civil disobedience by authoritarian jurists focused Habermas's mind on how close the spheres of legality and morality stood to each other. Civil disobedience was no "normal crime," Habermas argued, because it derived a specific "dignity" from the highest legitimation claims of the democratic *Rechtsstaat*. Judges and prosecutors who failed to "respect this dignity" by applying the normal criminal penalties fell "… into an *authoritarian*

[135] Habermas, "Recht und Gewalt," 112–3.
[136] Habermas, "Testfall," 43.
[137] Habermas, "Testfall," 38. See also Habermas, "Modernity's Consciousness of Time," in *PDM*, 7, 12.

legalism." Convinced of the specific dignity of the practice, Habermas sought to understand this moral intuition. Following Rawls's usage, Habermas named civil disobedience a "touchstone [*Prüfstein*] for the ripeness of a political culture."[138] By explicating the specific dignity of civil disobedience, he reenchanted the *Rechtsstaat*. This reenchantment in the Weberian sense – drawing the link to morality closer – served Habermas's political need to effectively counter the right's effort to monopolize the moral high ground. Further, reenchanting the *Rechtsstaat* suited Habermas's perennial need to rectify the moral deficit in Weber's theory of modernity.[139] But this was a delicate undertaking because collapsing the distinction between the two would flirt with a revival of natural law thinking, which represented a philosophical regression from the perspective of the secular status of modernity.[140] Nonetheless, the greater threat to Habermas' mind clearly was that posed by legal positivism's reduction of legitimacy to legality. Habermas sought a middle path between legal positivism and natural law, each of which was associated with a different dimension of German statism. He sought a way to draw legality and morality closer together without collapsing the two.

Habermas found his solution via a critique of the authoritarian vision of law. Its shortcomings appear to have spurred Habermas's insights. Authoritarian legalism was blind to the productive tension that connected the rule of law to democratic practice. Habermas twice repeated the notion that there was "no room" or "space within" this vision for his insight. His use of this evocative spatial metaphor suggests that he had experienced the German tradition in question as a constraining one:

> Such a theory [the authoritarian-legalistic]...must consider political culture as unimportant. For it, where legal order stops, sudden rebellion, if not revolution, begins. *There is no room* for an in-between, a political culture [*politischen Kultur*] ... where, as Hegel would have said, the ethical-moral life [*Sittlichkeit*] of a people is played out. *There is no room* for a place where the legitimation beliefs

[138] Habermas, "Testfall," 36.

[139] Habermas correspondence with author, May 30–June 7, 2005: Question: "Would you agree that throughout your career, you have been concerned with the democratic deficit in the thinking of Max Weber?" Answer: "More or less so, yes."

[140] See Chapters 1 and 2 for further discussion of natural law in jurisprudence.

> of the citizens regenerate from moral convictions. This sphere of life is normatively structured underneath the threshold of legal norm-foundation; it is the ground in which the *Rechtsstaat* is morally rooted.[141]

Habermas thus envisioned the relationship between legality and morality along a vertical axis with legality above and morality below. With his choice of the organic imagery of legality being "rooted" in morality and thus furnishing its "ground," Habermas thought he had solved the paradoxical task of the *Rechtsstaat*:

> The paradox of the *Rechtsstaat* is that it must embody positive law, but also stand for principles which transcend it, and by which positive law may be judged. The *Rechtsstaat*, wanting to remain identical with itself, stands before a paradoxical task. It must protect ... against injustice that may emerge in legal forms, although this mistrust cannot take an institutionally secured form. With this idea of a non-institutionalizable mistrust of itself, the *Rechtsstaat projects itself over* the entirety of its positive law.[142]

Habermas claimed that the paradox can be resolved by citizens of a "mature" political culture because they alone show the "sense of judgment" necessary to decide how to act in relation to unjust laws, or majority decisions, with which they disagree. Civil disobedience was thereby figured as a necessary component of a successful *Rechtsstaat*.

Habermas thus arrived at a new formulation of an old conviction, namely, that democracy has moral foundations. Now civil disobedience became the privileged site from which to know them. This was an updated vision of the classical doctrine of politics that had been obscured, Habermas had argued around 1960, by the elite theorists of democracy. In the place of the closure afforded by a revolutionary proletariat – what philosopher Georg Lukàcs had called the "identical subject-object" of history understood in the Hegelian-Marxist sense – Habermas substituted the dissenting citizen.[143] Through correct insight into the relationship of legality to legitimacy, the dissenting citizen perceives that the *Rechtsstaat* is "nonidentical"

---

141 Habermas, "Recht und Gewalt," 109 (emphasis added).

142 Habermas, "Testfall," 39 (emphasis added).

143 See Georg Lukàcs, *History and Class Consciousness: Studies in Marxist Dialectics*, trans. Rodney Livingstone (London: Merlin Press, 1971).

with itself. Thus Habermas concluded that there could be no formal "legal right" to civil disobedience: "The sense of the law and the existence of legal procedure must remain intact. It follows that civil disobedience cannot be legalized as such."[144] Legalization would collapse moral legitimacy into positive legality. By maintaining the tension between legality and legitimacy, however, the practice of civil disobedience could become the marker for Germany's maturity. Secure enough to tolerate the "space in-between" – the moral ambiguities created by historical change – the polity could become "mature." At the same time, Habermas conceived this maturity not only conservatively as an achieved state but also as the precondition of future growth. It was to be not only the "touchstone" of its maturity but the "pacesetter" of its evolution too. Criminalization and legalization of civil disobedience were equally destructive of the *Rechsstaat*'s "paradoxical task" and its "nonidentity." Civil disobedience rightly understood was the signature practice of a mature political culture because in it the paradoxical character of modern law is performed.

Habermas was, in the mid-1980s, engaged in a series of struggles over German national identity. But his greatest contribution to the resolution of West German identity was to describe it in terms of a series of nonidentities. West Germany did not need to be anchored in the West through an unambiguous friend-enemy logic of *Westbindung*, nor in the terms of older German nationalisms. For Habermas, German identity was, like modernity and the *Rechtsstaat*, an unfinished project. It is remarkable how the terms he used to describe "modernity" and the *Rechtsstaat* so closely resemble one another. Habermas's account of the *Rechtsstaat* puts great emphasis on its fallible, revisable character:

> The history of the development of basic rights in Europe is best understood as the history of a learning process. Who will claim that this learning process is at an end? Even today, we need not consider ourselves merely its lucky heirs. From this perspective, the *Rechtsstaat* appears not as a closed structure but rather, a fragile undertaking.[145]

The civil disobedience campaigns of the early 1980s were the crucible of this realization. Habermas saw the *Rechtsstaat* as a kind of

[144] Habermas, "Testfall," 51.
[145] Ibid., 39–40.

self-revolutionizing project, animated by a "non-institutionalizable mistrust of itself." This project had three dimensions of "nonidentity." First, by remaining nonidentical with itself, the *Rechtsstaat* refused the legal closure of its moral horizon. Second, by making the constitution nonidentical with the political culture, the values of society could evolve. Third, the idea of the West was not reducible to the "Atlantic value community" of NATO and therefore was not identical to it. Constitutional patriotism could be attained without a heightened climate of internal and external "security."

In a remarkable passage from 1983, Habermas drew a link between the spheres of foreign policy, historical writing, and law that confirms the suspicion that Habermas's interventions in the debates over civil disobedience, the Euromissiles, and the historians' accounts of the Nazi past were united by a common denominator. For Habermas, this was the inability of his antagonists to tolerate ambiguity:

> It is the same mentality, in the military, historical, and juristic professions, which cling to unambiguities all the more when the people involved feel that the rug is being pulled from under their feet.... If it is true that the superpowers even in the atomic age are preparing a return to the unambiguousness of winnable wars, then it repeats in this security-utopia the same thought-structure which occurs in the legal positivist misunderstanding of militant democracy, which seeks to do away with the *ambiguity* of civil disobedience. Authoritarian legalism denies the humane substance of the nonidentical, exactly at the point where the democratic *Rechtsstaat* draws its substance.[146]

This passage illuminates the nature of Habermas's integrated philosophical-political project in the mid-1980s. Habermas viewed Kohl as a politician who had been able to translate neoconservative theoretical positions into electoral success. Habermas responded with a redefinition of *Westbindung*. Together Habermas's positions on civil disobedience, constitutional patriotism, and modernity articulated a moral language of *Westbindung* that could compete with the neoconservative discourse. The two most celebrated concepts Habermas developed in the 1980s were that of modernity as

[146] Habermas, "Testfall," 52: "... wiederholt sich in dieser Utopie der Sicherheit die gleiche Denkstruktur wie in jenem rechtspositivischen Missverständnis der wehrhaften Demokratie."

an incomplete project and the notion of constitutional patriotism. These positions were strongly conditioned by his efforts during the critical years before and after *die Wende* to negotiate West Germany's relationship with both the security framework and the political culture of the West.

5 Learning from the Bonn Republic: Recasting Democratic Theory, 1984–1996

> But moods – and philosophies in a melancholic "mood" – do not justify the defeatist surrender of the radical content of democratic ideals … If defeatism were justified, I would have had to choose a different literary genre, for example, the diary of a Hellenistic writer who merely documents, for subsequent generations, the unfulfilled promises of his waning culture.[1]

On this proudly defiant note, Jurgen Habermas prefaced his magnum opus in political and legal theory, *Between Facts and Norms: Contributions to a Discourse Theory of Democracy* (1992). The tone provides a useful clue for situating and contextualizing his mature political thought. Because Habermas began the work in 1985 but completed it only in 1991, the work sits astride a historical chasm – represented by the collapse of the East German state in 1989 and the reunification of the East with West Germany in 1990 – making contextual interpretation of the work difficult. But keeping both eras in mind – both pre- and post-1989 – makes it possible to fundamentally reinterpret the work. *Between Facts and Norms* (*BFN* hereafter) wears a Janus face: Facing backwards, it culls the constitutional history of the Bonn Republic in search of its lessons; facing forward, it inaugurates a new chapter in left political theorizing after the end of the Cold War. It is therefore both epitaph and manifesto: epitaph for the Bonn Republic – a résumé of the achievements and limits of West German constitutionalism – and manifesto for the Berlin Republic.

The most common critiques of *BFN* suggest that it is an expression of a post-1989 European mood, that is, a document of a left that

[1] Jürgen Habermas, "Preface," *Between Facts and Norms: Contributions to a Discourse Theory of Law and Democracy*, trans. William Rehg (Cambridge, MA: MIT Press, 1996), xliii (*BFN* hereafter).

has either "abandoned" Marx,[2] resigning itself to liberal constitutionalism, or relinquished a utopian horizon. *BFN* has been said to mark a turn in Habermas's work: signifying a final capitulation to an ascendant neoliberal capitalism,[3] substituting ethics for politics,[4] representing the final abandonment of Critical Theory, or implicitly endorsing Western European parliamentary democracy as the unsurpassable framework of contemporary politics. One political theorist argues that *BFN* "... offers at times a surprisingly moderate and even conciliatory picture of 'real-existing' democracy... [It is] an inadequately critical assessment of capitalist democracy."[5] As Habermas acknowledged, "Even if readers do not always see the 'end of critical theory' in this project, they frequently think it defuses the critique of capitalism and just gives in to political liberalism."[6] This chapter argues, by contrast, that Habermas's 1992 work represents an important restatement of the radical democratic project of reform to which Habermas has been committed since the 1960s. In support of this project, Habermas supplies an investigation of the lessons of German intellectual history – specifically of its legal theory and jurisprudence.

The inventory Habermas takes in *BFN* of his own evolution as a political and legal thinker since the late 1950s permits a reading of the work as a kind of fragmented intellectual autobiography. The autobiographical character of Habermas's mature political testament reveals how pervasively the traditions of twentieth-century German legal theory influence his work. Where other scholars have characterized *BFN* as a decisive marker of a "legal turn" or "liberal turn" in Habermas's thought, in fact, no such turn exists.[7] The

---

[2] Chris Thornhill, *Political Theory in Modern Germany* (London: Blackwell, 2000), 173.

[3] See, for example, Chantal Mouffe, "Introduction: Schmitt's Challenge," in *The Challenge of Carl Schmitt*, ed. C. Mouffe (New York: Verso, 1999).

[4] Slavoj Žižek, "Carl Schmitt in the Age of Post-Politics," in Mouffe, *Challenge*.

[5] See William Scheuerman, "Between Radicalism and Resignation: Democratic Theory in Habermas's *Between Facts and Norms*," in *Habermas: A Critical Reader*, ed. Peter Dews (Oxford, England: Blackwell, 1999), 155–6.

[6] Habermas, "Reply to Symposium Participants," in *Cardozo Law Review* 17:4–5 (1996), 1545.

[7] For example, John McCormick writes that Habermas's *BFN* "... is something of a culminating moment in the absorption in recent years by social democratic political theory of liberal institutional, legal and ethical theory." McCormick, *Carl Schmitt's Critique of Liberalism: Against Politics as Technology* (Chicago: The University of Chicago Press, 1995), 306. Also see Kenneth

thesis of a legal or liberal turn obscures a significant continuity in Habermas's work, namely, his political analysis since publication of *The Structural Transformation of the Public Sphere* (1962) has been framed in the language of German legal theory. This reading of *BFN* thus is in accord with this broad feature of Habermas's own self-understanding as a radical reformer. Habermas's emplotment of German intellectual history as a series of dead ends helps him to legitimate his procedural (or discourse) theory of politics and law as the best remaining option for a progressive left after the Cold War's end. Both introspective and strategic, Habermas's *BFN* constructs a usable past for his distinct political project.

While *BFN* has been thoroughly appraised by scholars of constitutional law and political philosophy on both sides of the Atlantic, it has not been considered historically.[8] Much of the scholarship takes its cue from Habermas's hope that he would contribute to the resolution of the "liberalism-communitarianism" debate in Atlantic political theory. However, this academic conversation was a far less significant context informing the work than the dynamic shifts in postwar German political culture in the 1980s and 1990s. Habermas first sketched his mature political project in a 1984 lecture on what he called the "exhaustion of utopian energies" in Western European politics. In 1989–90, he aligned himself with the progressive wing of the jurists in the constitutional debates of the years 1989–90, who hoped a new constitution-giving assembly would serve to "refound" the republic. But Habermas was highly ambivalent about German reunification. His ambivalence offers a new perspective on the tension between the liberal and republican dimensions in his thought. For all his celebrated bridge-building between Continental and Anglo-American social and political thought, therefore, *BFN* is profoundly rooted in German intellectual traditions and its tumultuous political landscape. Situating Habermas this way recasts the meaning of his career: Reading *BFN* as his *summa* of the problems of German

Baynes, "Democracy and *Rechtsstaat*: Habermas's *Faktizität und Geltung*," in *The Cambridge Companion to Habermas*, ed. Steven White (Cambridge, England: Cambridge University Press, 1995), 201.

8 There are only two exceptions: Matůstìk, *Profile*, 202–18, and Dick Howard, "Law and Political Culture," *Cardozo Law Review* 17:4–5 (1996): 1391–1430. For a representative overview of the reception of *BFN* by political philosophers and constitutional lawyers, see *Discourse and Democracy: Essays on Habermas's Between Facts and Norms*, eds. Kenneth Baynes and René von Schomberg (Albany, NY: SUNY Press, 2002).

history and politics dramatically underscores his significance as *the* public philosopher of the Federal Republic of Germany.

NEITHER LIBERALISM NOR REPUBLICANISM: THE PROCEDURAL THEORY OF LAW AND DEMOCRACY

The central tension in modern Western political philosophy, as Habermas stages it, was the tension between the "freedom of the ancients," which he encapsulates with the term "popular sovereignty," and the "freedom of the moderns," which he denotes by the concept of "human rights."[9] While Habermas uses the term "republicanism" to refer to a tradition of thought exemplified by Rousseau but rooted in Aristotle and the traditions of Renaissance humanism, he uses modern "liberalism" to refer to a tradition whose exemplars are Locke and Kant. Elsewhere he emphasizes the parameters of a "narrow" tradition tracing its roots to Locke: "'Liberals' such as Dworkin and Rawls cannot be confined to this tradition."[10] What is absent from his explicit definitions, however, is the German historical experiences congealed and concealed within his characterizations of the "liberal" and "republican" traditions. That Habermas understands his procedural theory as an alternative to "liberal" accounts also reveals his discomfort with the label and affords us grounds for scepticism about the thesis that *BFN* is the signature of a liberal turn in Habermas's thought.

Habermas's ideal types are designed to suggest that where republicans tend to prioritize "public autonomy" – or the principle of popular sovereignty – liberals tend to fear tyrannical majorities and use human rights to erect barriers to encroachment by the sovereign will of the people. The problem is that "[o]nce the issue is set up in this way, either idea can be upheld only at the expense of the other. The intuitively plausible co-originality of both ideas falls by the wayside."[11] Habermas argued that his procedural or discourse theory of democracy is the ideal mediator because it "... takes elements

[9] Habermas, "Three Normative Models of Democracy," in idem, *The Inclusion of the Other: Studies in Political Theory*, eds. Ciaran Cronin and Pablo De Greiff (Cambridge, MA: MIT Press, 1998), 258; orig. *Die Einbeziehung des Anderen. Studien zur politischen Theorie* (Frankfurt/Main: Suhrkamp, 1996).

[10] Habermas, *BFN*, 549, note 10.

[11] Habermas, "Normative Models," 258.

from both sides and integrates them."[12] Understanding the goals Habermas articulated in his 1996 essays helps us to grasp the import of what he considers his central thesis in the 1992 *BFN*, namely, that the Western ideals of the rule of law and democracy are "internally connected."[13] Democracy and rule of law are "co-original" or "equi-primordial" (*gleichursprünglich*), he argued: The two "mutually presuppose each other."[14]

The strength of the republican model, Habermas explained, is that it alone preserves the meaning of radical democracy, that is, of a society that organizes itself. As such, it transcends the liberal model's definition of collective goals as the mere aggregation of private interests.[15] Its corresponding weakness is that it is overly dependent on virtuous citizens who are devoted to the public good.[16] Habermas claimed that his procedural model steered a middle course between what we may call "thicker" and "thinner" models of democracy. The republican concept of the state as "an ethical community" was too thick, whereas the liberal concept of the state as "the guardian of a market society" was too thin.[17] Habermas's procedural turn was prompted by his belief that only theoretical reconstruction could rescue the insights of republicanism and liberalism from their too concrete embodiments.

Historical contextualization of Habermas's critiques makes it clear why in the end he is more convincingly viewed as a species of civic republican than a liberal: He puts his faith in popular sovereignty, not human rights, as the ultimate basis for the legitimacy of the laws. Habermas acknowledged his partiality to republicanism in referring to his procedural theory as a "communicative account of *republicanism*."[18] According to Habermas, a "proceduralist," or

---

[12] Ibid., 246.

[13] William Rehg, "Translator's Introduction," in *BFN*, xxiv. For the core argument, see *BFN*, 84–104. Habermas published summaries of the main ideas of *BFN* in a 1994 "Postscript" and in two of the essays in *The Inclusion of the Other*. Thus the thesis he worked out in *BFN* remained central to his thinking through at least 1996.

[14] Habermas, *BFN*, 93, 122.

[15] Habermas, "Normative Models," 246.

[16] Ibid., 244.

[17] Ibid., 246.

[18] Habermas, "On the Relation between the Nation, the Rule of Law and Democracy," in idem, *Inclusion of the Other*, 139 (emphasis added). Compare Larmore, *The Morals of Modernity* (Chicago: the University of Chicago Press, 1999), 217–9, and Werner-Müller, *A Dangerous Mind*, 195.

"formal," turn was the sole means for salvaging the content of utopia from its twentieth-century embodiments. Proceduralism was the best alternative to overly "concrete" political ideologies. State socialism, Western European social democracy, and Western European liberalism all were "too concrete." The problem with Marx and Engels's thought, for example, was that

> ... they read Rousseau and Hegel too much through the eyes of Aristotle.... [T]heir idea of a liberated society was too *concrete*. They conceived socialism as a historically privileged form of *concrete* ethical life [*Sittlichkeit*] ... [rather than as] the set of necessary conditions for emancipated forms of life about which participants themselves would have to reach an understanding.[19]

To mark the distinction between discredited past utopias and the possibility of future ones, Habermas used different words: "*Entwurf*" and "*Projekt*."

> After the collapse of state socialism and the end of the "global civil war," the theoretical error of the defeated party is there for all to see: it mistook the socialist project [*Projekt*] for the design [*Entwurf*] – and violent implementation – of a *concrete* form of life.[20]

Borrowing from contemporary German legal theorists such as Ulrich Preuss, Habermas offered an alternative to the traditional socialist utopia: the image of the constitution as ongoing and infinitely revisable learning process. "If a utopia is equivalent to the ideal projection [*Entwurf*] of a concrete form of life, then the constitution taken as a project [*Projekt*] is neither a social utopia nor a substitute for such."[21] The German constitution was an unfinished project: It opened a discussion rather than finishing the design of the good society once and for all.

Since the mid-1980s, Habermas has more than once described the arc of his intellectual development since the late 1950s as a movement away from the "holism" and "cryptonormativism" of Western Marxism:

> You know that I grew up in the tradition of what Merleau-Ponty named "Western Marxism." ... I have tried to free myself from the

[19] Habermas, *BFN*, 478 (emphasis added).
[20] Ibid., xvi (emphasis added).
[21] Ibid., 444–5.

> teleological view of history and the cryptonormative assumptions built into it. Instead of the rationality of productive forces, including natural science and technology, I trust in the productive force of communication.[22]

In a number of writings composed between 1985 and 1990, Habermas developed this theme theoretically. He interpreted the French Revolution as an expression of the idea that "the people" could collectively author their destiny but asserted that this idea had since become problematic.[23] Habermas's concern was how to save the core of this idea of collective authorship under modern conditions. He believed that the left should acknowledge that societies are not higher-level "selves" that can know and steer themselves, whereas the right should acknowledge the validity of the public expectation of popular sovereignty.[24] Habermas argued that societies cannot have one "steering center."[25] Society cannot be grasped as a "macro-subject," be it that of a class (the proletariat) or a unitary conception of "the people."[26] As he had already written in his lectures on the philosophical discourse of modernity, "In modern societies … there is no equivalent for the philosophy of the subject's model of self-influence in general and for the Hegelian-Marxist understanding of revolutionary action in particular."[27] His solution to this quandary was that popular sovereignty should be "intersubjectively dissolved" or "proceduralized." But what did these terms of art mean?

Proceduralized popular sovereignty, he explained, would eschew the problem of the "unitary macrosubject" by breaking up sovereignty into a plurality of locations. Sovereignty therefore would have to "find its placeless place in the interactions between" parliament ("legally institutionalized will-formation") and culturally mobilized public spheres.[28] Habermas used words such as

[22] Interview with Hans-Peter Krüger (November 1988), in *DNU*, 85. Maurice Merleau-Ponty (1908–61) was a French existentialist-Marxist philosopher.

[23] Habermas, "Popular Sovereignty as Procedure" (1988), reprinted in *BFN*, 468.

[24] Habermas, "Lecture XII: The Normative Content of Modernity," in *The Philosophical Discourse of Modernity: Twelve Lectures*, trans. Frederick Lawrence (Cambridge, MA: MIT Press, 1987), 358, 363.

[25] Habermas, *Die nachholende Revolution: Kleine Politische Schriften VII* (Frankfurt/Main, 1990), 196 (*NR* hereafter); Habermas, *PDM*, 357.

[26] Habermas, *PDM*, 361.

[27] Ibid.

[28] Habermas, "*Nachholende Revolution linker Revisionsbedarf. Was heisst Sozialismus heute?*" in Habermas, *NR*, 196; idem, *BFN*, 442.

"desubstantialized," "disembodied," and "fully dispersed" to characterize a popular sovereignty that has "withdrawn into democratic procedures."[29] Habermas believed that breaking up legislative power into institutionalized and noninstitutionalized spaces – the parliament and a plurality of public spheres – was the best way to preserve the democratic ideal of popular self-determination while eschewing the holism that he believed connected Aristotle to Rousseau, Hegel, and Marx. Habermas thereby updated his idea of political culture as the "space in-between" and the "non-institutionalizable" mistrust of the citizens he had posited as the critical ingredient in the "non-identical *Rechtsstaat*" in his 1983 writings on civil disobedience.[30] He repeatedly used the metaphor of "withdrawal" to describe the sublimation of core liberal and republican ideals (human rights and popular sovereignty, respectively) into discursive "rules of procedure":

> [Proceduralism] ... relieves citizens of the Rousseauian expectation of virtue – the orientation to the common good only needs to be extracted in small increments insofar as practical reason *withdraws* from the hearts and heads of collective or individual actors into the procedures and forms of communication of political opinion and will formation.[31]

Similarly, Habermas substituted the rules of discourse for the more "concrete" (*sittlich*) features of universal human rights:

> According to [the] proceduralist view, practical reason *withdraws* from universal human rights or from the concrete ethical life of a specific community into the rules of discourse.[32]

Treating human rights as an example of excessive concreteness is a striking feature of *BFN* and Habermas's mature political thought generally. It reflects his skepticism toward one version of human rights politics, not human rights per se. Treating human rights as a foundational moral a priori, beyond reflection, reifies them in a manner Habermas finds unacceptable. Popular sovereignty, not

[29] Habermas, *BFN*, 486.
[30] Habermas, "Testfall," 53.
[31] Habermas, "Reply to Symposium Participants," 1481–2 (emphasis added).
[32] Ibid. For Habermas's definition of practical reason, see "On the Pragmatic, the Ethical and the Moral Employments of Practical Reason," in Habermas, *Justification and Application: Remarks on Discourse Ethics*, trans. Ciarin Cronin (Cambridge, MA: MIT Press, 1993); orig. *Erläuterungen zur Diskursethik* (Frankfurt/Main: Suhrkamp, 1991), 100–18.

human rights, is Habermas's ultimate priority, and this choice of priorities contradicts the notion of a "liberal turn" in his thought.

REENCHANTING THE *RECHTSSTAAT*: HABERMAS ON THE OFFENSIVE, 1984–8

The years 1984 to 1988 form a distinct chapter in Habermas's thought. The fact that Habermas had by 1988 completed a draft of *BFN*[33] alerts us that the key contexts informing the work predate the revolution of 1989. Emphasizing this pre-1989 context for *BFN* highlights the anachronism of reading the 1992 work as an exemplary document of political resignation, a farewell to alternatives. On the contrary, it was a sense of confidence that the West German *Rechtsstaat* was secure and reliable that seems to have permitted Habermas to go on the intellectual "offensive." The term comes from Habermas's own writings and captures his optimism in this period. His goal: to ambitiously synthesize the two elements of political theory most precious to him – the dynamic future orientation of Western Marxist tradition with the achievements of *Rechtsstaatlichkeit* (the rule of law).

In a December 1984 lecture delivered to the newly elected Spanish Socialist Parliament, he surveyed the political landscape in Western Europe.[34] With the development of the welfare state (*Sozialstaat*) at a "dead end," European social democracy had become conservative, Habermas argued: Its vision was excessively "defensive," and it expressed a historical consciousness denuded of its "utopian dimension." The left could seize "the offensive" only if the welfare state project were reimagined.[35] From Habermas's diagnosis of the exhaustion of utopian energies came his plan for reviving them: to shift the "utopian accent" of social theory from the idea of work to the idea of communication.

The outlines of the more extensive critique of the German welfare state he elaborated in *BFN* are clearly present in the lecture

[33] Conversation with Klaus Günther, J. W. Goethe University, Frankfurt am Main, June 10, 2005.

[34] Habermas,"Die Krise des Wohlfahrtstaates und die Erschöpfung utopischer Energien," in idem, *Die Neue Unübersichtlichkeit. Kleine Politische Schriften VII* (Frankfurt/Main: Suhrkamp, 1985).

[35] Ibid., 157, 160.

to the Spanish Parliament. Habermas introduced his procedural paradigm of law as an alternative to the two postwar paradigms (liberal and social-welfare state), the errors of which were analogous: "Both views are fixated on the question of whether it suffices to guarantee private autonomy through individual liberties or … whether [private autonomy] … must be secured by granting welfare entitlements."[36] The lecture also tested the metaphor of concreteness that was so important in *BFN*: "The proceduralist legal paradigm … presupposes that the welfare and liberal models of law construe the realization of rights in overly *concrete* terms and conceal the internal relation between private and public autonomy."[37] The welfare state "still draws its power" from the utopian idea of liberation from alienating work, Habermas acknowledged. But he argued that liberation had always been envisioned too "concretistically"; that is, classical utopias had tried to "paint" too detailed a picture of the good life.[38] Habermas's goal was to preserve the spirit of the "utopia of a workers' society" (*arbeitsgesellschaftliche Utopie*) but to transpose its core values – freedom, equality, and solidarity – into a new, less concretely pictured framework. Habermas asserted that what made his utopia unprecedented was that it restricted "itself to the formal aspects of undistorted intersubjectivity."[39] He explained that the "ideal speech situation" he had worked out in the 1970s did not depict a "concrete form of life": Rather, it only created the necessary "formal" or "procedural" framework within which the public could deliberate and collectively fill in the picture of the good society.[40] Through a defined procedural framework, participants themselves would decide which "concrete possibilities" of social organization they desired. Only by shifting the utopian accent from work to communication, he wrote, could a new "division of powers" between the three resources of modern societies – money, power, and solidarity – be pursued.[41] Habermas's first formulations of the proceduralist paradigm, the signature of his mature political thought, were rooted in this context of being on the political offensive.

---

[36] Habermas, *BFN*, 408.
[37] *BFN*, 437 (emphasis added).
[38] Habermas, *NR*, 195.
[39] Habermas, "Krise des Wohlfahrtstaates," 161.
[40] The concept of the "ideal speech situation" dates back to at least the Gauss Lectures of 1971. See Habermas, *On the Pragmatics of Social Interaction*, 97.
[41] Habermas, "Krise des Wohlfahrtstaates," 158.

That Habermas felt that there was positive historical momentum in the mid-1980s is also evident in one of his 1988 essays: "Under the banner of postmodern farewells," he wrote, "we are now supposed to distance ourselves from that exemplary event [the French Revolution] whose effects have been felt for the last two hundred years."[42] But Habermas resisted the postmodern critiques of Enlightenment ideals by "endeavor[ing] to translate the the normative content" of the ideals of 1789 into new forms.[43] Reconceptualizing democratic republics as a dynamic "project"(*Projekt*) rather than a static "possession" was critical to this act of translation:

> A republic of this sort is not a *possession* we simply accept as our fortunate inheritance from the past. Rather it is a *project* we must carry forward in the consciousness of a revolution both permanent and quotidian.[44]

Habermas was dissatisfied with the West German citizenry's relationship to its constitution, seeing in it a kind of passivity or, to recall Kant's phrase, a self-incurred immaturity. By contrasting two views of the constitution – as "possession" or "project" – Habermas reenchanted the *Rechtsstaat* with a utopian, revolutionary aura. By treating the constitution as something static – the "fortunate inheritance" from 1949 – the public forfeited what Habermas valued: an understanding of the constitution as a dynamic, unfinished project:

> In view of the double anniversaries of 1789 and 1949 ... a leftist in the Federal Republic must consider this undertaking an imperative: the principles of the constitution will not take root in our souls until reason has assured itself of those principles' orienting, future-directed contents.[45]

The statement that the constitution would not be "rooted in our souls" until "reason" has been reassured that the content of the constitutional principles is "future-oriented" appears at first to signify an uncharacteristic romanticism. But the ambiguous subjects – "our souls" and "reason" – were not only aimed at West Germans generally

---

[42] Habermas, "Popular Sovereignty as Procedure"[1988], in idem, *BFN*, 463. He is referring to François Furet's *Penser La Révolution Française* (Paris: Gallimard, 1978).

[43] Ibid., 477.

[44] Habermas, *BFN*, 471 (emphasis added).

[45] Ibid.

but also refer to the West German left, which he had urged since the late 1960s to identify more with the constitution. With his idea of the democratic constitutional state as an "unfinished project," Habermas tried to reorient the goals of the German left.

His key maneuver was to break down the antinomy of "constitution" and "revolution" by arguing that constitutions are "self-revolutionizing" entities. For Habermas, being a leftist "loyal to the constitution"[46] meant rejecting the claim that the "orienting power" of the French Revolution was exhausted. The single most important legacy of the French Revolution for Habermas was the constitutional state because in it the utopian core of "revolution" – the universally valid ideas of democracy and human rights – was preserved.[47] In contrast to nearly all of his critics, Habermas saw (and still sees) himself as part of a Marxian tradition of social theory that seeks to preserve such key Marxist-humanist ideals as solidarity and liberation from coercion by reconstructing them.[48] This thought is evident in his chapter on contemporary Marxist theory in *The Philosophical Discourse of Modernity*, in which he explains that retrieving the "normative content" of modernity means moving away from the "… concepts of praxis philosophy if not its intentions":[49]

> I've quite fiercely decided to defend [social theory in the Marxian tradition] … as a still meaningful enterprise; … I do think that I have been a reformist all my life, and maybe I have become a bit more so in recent years. Nevertheless, I mostly feel I am the last Marxist.[50]

Whether or not Habermas can be categorized as a Marxist, if an extremely unorthodox one, need not detain us here. The point is that Habermas's mature work can hardly be characterized as a document of political resignation. In *BFN*, Habermas imagines a constitutionalism capacious enough to absorb the full force and breadth of the French revolutionary project.

What is significant about these formulations is that Habermas was arguing that that no *Verfassungspatriotismus* (patriotism centered on

---

46 Author's private correspondence with Habermas, June 7, 2005.
47 Habermas, *BFN*, 465.
48 Habermas, "Excursus on Cornelius Castoriadis: The Imaginary Institution," in *PDM*, 347.
49 Ibid. He is using "praxis philosophy" as a synonym for Western Marxism.
50 Habermas, "Further Reflections on the Public Sphere," [1992] 464, 469.

the constitution) could be justified without a complementary notion of the constitution as an instrument for realizing a more democratic society. By sublimating the spirit of revolution, as it were, into the concept of constitutionalism as a self-revolutionizing or "fallible learning process," society could become more free, equal, and solidaristic. Here Habermas followed Preuss: "Preuss defines 'constitution' as the establishment of a fallible learning process through which a society gradually overcomes its ability to engage in normative reflection on itself."[51] Habermas elaborated on what he meant by the claim that the constitution should be understood "dynamically" as an "unfinished project":

> … [T]he constitutional state does not represent a finished structure but a delicate and sensitive – above all fallible and revisable – enterprise, whose purpose is to realize the system of rights *anew* in changing circumstances, that is, to interpret the system of rights better, to institutionalize it more appropriately, and to draw out its contents more radically.[52]

By contrasting static and dynamic concepts of the constitution, Habermas outlined the minimum conditions, as it were, "… for the constitution's principles to take root in our souls." On the eve of the revolution of 1989, Habermas was crafting a compelling reinterpretation of the classic Marxist notions of utopia and revolution. However, the dynamic unleashed by the revolution of 1989 changed everything. Soon, Habermas was on the defensive again, anxious about the illiberalism of the citizens of the new German *Länder.*

A MISSED OPPORTUNITY TO REFOUND THE REPUBLIC: HABERMAS ON THE DEFENSIVE

The revolution of 1989 reopened the question of the status of the German Basic Law, a document that had never been intended to be more than provisional. Habermas and other progressives began to contemplate convoking a constitutional assembly that would have the power to symbolically refound the republic. By the beginning of 1990, though, Habermas worried that the quick absorption of the

[51] Habermas, *BFN*, 444.
[52] Ibid., 384 (emphasis added).

old German Democratic Republic (GDR) posed a dire threat to the progress achieved in liberalizing West German political culture – an achievement with which he was by now deeply identified. Democracy was an undisputed good for Habermas, but he wondered: Could democracy function without a liberal political culture that could "meet it halfway"?[53] During this period, Habermas's republican commitment to a robust form of popular sovereignty vied for primacy with his liberal anxieties that citizens of the former GDR might not be equipped for the challenges of self-government. The difficulties Habermas had in negotiating his response to the East German revolution of 1989 are visible in *BFN*. The tension between its civic republican and liberal impulses expresses Habermas's contradictory reactions to the changing landscape of German politics in the years 1989–90.

In interviews and essays both published and circulated privately, Habermas complained that reunification was an "annexation" of the East by the West. A historic opportunity was missed for the two states to choose a common future together, he argued. The frantic pace and authoritarian mode of reunification would only reinforce the cultural and economic asymmetry between the two states and pose dangers to both. Perhaps most disturbing to Habermas was the way the revolution appeared to undermine an imminent West German progressive electoral majority that seemed for the first time within grasp: "... [T]he old Federal Republic was well on the way towards [becoming] a modern democratic society with strengthened political participation and towards a protest culture,"[54] he argued. Habermas interpreted the results of the elections of March 1990 as a critical reversal of this positive trend: "There is a mentality predominating in the new states that we recognize from the Adenauer period. The GDR has *not yet caught up with* the dramatic transformations of value-orientations that has occurred in the Federal Republic since the '60s."[55] Habermas thus was engaged in a tricky balancing act: He could not ignore the threat he saw of intellectual contamination by the GDR – he spoke of the potential

---

[53] See the "Postscript" (1994), in *BFN*, 461, for one of his frequent uses of this phrase.

[54] Michael Haller, *The Past as Future*, trans. and ed. Max Pensky, Foreword, Peter Hohendahl (Lincoln, NE: University of Nebraska Press, 1994), 57; orig. *Vergangenheit als Zukunft* (Zurich: Pendo, 1990).

[55] Ibid., 58 (emphasis added).

ruin to West Germany's "spiritual hygiene" – but neither did he consider it acceptable to assume the "role of judge in this waste-disposal project."[56] To the question *Was bleibt?* – What remained worth preserving in the history of the GDR? – Habermas argued that it had left no positive legacy at the level of institutional design.[57] Habermas thereby oscillated between affirming the legitimacy of GDR citizens' experiences and culture and fearing that absorption of the GDR risked weakening the relatively liberal political culture attained in the Bonn Republic. Meanwhile, however, the GDR political culture could not be neglected without risk, he warned:

> Self-understanding, the political self-consciousness of a nation of citizens, forms itself only in the medium of public communication. And this communication depends on a cultural infrastructure which is at this moment being allowed to fall into ruins in the new states.[58]

Habermas was concerned that if the GDR's cultural infrastructure – universities, museums, theater, film, and literature – were handled roughly and recklessly, there was a politically worrisome possibility that East Germans could be humiliated. Treating all of GDR culture cavalierly as "waste" to be disposed of risked weakening the ground into which the institutions of the *Rechtsstaat* were to be transplanted. In a formula that echoed his more abstract reflections in *BFN*, he explained: "Political culture is made up of a delicate fabric of mentalities and convictions that can neither be invented nor manipulated through administrative measures."[59] Habermas seemed split between his respectful concern for GDR citizens's experiences and anxiety about its fundamental illiberalism: "The institutions of the Basic Law can only function as well as they are allowed by the civil consciousness of a population accustomed to institutions of freedom."[60] When Habermas lent his support to the project of a new constitution-giving assembly, therefore, he expressed his republican convictions that political community should be formed through public communication. But this plan did not resolve his liberal anxieties that a democracy could not be built without democrats.

---

[56] Ibid., 51.
[57] Ibid., 34.
[58] Ibid., 47, 51.
[59] Ibid.
[60] Ibid.

Habermas believed that East Germany should have a founding constitutional moment to compensate for West Germany's lack of one. In 1949, there had been no constitution-giving assembly but rather a parliamentary council elected by the regional parliaments. The council deliberated under Konrad Adenauer's chairmanship and submitted its draft constitution to the Allied military governors for approval. "I do not undervalue the weight of reasons for conserving our constitution," he explained, but practical considerations for "stability" could not substitute for normative considerations.[61] He thought that a founding moment would help to constitute a future collective memory for all Germans. A founding act – of "conscious will and decision" – would form a historical event around which the republican self-understanding of future generations could crystallize.[62] Habermas appears to have been at least as concerned that future generations have a coherent memory of a founding moment as that the current generation experience it.

Habermas therefore sided with the group of professional jurists who advocated a new constitution-giving assembly. He especially admired the efforts of the "Round Table," advised by Preuss. But their work was outpaced by the Christian Democratic Union's (CDU's) effectiveness in winning over East Germany to its plan for quick reunification. By the end of September 1989, Chancellor Helmut Kohl had seized the initiative with his "Ten Point Program" for reunification. New elections to the East German Parliament (*Volkskammer*) were set for March 18, 1990. The Western parties moved into the East and mobilized voters. The CDU-allied party, "Alliance for Germany," with Lothar de Mazière at its head, won the elections with 48 percent of the popular vote. In April, de Mazière announced that the East would seek to join the Federal Republic under Article 23, the option for "accession" – thereby rejecting the alternative constitutional route to German reunification, Article 146, which mandated a new constitution-giving assembly. On July 1,1990, monetary union was established; on August 23, the *Volkskammer* voted to accede to the Federal Republic of Germany.

Before 1989, constitutional lawyers and politicians were nearly unanimous that reunification would be achieved by means of Article 146 and that a new constitution would be required. Article

61 Ibid., 216.
62 Ibid., 218.

146 stated that on unification, the Basic Law would cease to exist, and a new constitution would be adopted "by the free decision of the German people."[63] Once reunification became a real possibility, though, many German lawyers argued that Article 23 – an article designed originally for accession of areas still under Allied occupation in 1949 such as the Saar Region – was the more efficient vehicle: Under Article 23, a new region simply would come under the jurisdiction of the Basic Law, thus obviating the need to convene a time-consuming, constitution-giving assembly.[64]

Habermas sided with the jurists led by Helmut Simon who advocated applying the route outlined in Article 146. Josef Isensee was the leader of an opposing group of 100 constitutional law professors who defended reunification through Article 23. The main arguments of the conservatives were that one should not tamper with successful institutions such as the Basic Law because it deserved the lion's share of credit for the stability of West German democracy. They also argued that the GDR constitutions of 1969 and 1974 hardly deserved emulation because the guarantees of civil and political rights in those constitutions were contradicted by the state's totalitarian practices.[65] *Sozialsstaat* it may have been, but *Rechstsstaat* never.

The left argued, by contrast, that that the GDR's constitutional history was "not a blank page" and that the Basic Law was antiquated and in need of updating. New explicit state-goals such as ecological security could be added. A metaphor was commonly employed to underscore their point: that of building a common house. "When a couple is in love," wrote one GDR activist, "they should build a new house together. One partner should not move into the other's house."[66] Habermas too used a version of the metaphor: "Unification hasn't [yet] been understood as a normatively willed act of the citizens of both states, who ... decided upon a common civil union."[67]

---

[63] Basic Law, Article 23.

[64] Article 23 had been used for the accession of the Saarland in 1957.

[65] Robert Leicht, *Die Zeit* (February 3, 1990). Reprinted in Bernd Güggenberger and Tine Stein, eds. *Die Verfassungsdiskussion im Jahr der deutschen Einheit: Analysen – Hintergründe – Materialien* (München: C. Hauser, 1991).

[66] Karl-Heinz Ladeur, "Verfassungsgebung als Katharsis: Der Entwurf des 'Runden Tisches,'" and Gerd Roellecke, "Dritter Weg zum zweiten Fall. Der Verfassungsentwurf des Runden Tisches würde zum Scheitern des Staates führen."

[67] Haller, *Past as Future*, 44.

Ultimately, when the Round Table advanced its draft constitution in April 1990 – with a preamble penned by novelist Christa Wolf – it won only a minority of the East German *Volkskammer* vote. But the issue had already been mooted by the victory of the CDU in March.

Habermas viewed these developments bitterly: He used the word "annexation" (*Anschluss*) instead of accession (*Beitritt*), thereby invoking Nazi Germany's absorption of Austria in 1938. Kohl's determination to be "lord" of the process, wrote Habermas, meant that there had been no time for the East's own public sphere to develop. Habermas viewed the March elections as nothing more than a struggle between the Western parties for control of the East.[68] What galled Habermas most about those who advocated swift accession was their hypocrisy: "It is curious that those who now support accession through Article 23 for decades were against the reunification clauses in the preamble of the Basic Law."[69] Habermas was pointing to a revanchism implicit in the case for Article 23: "When will the day foreseen by Article 146 come, if not now? Are we still waiting for the East Prussians and Schleswig?"[70] Only those with revanchist hopes for German territory surrendered in 1945 could support Article 23 and reject the applicability of Article 146, he alleged; if Article 146 were used, it would preclude any future claims that the German *Volk* was still dispersed and incomplete.[71] Further, reunification under Article 23 would "leave Article 146 empty.... [I]t contradicts the methodological principle of interpreting the constitution as a unified whole."[72] Clearly, Habermas was becoming quite involved with constitutional jurisprudence and methods.

Unification did not close the question of a new constitution completely. The reunification treaty merely postponed debate on Article 146. The Joint Constitutional Commission was established to discuss the reforms reunification might require. The lawyers who remained opposed to a new constitution developed three new arguments for why the Basic Law should remain legitimate in reunified

---

[68] Habermas, "Nochmals: Zur Identität der Deutschen. Ein einig Volk von aufgebrachten Wirtschaftsbürgern," in *NR*, 212.

[69] Habermas put "accession" (*Beitritt*) in quotation marks to underscore his critique.

[70] Ibid.

[71] Ibid., 216.

[72] Ibid., 217.

Germany. First, the Basic Law already had popular endorsement because every national election since 1949 could be considered a ratification of the constitution and its legitimacy. Second, the March 1990 elections were evidence that the majority of East Germans had supported it. Third, it was an excellent constitution by any conceivable standard. One scholar has described this third position as an appeal to "*hypothetical* popular sovereignty"; that is, the Basic Law contained those principles that free and rational individuals *would* choose had they had the opportunity.[73] The opposing side, including Habermas, argued that neither the March 1990 elections in the East nor the four decades of federal elections in the West had addressed constitutional issues explicitly. Without a founding moment, a constitutional tradition could not take root. In the end, the reformers lost. Instead of a broad constitutional convention, a commission, comprised of thirty-two members of Parliament, divided along party lines, was established to engage public proposals; no major public forum took place.[74]

Habermas's disappointment with the outcome of the Round Table's quest was clearly an important factor shaping the argument of *BFN* although he does not acknowledge this. When asked in an interview if he thought "traces" of disappointment were evident in the work, he said that he didn't know.[75] Nevertheless, the imprint of history on Habermas's theory could not be clearer than in the following example: Disputes over the shape of the constitution in a democracy

> ... [concern] all participants, and it must be conducted not only as an esoteric discourse among experts apart from the political arena.... Legal experts participate in this contest of interpretations in a privileged way, but they cannot use their professional authority to impose one view of the constitution on the rest of us. The public must itself find such a view convincing.[76]

In a concurrent interview from late 1990, he wrote angrily of the "near hysterical fear of a forum on the constitution itself" and

[73] Simone Chambers, "Democracy, Popular Sovereignty, and Constitutional Legitimacy," *Constellations* 11:2 (June 2004), 167 (emphasis added).
[74] Ibid.
[75] Author's private correspondence with Habermas, June 7, 2005.
[76] Habermas, *BFN*, 395.

defended the idea of a republican refounding.[77] A clear picture emerges of a Habermas who was frustrated and on the defensive: "Those who demanded it [a new constitutional assembly] were laughed at as utopians, or were saddled, as usual, with the reputation of a lack of loyalty to the constitution."[78] This is a familiar theme in Habermas's writing and refers to his experience of being challenged in the late 1970s by conservatives who sought to link the Frankfurt School to domestic West German terrorism. Habermas disputed the characterization of his project as utopian:

> Was it so utopian to expect that the federal government, or at least the SPD [Social Democratic Party], would take up the impulses set in motion by the Round Table?
>
> ... Is it too much to demand that an effort be made [to discuss these issues] in the medium of public communication?[79]

By May 1993, Habermas's outrage had yielded to resignation: It was certain that a republican refounding would not take place. "Today we're busy with other problems," Habermas lamented.

> These days ... small stories buried in the back pages of the newspapers report of what has come of the transfer of moral waste products into West German management; of the politically crippled discussions over a new constitution; of the vague appeals to dull national feeling that go straight past the republican consciousness of a nation of citizens.[80]

The West German milieu of 1984–8, which had enabled Habermas to challenge the exhaustion of utopian energies and to formulate the ideal of a revolutionary constitutionalism, had, quite ironically, vanished with the revolution of 1989. But the double loss – first, the evaporation of the longed-for progressive majority in the West, and second, the abortive failure to refound the republic – added another set of motivations and a new horizon of significance to Habermas's stocktaking of the Bonn Republic's history, an inventory he had begun before 1989.

---

77 Haller, *Past as Future*, 44.
78 Ibid., 52.
79 Ibid.
80 Haller, "Afterword" (May 1993), in Haller, *The Past as Future*, 150. The phrase "moral waste" is intended ironically.

STATISM AND ITS CRITICS: THE WEST GERMAN EXPERIMENT WITH LAW AND DEMOCRACY

While the ostensible objective of *BFN* was to dissolve tenacious antinomies in Western political thought – the rule of law and democracy, human rights and popular sovereignty, public and private autonomy – it also distilled lessons Habermas drew from German and West German historical experiences with statism. Because he did not explicitly foreground it in the architecture of the work, Habermas's reading of recent German intellectual history requires careful reconstruction before its shaping influence on his political theory can emerge. What remains in the text implicit and overshadowed by his theoretical argument is that Habermas's reading of German history strongly conditioned his thought.

According to Habermas, for two centuries Germany's legal intellectuals repeatedly failed to address – and thus exacerbated – the chronic problems of a German statism unbound by democracy. While residual elements of German statism persisted after the creation of the West German republic in 1949, the long-term trend was toward an erosion of this view of the state and maturation of a countervailing civil society. Habermas's critical exploration of the intellectual history of German legal theory focuses on two figures whose thought seemed to him most symptomatic of the problem of German statism: sociologist Max Weber (1864–1920) and Rudolf Smend (1882–1975), the Weimar jurist whose writings were a dominant influence on West German jurisprudence in the 1950s. Weber's formalism and Smend's moral a priorism were the two theoretical positions that most exacerbated the legacies of German statism in West Germany. The theory articulated in *BFN* is the precipitate that remained, as it were, after Habermas pressed German intellectual traditions through his proceduralist filter.[81]

It is a recurring argument of this book that many of Habermas's most challenging abstractions conceal hidden historical referents; once decoded as references to German historical experience, the most cryptic become revelatory. The following statement, for example – "The law receives its full normative sense neither through its legal *form* per se, nor through an a priori moral *content*, but through

[81] For Habermas's use of this metaphor, see Habermas, *BFN*, 99.

a procedure of lawmaking that begets legitimacy"[82] – implicitly alludes to two of the most significant theoretical positions in twentieth-century German political or legal thought. By the "formalist error," Habermas designated the family resemblances he finds in the thought of Max Weber, Carl Schmitt, Franz Neumann, and the Schmittian school – despite their fundamental differences, such as that of the political orientations of Neumann and Schmitt, for example. By the "moralistic error," Habermas implicated Rudolf Smend's positions. Read in the light of these reflections on German legal traditions, Habermas's procedural turn appears to be the fruit of a passionate effort to eschew what he considered to be the worst dead ends and wrong turns in German intellectual history. German liberalism erred in two ways according to Habermas: It was either too formalistic – denuded of democratic content – or too moralistic – and thereby insulated from democratic discussion.

The root deficiencies of the German liberal tradition lay in the intellectual history of nineteenth-century German constitutionalism, Habermas argued. His republican inclination to value popular sovereignty over human rights stemmed from his deep investment in the historical diagnosis of the weaknesses of nineteenth-century German liberalism. Following the eminent legal scholars Ernst Wolfgang Böckenförde and Ingeborg Maus, Habermas asserted that the connection between individual liberty and state power in the tradition of the nineteenth-century *Rechtsstaat* tradition was "too direct."[83] Habermas traced a tradition from the early nineteenth century (Savigny, Puchta, and Windschied) to the late nineteenth century (Ihering and Kelsen) to the 1950s in West Germany (*Ordo*-liberalism),[84] the defining characteristic of which was that liberties were conceived as grants of the state. For Habermas, however, rights attained in this manner were deeply insufficient: Law that treats rights as "possessions" granted by the state rather than as something that emerged from citizens' recognition of each other as equals under the law is a signature of the German statist approach to law.[85]

[82] Ibid., 135.
[83] Ibid., 134.
[84] Ibid., 84–9. Friedrich Carl von Savigny (1799–1861), Georg Friedrich Puchta (1769–1845), Bernhard Windschied (1817–92), Rudolf von Ihering (1850–1930).
[85] Ibid., 88–9.

The weakness of German constitutional law stemmed from the hegemonic influence of its civil law, Habermas argued. The doctrinal history of civil-law jurisprudence from von Savigny to Kelsen "... has been decisive for the understanding of law [in Germany] *in general*."[86] By this, Habermas meant that it illustrates the persistent fallacies of German statism. Habermas highlighted a major problem with the tradition of German "liberalism" as embodied in the tradition of civil law. It "... got started with the idea of morally laden individual rights which claim ... a higher legitimacy than, the political process of legislation."[87] Even the *Ordo*-liberalism associated with Adenauer and Erhard's social-market economy, of which Habermas had been critical in the 1950s, seemed an expression of these same distortions: *Ordo*-liberals "only rehabilitated [an] individualistically truncated understanding of rights."[88] As discussed in Chapter 1, it was the *Ordo*-liberals associated with the Freiburg school that helped drive the Social Democratic Party (SPD) to the right at Bad Godesburg and resulted in Abendroth and Habermas's exit from the SPD.

German liberalism also erred by its excessive formalism. At the feet of one of the most important German liberals, Max Weber, Habermas placed a substantial burden: the German legal profession's unproductive and undemocratic obsession with legal "deformalization."[89] The formal equality of subjects under law was compromised, Weber had noted in *Economy and Society*, by statutes that treated different social classes unequally.[90] Weber's legacy, Habermas asserted, was a strict legal formalism that caused its adherents to discern in the policies of every German welfare state

[86] Ibid., 84 (emphasis added).

[87] Ibid., 89.

[88] Ibid., 87 (emphasis added). *ORDO: Jahrbuch fur die Ordnung von Wirtschaft und Gesellschaft* was a journal first published in May 1948 and was edited by economists Friedrich Hayek, Walter Eucken, Franz Böhm, Wilhelm Röpke, and Alexander Rüstow.

[89] Ibid., 389. "A trend already bemoaned by Max Weber, that fully asserted itself ... only at the end of WWII." Habermas links Forsthoff and Weber closely. See Habermas, "Recht und Moral" (a German translation of the Tanner Lectures of 1986), reprinted in idem, *Faktizität und Geltung*, 541–99: "Forsthoff [merely] continued Weber's critique with legal dogmatic means." For the English version, see *The Tanner Lectures on Human Values*, vol. VIII (Salt Lake City, UT: 1988), 217–80.

[90] See Max Rheinstein, ed., *Max Weber on Law in Economy and Society* [1925], trans. Edward Shils (Cambridge MA.: Harvard University Press, 1954).

since the 1880s a crisis that threatened the legitimacy of law. "With his distinction between 'formal' and 'material,' Weber shaped the relevant discussion up to the present day – and in my opinion steered it in the wrong direction," Habermas wrote in a 1986 sketch of his emerging legal theory.[91] "German jurisprudence perceived this long-standing process (of the social transformation of law) which dissolved the classical unity and systematic organization of the only legal order that appeared rational, as a 'crisis of law.'"[92] The formalist error consisted in an overly literal interpretation of the concept of law's "generality," to which Habermas admitted that he also had succumbed. In Germany, a narrow interpretation of the meaning of the generality of statute prevailed, according to which a law "… [owed] its legitimacy not to the democratic procedure [behind its genesis] but to its grammatical form."[93] Habermas renarrated his past error as a "semanticist abstraction" for which Weber and the tradition of German liberalism were ultimately responsible. To understand why Habermas was so passionate about such a seemingly obscure point – how Weber's dichotomy between legal "form" and legal "material" had produced a crisis for German law – one needs to consider the broader context to which Weber's "formalist error" referred.

That context was the 1950s debate over the constitutional legitimacy of the West German social welfare state discussed in Chapter 2. Habermas was drawn into the debate, adopting Forsthoff's critique of legal deformalization as an integral part of his critique of liberal democracy in his *Students and Politics* (1961) and *Transformation* (1962). Buried in a footnote is Habermas's acknowledgment that by doing so, he had failed to "escape" the influence of this tradition:

> In Germany the discussion over the generality of legal statutes is still colored by the extreme views found in Carl Schmitt's 1928 *Verfassungslehre* [Constitutional Theory]. This view became influential in the Federal Republic through the direct efforts of Forsthoff and indirectly through Franz Neumann. *I did not escape this influence myself* at the end of the 1950s.[94]

[91] Habermas, "Recht und Moral," 543.
[92] *BFN*, 389–90. Compare Habermas, "Further Reflections on the Public Sphere," 435.
[93] Habermas, *BFN*, 189.
[94] Ibid., 563–4, n.75 (emphasis added).

BFN thus records a very personal process of coming to terms with his intellectual past but also attempts to derive conclusions of general theoretical significance.

Habermas's key statement was that law's legitimacy depends neither on its grammatical form nor on an a priori moral content. This enables us to turn from one error in German legal thought to another: from the formalist error to the error of moral a priorism. Proceduralism was Habermas's effort to eschew these two primary defects of twentieth-century German legal thought. In contextual terms, Habermas's procedural turn against "concreteness" was a defensive maneuver to protect his radical reform agenda from threats on multiple fronts in German politics between the mid-1980s and the mid-1990s. But his procedural turn also depends to a significant extent on his acquisition of terms of art internal to his system, which he introduced for the first time in his writings on discourse ethics in the early 1980s.[95]

The key conceptual distinction he introduced was between "moral" and "ethical" discourses. Moral discourses differ from ethical discourses in that the former are universal in scope, whereas the latter are particular. As one philosopher explained:

> Ethical discourses are concerned with the life-history of an individual or a group. They seek to answer the question, "What is good for me?" ...
>
> [Moral discourses by contrast] ... are concerned with questions of justice and right, not with good and value.... [They] are not particularistic – limited to a particular historical group. They are genuinely universal and concern the equal respect and rights of all human beings.[96]

While this philosopher finds unconvincing Habermas's claim that his procedural model of democracy does not presuppose any "substantial-ethical" commitment, he apprehended the reasons for Habermas's insistence on the distinction between moral and ethical discourses: "For if discourse theory were dependent on a substantive ethos, then this would mean it could never achieve the

[95] See Habermas, *Erläuterungen zur Diskursethik* (Frankfurt/Main: Suhrkamp, 1991).

[96] Richard Bernstein, "The Retrieval of the Democratic Ethos," *Cardozo Law Review*, 17:4–5 (1996), 1139–40.

type of universality required to justify a universal point of view."[97] The factors that made Habermas nervous about the "thickness" of ethical life are accurate, but Habermas's anxieties also have a more proximate historical explanation.

Habermas's insistence on a strict distinction between norms and values responds to the hegemonic discourse of common "values" introduced by the post–World War II Federal Constitutional Court as a means of integrating West German society. Its so-called value jurisprudence was dominant from the early 1950s through the early 1970s and was shaped decisively by the Weimar-era writings of jurist Rudolf Smend, as discussed in Chapter 2. In a neglected section of *BFN* entitled, "Norms vs. Values: Methodological Errors in the Self-Understanding of the Constitutional Court," Habermas put forth a strongly worded critique of value jurisprudence. Smend's strand of legal theory and the practices of the postwar Federal Constitutional Court it inspired are the concealed historical referent that animates Habermas's rigid insistence on strict binary distinctions between the moral and the ethical, the right and the good, and norms and values.

By conceiving of fundamental rights as "basic values" that expressed a social consensus on the notion of "the good," Smend's value jurisprudence elevated the highest West German court to a position of political power that was, in Habermas's view, beyond the reach of any democratically legitimated legislator. Habermas's efforts to theorize human rights and popular sovereignty as co-original thus are simultaneously a critique of the West German practice of value jurisprudence, a practice that appeared to him to enshrine human rights at the expense of the democratic sovereign.

Leading German scholars disagree as to whether value jurisprudence has had any impact on German jurisprudence since the early 1970s. Ingeborg Maus, a political scientist at the University of Frankfurt, was an integral member of the legal theory group that Habermas organized to meet regularly from 1985–90. Maus finds in the Federal Republic, but also in advanced democracies generally, "… an overwhelming consensus that today's societies should not so much be integrated through the law but by means of higher order 'material' values."[98] But one reviewer of *BFN* claimed:

---

[97] Ibid., 1141.

[98] Ingeborg Maus, "Liberties and Popular Sovereignty: On Jürgen Habermas's Reconstruction of the System of Rights," *Cardozo Law Review*, 17:4–5 (1996), 830.

> The [Federal Constitional Court's] value orientation is a myth. It is true that between the 1950s and 1970s [it] discussed fundamental rights as being values, and as forming a value-system. But it never meant this in a philosophically ambitious sense, in the sense of a material value ethics developed by Max Scheler or Nicolai Hartmann.... Since the Federal Constitutional Court's value-orientation is a fiction, Habermas's confrontation of principles as norms and principles as values must also miss the reality of constitutional adjudication.[99]

Habermas's response was brief: "Since I did not invent this interpretation but took it from the numerous writings of prominent scholars and even members of the Court itself, I would rather leave this to legal scholars to settle."[100] Whether or not Habermas is right about the intellectual filiations of the German constitutional court is less important here than the fact that Habermas believed it to be so.

In "the wording and tenor" of some important opinions of the Federal Constitutional Court, Habermas detected a tendency to treat the Basic Law "... not so much as a system of rules structured by principles, but as a 'concrete order of values.'"[101] Habermas's primary concern was that by treating constitutional principles as "values" rather than as "norms," value jurisprudence opened a door to "the talk of balancing interests or weighing values [*Güterabwägung*] which is common among lawyers."[102] From here, Habermas believed, a critical line was crossed: "Anyone wanting to equate the constitution with a concrete order of values mistakes its specific legal character; as legal norms, basic rights are, like moral rules, modeled after obligatory norms of action, and not after attractive goods."[103] Habermas worried that if rights were conceived as valuable goods, they could be weighed, balanced, and possibly rejected. This kind of relativization of the status of basic rights could lead the constitutional state to deteriorate into rule by the administration and judiciary, a concern of Habermas's since his first work in political theory in the late 1950s. The reflections of Ingeborg Maus echo and

99 Bernhard Schlink, "The Dynamics of Constitutional Adjudication," in *Cardozo Law Review*, 1234.
100 Habermas, "Reply to Symposium Participants," *Cardozo Law Review*, 1477–78.
101 Habermas, *BFN*, 254, 258.
102 Ibid.
103 Ibid., 256.

amplify Habermas's concern that government might "instrumentalize" basic rights for its own objectives and prize efficiency over legitimacy. In today's constitutional adjudication, she warned:

> [W]e find the prevalence of a "basic rights policy" based on a logic that suggests action by the state is legitimate if it is efficient in enforcing rights instead of being based on a democratic consensus. This version of rights taking on a life of their own is a typical feature of the paternalistic social welfare state that is immunized against a democratic constitutional process ... and ordains rights from above by an expertocracy.[104]

Maus's critique of rule by experts, be they welfare state administrators or judges, furnishes the context we need to understand Habermas's otherwise surprising claim that "[h]owever well grounded human rights are, they may not be paternalistically foisted, as it were, on a sovereign."[105] It may seem counterintuitive that Habermas criticizes and fears the "isolation" of individual rights from democratic majorities, which for many U.S. theorists is central to the practice of American liberal democracy. Moreover, the prominence of the basic rights catalogue in the constitutions of both the Bonn and Berlin Republics and their unalterability (the so-called eternity clause) reflect the postwar consensus of German political and legal elites that rights were inviolable, sacred, and central to the meaning of a secure liberal constitutional order. This position is known as "rights foundationalism."

But the lesson Habermas drew from German history about the relationship of rights to democracy is a very different one: that the fundamental idea of democracy is *autonomy*. Against rights foundationalism, Habermas takes the position that the addressees of law also must be its authors: "It would contradict [the idea of autonomy] if the democratic legislator were to discover human rights as though they were (preexisting) moral facts that one merely needs to enact as positive law."[106] Habermas was critical of value jurisprudence

[104] Maus, *Liberties*, 831. Maus takes the argument much further than Habermas, however. She explicitly compares value jurisprudence to the National Socialist claim to replace the formalistic rule of law with a rule of justice (*Gerechtigkeitsstaat*). See *Liberties*, 829–30.

[105] Habermas, "Internal Relation of Law and Democracy," in idem, *Inclusion of the Other*, 260.

[106] Ibid., 260. Compare "Postscript," in *BFN*, 454.

specifically and rights foundationalism more broadly because they seemed to arm judges – however enlightened or well-intentioned – with a dangerous form of morality: an a priorism that insulates rights from the reach of the democratic sovereign. These remarkable reservations about the status of rights in German political culture stem from his passionate convictions, expressed across decades of writing, about the illiberalism of the tradition of the German *Rechtsstaat* – and of the conservatism historically lurking within it: Liberal constitutionalism is not yet democratic constitutionalism, and rights foundationalism has a closer affinity to the former than to the latter.

Habermas's contemporary critique of the paternalism of judges is remarkably reminiscent of his critique of the "morally laden individual rights" that he identified as a weakness of German liberal legal theory in the nineteenth century.[107] As Habermas put it in his critique of contemporary U.S. legal scholar Michael Perry, overreliance on the notion of "substantive values pregiven in constitutional law" can produce a politics that is too communitarian, that is, too "thick." In Habermas's characterization, Perry represents a "neo-Aristotelian variant of the doctrine of objective values":

> [Perry] ... conceives of the text of the constitution as a founding charter that manifests the ethical self-understanding of a historical community...
>
> In a still more pronounced fashion than the German legal hermeneutics following Gadamer, Perry sees the constitutional judge in the role of a prophetic teacher, whose interpretation of the divine word of the Founding Fathers secures the continuity of a tradition that is constitutive of the community's life ... By assuming it should strive to realize substantive values pregiven in constitutional law, the constitutional court is transformed into an authoritarian agency.[108]

In sum, in his discussion of the "methodological self-understanding" of the Supreme Court in the United States and the Federal Constitutional Court in the former West Germany, Habermas critiqued the notion that judges should be viewed as an elite caste of interpreters. For example, he also argued that Ronald Dworkin's

[107] Habermas, *BFN*, 89.
[108] Ibid., 257–8.

"ideal judge" is a less reliable bulwark of democracy than an "open society of interpreters of the constitution."[109] Habermas's firm objection to the notion that judges and professional jurists should monopolize the interpretation of the constitution was a view augmented by his experience in the constitutional debates of 1989–91. But it also reflected his deep reservations about the democratic deficit in the application of the philosophy of rights foundationalism, reservations so deep that they threaten to eclipse recognition of the substantial contributions made by that jurisprudence to the liberalization of West Germany's political culture.

Habermas's procedural theory of law and democracy took shape in two distinct political contexts and bears the traces of each. Sedimented within the theory is a mood and a tempo: a Habermas who was on the offensive, as it were, in the pre-*Wende* period, from 1984 until the fall of the Berlin Wall in November 1989. In that period, he proposed the notion of a self-revolutionizing *Rechtsstaat*, a notion that reconstructed Western Marxist concepts of utopia and revolution. Viewing the constitution as an unfinished and infinitely revisable project rather than a fixed inheritance was Habermas's answer to a question with a long pedigree in German history: how to turn the *Rechtsstaat* from an object only a republican out of reason (*Vernunftrepublikaner*) could love into an anchor of national identity. Only then could a leftist in the Federal Republic finally embrace the constitutional state as the ne plus ultra of German politics, Habermas concluded.

But Habermas's mature political theory is also imprinted with a second set of historical experiences: the revolution of 1989–90 and the process of German reunification, completed in 1991. Initially, he viewed the revolution of 1989 as a threat to the emerging progressive majority he hoped would furnish the constituency for his vision of radical reform. The potential illiberalism of the East German citizenry threatened to undermine the "mature" political culture Habermas had nurtured in the West. A tension surfaced between Habermas's republican convictions and his liberal anxieties, which

[109] Habermas, *BFN*, 223. See Dworkin. Habermas adopts the phrase from the chapter of that title in Peter Häberle, *Die Verfassung des Pluralismus: Studien zur Verfassungstheorie der offenen Gessellschaft* (Königstein/Ts:Athenaüm, 1980).

he tried to resolve by embracing the progressive jurists' agenda of a new constitutional assembly for the Berlin Republic. His reactions to the German reunification process betrayed his ultimate conviction that republican institutions could survive only if they were complemented by a liberal political culture, a set of attitudes and dispositions that could meet institutions "halfway."[110]

Conversely, his critical stocktaking of the intellectual history of German legal theory in *BFN* revealed a Habermas who seemed ultimately to privilege popular sovereignty over human rights and thus implicitly a republican over a liberal model of political community. This was so because Habermas's reading of the history of judicial activism and a paternalistic welfare state in the Bonn Republic convinced him that the legitimacy of the laws in the end rested on the democratic conditions of their genesis rather than on their legal form or moral content. The procedural vision Habermas worked out between 1984 and 1992 – and which he has remained committed to since – is the mature statement of his political theory. It is hard to imagine him revising it in its fundamentals. *BFN* was consistent with Habermas's lifelong commitment to a radical reform of liberal constitutionalism; in this work, he adapted this project to the new circumstances of the 1980s and 1990s rather than abdicating something essential in Habermasian Critical Theory. By decribing itself as the antithesis of diverse incarnations of "concreteness," Habermas's procedural theory of law and democracy offered a powerful rhetorical reformulation of the utopian longings of the German Left. Far from a document of political resignation, *BFN* scrutinizes the Bonn Republic for instruction on Berlin's future: It is a bridge that links the two historical continents.

[110] See supra note 55.

Conclusion

Two major premises guided this study. The first is that Habermas's theoretical and political writings provide a unique vantage point from which to consider major developments in postwar German history. The second is that historical contextualization of Habermas within the postwar German frame yields an entirely new understanding of what is central to his theoretical project. We begin with the first. The recivilization of West Germany within the framework of Western liberal institutions and values was a historical process of great significance for Europe and the world. Habermas's career illuminates this transformation. Consider his statement from the early 1990s:

> In hindsight ... I recognize that as a student and in the immediate years thereafter, I didn't have an adequate assessment of the historical consequences of Adenauer's greatest achievement binding the Federal Republic strongly with the Western alliance and the Western social model ... Nevertheless, our radical opposition to [the] spirit [of restoration] of the Adenauer era appears to me to be still justified. Without [it] ... a sense of *zivilisierter Bürgersinn*, or a civic mentality as such, would never have been able to develop in the Federal Republic.[1]

In this passage, Habermas achieved a new historical perspective on the Federal Republic, the state with which his intellectual and political career had long been intertwined. For Habermas, Adenauer had long signified above all the "restoration spirit" of the 1950s – its hidden and not-so-hidden continuities with the Nazi past. But where Habermas once saw a contradiction between *Westbindung* and the cultivation of a civic mentality, Habermas later understood the two processes of integration with the West

[1] Haller, *The Past as Future*, 49.

as complementary – integration along dual tracks. The change in Habermas's perspective on Adenauer reflects the extent to which Habermas came to identify with a North Atlantic political model of liberal democracy. In bringing much of German academic and progressive public opinion along with him, he contributed to a liberalization of the German left.

Recall that in the 1950s debate over the social welfare state, it was the Schmittians who defended the ideal of the *Rechtsstaat*. In the context of the failed denazification of the universities, judiciary, and government, the ideal of the rule of law appeared to many leftists to be a mirage. Habermas's signature achievement as citizen of the Bonn Republic was to help the left reacquire an appreciation for the normative and institutional value of liberal constitutional order. By driving many of the most important representatives of the interwar Social Democratic traditions in legal theory into exile – Hans Kelsen, Hermann Heller, Karl Loewenstein, Ernst Fraenkel, Franz Neumann, and Otto Kirchheimer – the Third Reich severed the conceptual links between *Rechtsstaat*, welfare state, and democracy. Habermas's search for a method in the late 1950s was disoriented by this absence. His association with Wolfgang Abendroth was the key biographical fact that allowed him to pick up the thread of Weimar debates, going back to the classics of Schmitt and Smend and forward to the Schmitt school and Smend's influence on the Federal Constitutional Court. A series of high-profile court cases, especially the *Lüth* judgment of 1958, helped Habermas to consolidate his approach to Critical Theory on the postwar German terrain of Cold War and the Basic Law.

From Karl Marx, the writers of the Frankfurt School, and Wolfgang Abendroth, Habermas learned to be sceptical of the *Rechtsstaat* and its signatures – the separation of powers, the generality of the legal norm – as the political expression of bourgeois class interests. Because Habermas wrote *The Structural Transformation of the Public Sphere* in a framework contrasting state and civil society that he inherited from the thinkers Lorenz von Stein, Hegel and Marx, his text echoed the Marxian critique of legality. But *Transformation* also contained strong but previously neglected subterranean themes: a lament for the power of legal norms that had been eclipsed by the positivist cast of American political science and its German imitations, and the Marxian reduction of law to superstructure. Constitutional law appeared to Habermas as the refuge to which normativity had retreated. But the legal community was mired in anachronistic and conservative metaphysics: "On the one side, the guarantee of fundamental rights is the foundation of constitutionality … On the other side, Natural Law is devoid of any and every convincing philosophical justification."[2] Habermas found himself in the middle of an intellectual Cold War in which "the one side has taken up the heritage of revolution [and] the other the ideology of natural law."[3] Working through these aporia was Habermas's task. *Transformation* records his transition from skepticism to guarded optimism about the liberal idea of a constitutional order accountable to the public sphere. Habermas reenchanted the *Rechtsstaat* for leftists in his own generation sceptical of bourgeois legality and helped to steer younger generations away from the temptation of varied "great refusals" – be they of nonviolent struggle or the ideal of deliberative reason in the public sphere.

To steer the left onto the terrain of the *Rechtsstaat*, however, Habermas had to equip himself with the tools of the trade, to become what he once jokingly called a "lay jurist." The notion that jurists proper were a kind of modern clergy encodes Habermas's deep reservations about viewing jurists and judges as a class of Platonic guardians. In acquiring the tools of *Staatsrechtslehre* (constitutional theory and jurisprudence), Habermas expropriated the intellectual property of a highly conservative profession. The overwhelming majority of the West German constitutional lawyers had served the Third Reich unflinchingly, and there was no process of coming to terms with the past in the profession. Abendroth was an outsider among them. Moreover, the *Rechtsstaat* ideal had a long conservative pedigree in German history. Under the Kaiser, *Rechtsstaatlichkeit* had been disassociated from both the democratic Parliament and judicial review. In the Weimar Republic, too, the rule of law was weakened by a conservative judiciary. In the Third Reich, the ideal had been bastardized, drained of all sense.

In retrospect, we can see Habermas's intellectual project as a kind of grand bargain proposed to the German intellectual public: If the left would come to the *Rechtsstaat*, the right would come to accept the "internal connection" between the *Rechtsstaat* and democracy. No more would the constitution function as a moralistic superego

---

[2] Habermas, "Natural Law and Revolution," 113.
[3] Ibid.

for society, setting limits to democracy in the name of natural law or the Cold War. Jurists would no longer monopolize the interpretation of the constitution, and the constitution would be expected to evolve. The state would have to learn to tolerate civil disobedience. The legitimacy of legality would depend on expanded access to the public sphere and a more robust democratic genesis of the laws.

Habermas's description of the transformation of West German political culture as the result of an "opening without reserve"[4] is a myth, albeit a heroic and appealing one. The truth about West Germany's postwar transformation is more interesting, however. The contours of the opening were jagged. In the late 1950s and early 1960s, Habermas struggled to find anything redeeming in Adenauer's chancellor democracy. Prominent figures on the left rallied to the defense of the hitherto unloved *Rechtsstaat* in the *Spiegel* affair of 1962 and in the campaigns against the emergency powers-enabling amendment to the constitution. Habermas joined in the defense of the *Rechtsstaat* with other '58ers such as Jürgen Seifert, who together helped to reorient the German left toward a sympathetic view of liberal constitutionalism. As one scholar has written, "The danger of the forces of conservatism eroding democracy by legal means also sensitized many left-wing thinkers, who had previously been focused mainly on the economy, to the autonomy of the political."[5] Günther Frankenberg, who advised Habermas in questions of legal theory in the late 1980s, was, for example, first politicized in the campaigns of the 1960s against the emergency laws.[6] The threat of technocratic governance sharpened Habermas's focus on the question of how to secure democratic legitimation for decisions of public consequence. In the 1970s, the threat to popular sovereignty came from the paternalism of the welfare state (the "juridification of the lifeworld" in the *Theory of Communicative Action*) and a state that overreacted to the threat of domestic radicalism. These heightened Habermas's awareness of the ambivalent promise of law as a means of social integration.

Habermas was indeed a Westernizer of German political culture and a protagonist of its liberalization. But his embrace of the

---

[4] Habermas, "Die Neokonservativen," 54; Interview with Axel Honneth, "Dialektik," 161.

[5] See Müller, *A Dangerous Mind*, 186.

[6] Author's conversation with Professor Günter Frankenberg, June 25, 2005, Frankfurt am Main.

rule of law signified neither the end of Critical Theory nor the end of history in the neoliberal sense. As discussed in Chapter 4, the multidimensional political crisis of 1981–7 – from Euromissiles to *Historikerstreit* – was the theater in which Habermas worked out his own account of *Westbindung*, the key to which was his redefinition of the West as a fallibilistic, open, democratic experiment. The price exacted for constitutional patriotism was civil disobedience. By explicating the specific dignity of civil disobedience, he reenchanted the *Rechtsstaat*. By trying to draw legality and morality closer together without collapsing the two spheres, Habermas sought to chart a middle path between two historical variants of German statism: legal positivism and natural law jurisprudence. Ultimately, Habermas's reconstructive work on the concepts of modernity and constitutionalism in the 1980s staged a mutually transformative encounter between Germany and the West that has helped to keep the meaning of Western liberal democracy open for all its citizens. For that we are in his debt.

Habermas's career and corpus provide a privileged vantage point for thinking about postwar Germany because the reservations he had about the opening to the West were thoughtful and revealing of real problems in German public life. These included strong criticisms of the juridification of politics, the countermajoritarian power of judges, and the threat posed by human rights conceived metaphysically and implemented paternalistically. With his critical perspective on the value jurisprudence of the "Karlsruhe Republic," Habermas provided us with a new variant of the dialectic of enlightenment: a dialectic of legal enlightenment in which human rights can become a tool of state power rather than a barrier against it.

Habermas's search for a method for redeeming the original validity claim of the *Rechtsstaat* drove him to become an interdisciplinary thinker. No other figure in postwar German intellectual life reformulated such broad swaths of German philosophical and political discourse. His lengthy forays into jurisprudence led him to Carl Schmitt and his school and contributed to the belated process of *Vergangenheitsbewältigung* in the legal field. His career also sheds light on the critical generation of the '58ers, who did so much to reorient German political culture. Finally, Habermas is a representative of the broader West German literate public sphere of which the publishing house *Suhrkamp* is an emblem.

Habermas's interest in American pragmatism and appropriation of John Austin's speech-act theory have led many readers to consider Habermas a bridge-builder between the spheres of Anglo-American analytic and Continental philosophy. Habermas's description of the opening without reserve, too, addressed the German reception of American philosophers in particular. This book has shown, by contrast, that Habermas is preeminently a German thinker, but not in an essentialist sense. A major theme of this book is Habermas's decades-long struggle with the intellectual legacies of Max Weber, Karl Marx, and Carl Schmitt, thinkers who cast a long shadow over any effort to conceptualize the relationship between law and politics. Habermas's struggle required him to work through persistent antinomies in German intellectual traditions: the so-called formal versus the material elements in law, the *Rechtsstaat* and the *Sozialsstaat*, legal positivism and natural law, the state's monopoly on violence and the right of resistance.

From Max Weber and his mentors at the Institute for Social Research, Theodor Adorno and Max Horkheimer, Habermas absorbed a narrative of the history of the West as a story of decline. The ascent of instrumental rationality in the economic and political realms had yielded a net loss in human freedom. Weber's critique of the regulatory law of the German social welfare state set the agenda for a century of German legal theorists who worried about law's "deformalization" by considerations of social justice. Thinkers thus oscillated between the conceptual poles Weber's work codified – the "formal" and the "material." As shown in Chapters 2 and 3, Habermas in the 1960s confronted Max Weber's theory of legal positivism and the way technocratic and decisionist politics seemed to flow from the refusal to burden law with moral and political content. In the 1970s, Habermas developed his theory of communicative action in explicit opposition to the reductive account of rationality he believed was Weber's legacy to Horkheimer and Adorno. Finally, in the 1980s and early 1990s, Habermas identified Max Weber's thought as a major obstacle to the contemporary ability to grasp the internal connection between democratic deliberation and the rule of law.

Although Habermas insists on his filiation to Marxist tradition broadly conceived, it is clear that Marx's denigration of the rule of law was incompatible with Habermas's intellectual project in the 1980s. Marxism had exiled Habermas, as it were, to a discourse of political economy in which he had never felt "at home." Attacks on the German *Rechtsstaat* by the German right in the 1960s, 1970s, and 1980s enabled Habermas to transcend this limitation of much Marxist thought and to feel more "at home," as it were, with the liberal democratic West. As he explained in a recent interview, he has long considered himself a "left-liberal."[7] When asked whether his political theory displays a "legal" or "liberal" turn in the 1980s, he replied:

> No, the interest in legal theory stems from the 1950s, as I came to know the literature, and regretted not having studied law. The idea of a liberal turn isn't correct in my view: I was a "left-liberal, left of Social Democracy" in the '60s also. But my interest in political economy, in which I had never felt at home, declined.... I believe that I have been true to my basic political convictions.... You should not underestimate that in the '60s, a left loyal to the constitution existed that was left of the Godesburg SPD; I felt I belonged to this group: we took socialism seriously, if also in confrontation with Soviet Communism. If you had passed through the controls at the Bahnhof Friedrichstrasse on the way to the GDR [as Habermas had done in 1952 in order to see a Brecht piece at the Berliner Ensemble], one must be healed of all illusions.[8]

In March 1990, Habermas circulated an essay to friends addressing the question of how socialism should be rethought after 1989. Habermas believed that the collapse of East German communism vindicated positions he had held since the early 1960s. His description of "the West European left" as a homogeneous group that had only been burdened by Eastern Bloc distortions of socialism but never deceived by it was problematic as a general statement but fair as a self-description. His participation in annual discussions with the Yugoslavian "Praxis" group of nonaligned left theorists, which met throughout the 1970s on the island of Korcula, was consistent with his self-description as a representative of a non-communist left.

For this non-communist left, he argued, the appropriate reaction to the velvet revolutions of 1989 was neither melancholy, disillusionment, nor contrition. They had no reason, to cite his

[7] Author's private correspondence with Habermas, June 7, 2005.
[8] Ibid.

peculiarly religious metaphor, "to go around in sack and ashes."[9] "The destruction of Eastern Bloc socialism is trumpeted by Strauss [of the Christian Social Union] and overlooks the fact that "... this socialism was sharply criticized within the left – not least out of fear that socialism would be equated with ... Soviet Marxism."[10] The "non-communist left left of Social Democracy," Habermas asserted, had neither succumbed to illusions about communism nor failed to keep alive an awareness of the price European social democratic parties had paid for the achievement of their post–World War II welfare states.[11] It thus was uniquely positioned to bear a new progressive agenda. This left is today the "bearer of the memory" that "more was meant" by socialism than state-driven social policy.[12] East German intellectuals would have to learn what "... we in the West learned decades ago: to develop a self-critique of the capitalist, mass democratic, constitutional welfare state, with its strengths and weaknesses."[13] After the expiration of state socialism, this mode of critique was "... the single eye of the needle through which all must pass."[14] Habermas's reading of the significance of 1989 is but one part of his larger corpus of reflections on the postwar European welfare state, its material successes and institutional shortcomings. His reconstructive history of modern legal and political theory offers today's radical reformers a usable past.

While Habermas ultimately came to view the Marxian and Weberian views of law as too "thin," he also arrived at the conclusion that the Schmittian and Smendian versions of law were too "thick." This book presents the constitutional and political theory of Carl Schmitt as a constitutive element of major public debates: the Schmittian critique of the Basic Law and the welfare state in the 1950s, the turn to theories of technocracy by German conservatives in the 1960s, and the arguments developed by conservative jurists in the 1980s against civil disobedience. In each of these contexts, Habermas saw different versions of the same threats: the dangers of

---

[9] Habermas, "*Was heisst Sozialismus heute?*" in idem, *Die nachholende Revolution: Kleine Politische Schriften VII* (Frankfurt/Main, 1990), 188 (*NR* hereafter).

[10] Habermas, "Die Stunde der nationalen Empfindung. Republikanische Gesinnung oder Nationalbewusstein?" in *NR*, 164.

[11] Habermas,"*Was heisst Sozialismus heute?*," 192–3.

[12] Ibid.

[13] Ibid., 203.

[14] Ibid.

authoritarian legalism, a bias toward the state, and an occlusion of the public sphere. In Chapters 2 and 5, Habermas's critical evaluation of the Smendian strand of German legal tradition was portrayed as the medium through which he assessed the dangers of welfare state paternalism and judicial activism by conservative judges.

After 1989, Habermas promoted his procedural version of democratic theory as a "thin" alternative to a variety of errors of "concreteness," which included the excessive thickness of both Smendian value jurisprudence and Schmittian statism. Habermas's procedural reinterpretation of the republican tradition was in large part designed as a rebuttal of Schmitt's antirepublican stance. Schmitt's theory of a homogeneous nation, anchored in a consciousness of its past, was the key position against which Habermas defined his procedural theory. As he asserted in 1996, "The idea of a procedural, future-oriented popular sovereignty along these lines renders meaningless the demand to tie political will-formation to the substantive a priori of a past, pre-politically established consensus among homogeneous members of a nation."[15] Habermas characterized Schmitt as a figure who conceived the people as a "prepolitical datum," that is, who existed before any social contract, and thus failed to appreciate the significance of the decision to engage in "constitution-founding praxis."[16] Habermas saw himself providing an alternative to Schmitt's theory: "In contrast with Carl Schmitt's account, on this conception, popular sovereignty and human rights, democracy and the constitutional state, are conceptually intertwined."[17] In order to reach his mature political account of the co-originality of democracy and the rule of law, therefore, Habermas had to navigate and surmount visions of law and politics that were either too "thick" or too "thin."

Over decades of critical encounters, Habermas met the challenges of Marx and Weber, Schmitt and Smend. His trajectory from outsider to insider in the history of the Federal Republic should not obscure from view the significance of his accomplishments in reconstructing German political and intellectual tradition. Habermas's grappling with the theoretical concepts of state, constitution, and law not only succeeded in transcending tenacious antinomies in

[15] Habermas, "The Nation, the Rule of Law, and Democracy," 137.
[16] Ibid.
[17] Ibid.

German tradition but by doing so also helped anchor West Germany in the West. As such, his thought played a dramatic part in the intellectual reconstruction and recovery work of the Bonn Republic, a polity whose historical contours are now becoming clearer. Making good on the promise of the *Rechtsstaat* was an agenda rooted in Habermas's biographical circumstances – his generational identity as a '58er. Not only his explicit political and legal thought but also his social theory bear the unmistakeable imprint of its genesis over four decades in the Bonn Republic.

Bibliography

Archives Consulted

Friedrich-Ebert Stiftung, Bonn
  Willy Brandt Archiv
  Helmut Schmidt Archiv
Berlin Newspaper Archive
International Institute for Social History, Amsterdam
  Nachlass Wolfgang Abendroth
Horkheimer Archiv, Frankfurt am Main
  Nachlass Alexander Mitscherlich
  Nachlass Herbert Marcuse
  Nachlass Max Horkheimer
Main State Archives Nordrhein-Westfalen
  Nachlass Carl Schmitt

Interviews

Jurgen Habermas, July 3, 2004; June 7, 2005; June 20, 2005
Günter Frankenberg, June 25, 2005
Elizabeth Abendroth, July 1, 2005
Klaus Günther, June 10, 2005
Wilhelm Hennis, June 18, 2005
Lutz Wingert, May 20, 2005
Joachim Perels, February 14, 2005
Detlev Horster, July 28, 2001
Ulrich Preuss, July 20, 2001
Jürgen Seifert, July 10, 2000
Ingeborg Maus, June 15, 2000

Ludwig von Friedeburg, June 16, 2000

Aarnio, Aulis & K. Tuori. *Law, Morality and Discursive Rationality*. Helsinki: Hakapaino, 1989.

Abelshauser, Werner. *Die Langen Fünfziger Jahre: Wirtschaft und Gesellschaft der Bundesrepublik Deutschland, 1949–66*. Düsseldorf: Schwann, 1987.

Abendroth, Wolfgang. *Das Grundgesetz: Eine Einführung in seine politischen Probleme*. Pfüllingen: Verlag Gunther Neske, 1966.

"Zum Begriff des demokratischen und sozialen Rechtsstaates im Grundgesetz der Bundesrepublik Deutschland." In *Rechtsstaatlichkeit und Sozialstaatlichkeit: Aufsätze und Essays*, ed. Ernst Forsthoff, 114–43. Darmstadt: Wissenschaftliche Buchgesellschaft, 1968; originally published 1954.

"Zur Funktion der Gewerkschaften in der westdeutschen Demokratie." In Herbert Sultan and Wolfgang Abendroth, *Bürokratischer Verwaltungsstaat und soziale Demokratie*, 59–68. Hannover: Norddeutsche Verlagsanstalt Goedel, 1955.

"Staatsverfassung und Betriebsverfassung." In Herbert Sultan and Wolfgang Abendroth, *Bürokratischer Verwaltungsstaat und soziale Demokratie*, 103–10. Hannover: Norddeutsche Verlagsanstalt Goedel, 1955.

"Bundesverfassung und Widerstandsrecht," in *Antagonistische Gesellschaft und Politische Demokratie*. Neuwied: Luchterhand, 1967; originally 1955.

"Das KPD-Verbotsurteil des Bundesverfassungsgerichts. Ein Beitrag zum Problem der richterlichen Interpretation von Rechtsgrundsätzen der Verfassung im demokratischen Staat." In *Antagonistische Gesellschaft und Politische Demokratie*. Neuwied: Luchterhand, 1967; originally 1955.

Festschrift für Adolf Arndt zum 65. Geburtstag, ed. Horst Ehmke, Carlo Schmid, & Hans Scharoun. Frankfurt am Main: Europäische Verlagsanstalt, 1969.

Der Kampf um das Grundgesetz: Über die politische Bedeutung der Verfassungsinterpretation. Referate und Diskussionen eines Kolloquiums aus Anlass des. 70. Geburtstages von Wolfgang Abendroth. Frankfurt am Main: Syndikat, 1977.

"Was ist heute 'links' in der BRD?" In *Die Linke. Bilanz und Perspektiven für die 80er*, ed. Hermann L. Gremliza & Heinrich Hannover, 9–38. Hamburg: VSA-Verlag, 1980.

"Die Funktion des Politikwissenschaftlers und Staatsrechtslehrers Hermann Heller in der Weimarer Republik und in der Bundesrepublik Deutschland." In *Staatslehre in der Weimarer Republik: Hermann Heller zu ehren*, ed. Christoph Müller & Ilse Staff. Frankfurt am Main: Suhrkamp, 1985.

Abendroth, Wolfgang, R. Kessler, J. Perels, H. Rottleuthner, & J. Seifert. "Diskussion über Probleme sozialistischer Rechtspolitik. Ein Gesprächsprotokoll." In *Probleme der Marxistische Rechtstheorie*, ed. Hubert Rottleuthner, 392–417. Frankfurt am Main: Suhrkamp, 1975.

Abendroth, Wolfgang, & Herbert Sultan. Bürokratischer Verwaltungsstaat und soziale Demokratie: Beiträge zu Staatslehre und Staatsrecht der Bundesrepublik. Hannover: O. Goedel, 1955.

Aboulafia, Mitchell, Myra Bookman, & Catherine Kemp, ed. *Habermas and Pragmatism*. London: Routledge, 2002.

Adorno, Theodor. "Marginalien zu Theorie und Praxis." In *Stichwörte*. Frankfurt am Main: Suhrkamp, 1969.

Albrecht, Clemens. *Die Intellektuelle Gründung der Bundesrepublik: Eine Wirkungsgeschichte der Frankfurter Schule*. Frankfurt am Main: Campus Verlag, 1999.

Alexy, Robert. *Theorie der juristische Argumentation*. Frankfurt am Main: Suhrkamp, 1978.

A Theory of Constitutional Rights. Trans. Julian Rivers. Oxford: Oxford University Press, 2002.

Altmann, Rüdiger. "Zur Rechtstellung der Öffentlichen Verbände." *Zeitschrift für Politik* 2:3 (1955), 211–27.

"Eierköpfe für Erhard? Diskussion um den Beraterstab des Kanzlers." *Die Zeit* (November 22, 1963).

Arndt, Hans-Joachim. "Öffentlichkeit als Staatsersatz." *Archiv für Rechts- und Sozialphilosophie* 42: 2 (1956), 239–47.

Augstein, Rudolf, ed. "Historikerstreit." Die Dokumentation der Kontroverse um die Einzigartigkeit der Nationalsozialistische Juden Vernichtung. München: Piper, GMBH, 1987.

Badke, Rolf. "Feind oder Gegner?" *Geschichte in Wissenschaft und Unterricht*, 9 (1958), 686–95.

Badura, Peter. "Staat, Recht und Verfassung in der Integrationslehre. Zum Tode von Rudolf Smend." *Der Staat* 16 (1977).

Bahrdt, Hans P. "Helmut Schelskys technischer Staat." *Atomzeitalter* 9 (1961).

Barion, Hans, Ernst Forsthoff, & Werner Weber. *Festschrift für Carl Schmitt zum 70. Geburtstag.* Berlin: Dunckler & Humblot, 1959.

Baynes, Kenneth & René von Schomberg, eds. *Discourse and Democracy: Essays on Habermas's* Between Facts and Norms. Albany, NY: State University of New York Press, 2002.

Baynes, Kenneth. "Democracy and *Rechtsstaat*: Habermas's *Faktizitat und Geltung*." In *The Cambridge Companion to Habermas*, ed. Steven K. White, 201–32. Cambridge, England: Cambridge University Press, 1995.

Becker, Jürgen. "Die Wehrhafte Demokratie des Grundgesetzes." In *Handbuch des Staatsrechts VII*, 1992: 309–88.

Berghahn, Volker R. *The Americanization of German Industry, 1945–1973.* Leamington Spa: Berg, 1986.

Bernstein, J. M. *Recovering Ethical Life: Jürgen Habermas and the Future of Critical Theory.* London: Routledge, 1995.

Bernstein, Richard J., ed. *Habermas and Modernity.* Cambridge, England: Polity Press, 1985.

ed. "The Retrieval of the Democratic Ethos." In "Habermas on Law and Democracy: Critical Exchanges," ed. Michel Rosenfeld, Special Issue. *Cardozo Law Review* 17: 4–5 (March 1996), 1127–46.

Beyme, Klaus von. "Der Neokorporatismus und die Politik des begrenzten Pluralismus in der Bundesrepublik." In *Stichwörte zur geistige Situation der Zeit*, Vol I: *Nation und Republik*, ed. Jürgen Habermas, 229–62. Frankfurt am Main: Suhrkamp, 1979.

Birnbaum, Norman. *After Progress: American Social Reform and European Socialism in the Twentieth Century.* Oxford, England: Oxford University Press, 2001.

Blair, Philip. "Law and Politics in Germany." *Political Studies* 26: 3 (1978), 348–62.

Blanke, Thomas, & Dieter Sterzel. "Demonstrationsrecht und Demonstrationsfreiheit in der BRD." In *Demonstrationsrecht und gewaltfreier Widerstand: Argumente zur aktuellen Diskussion*, ed. Kommittee für Grundrechte und Demokratie. Sensbachtal: Dietelhoff, 1983.

Bleek, Wilhelm, & Hans J. Lietzmann, eds. *Schulen der deutschen Politikwissenschaft.* Opladen: Leske and Budrich, 1999.

Böckenförde, Ernst-Wolfgang. *Gesetz und gesetzgebende Gewalt: Von den Anfängen der deutschen Staatsrechtslehre bis zur Höhe des Staatsrechtlichen Positivismus.* Berlin: Duncker & Humblot, 1957.

"Die deutsche Staatsrechtslehre in der Zeit des Nationalsozialismus." *Veröffentlichungen der Vereinigung der Deutschen Staatsrechtslehrer*, 60. Berlin: de Gruyter, 2001.

Bloch, Ernst. *Natural Law and Human Dignity*. Cambridge, MA: MIT Press, 1986; originally published 1961.

Bourdieu, Pierre. "Intellectual Field and Creative Project." *Social Science Information* 8 (April 1969), 89–119.

Brandt, Willy. "'Mehr Demokratie wagen.' Innen- und Gesellschaftspolitik 1966–1974." Bearb. Wolther von Kieseritzky. Berliner Ausgabe, Nr. 7. Bonn: Dietz, 2001.

Braunthal, Gerhard. *The West German Social Democrats, 1969–82*. Epping, England: Bowker, 1983.

Brunkhorst, Hauke. "Critical Theory and the Analysis of Mass Society," 248–79. In *The Cambridge Companion to Critical Theory*, ed. Fred Rush. Cambridge, England: Cambridge University Press, 2004.

Brunkhorst, Hauke, & Peter Nielsen, eds. *Das Recht der Republik*. Frankfurt am Main: Suhrkamp, 1991.

Bubner, Rüdiger. "Das sprachliche Medium der Politik." In *Antike Themen und ihre moderne Verwandlung*, 188–202. Frankfurt am Main: Suhrkamp, 1992.

Bubner, Rüdiger, et al., eds. *Hermeneutik und Dialektik. Festschrift fur H.G. Gadamer*, Pt. 1. Tübingen: 1970.

Buchstein, Hubertus. "Franz Neumann im Schatten der Kritischen Theorie. Eine Bemerkung zum Verhältnis von Kritischer Theorie und Politikwissenschaft mit drei bisher unbekannten Texten Neumanns." *Internationale wissenschaftliche Korrespondenz zur Geschichte der deutschen Arbeiterbewegung* 25, (1989), 490–520.

Bude, Heinz, & Bernd Greiner, eds. *Westbindungen: Amerika in der Bundesrepublik Deutschland*. Hamburg: Hamburger Edition, 1999.

Bulla, E. "Die Lehre von der streitbaren Demokratie." *Archiv des Öffentlichen Rechts* 98, 3 (1973), 340–60.

Caldwell, Peter C. *Popular Sovereignty and the Crisis of German Constitutional Law: The Theory and Practice of Weimar Constitutionalism*. Durham, NC: Duke University Press, 1997.

Caldwell, Peter C. & William Scheuerman, eds. *From Liberal Democracy to Fascism: Legal and Political Thought in the Weimar Republic*. Leiden: Humanities Press, 2000.

Calhoun, Craig. *Habermas and the Public Sphere*. Cambridge, MA: MIT Press, 1992.

Cammann, Alexander. "Uber die Zaune und Sperren hinweg. Zum Tod von Jurgen Seifert," *Vorgänge: Zeitschrift für Bürgerrechte und Gesellschaftspolitik* 170, 44 (2005), 128–9.

Chambers, Simone. "Democracy, Popular Sovereignty, and Constitutional Legitimacy," *Constellations* 11, 2 (2004), 153–73.

Chatzoudis, Georgios. *Die Deutschlandspolitik der SPD in der zweiten Hälfte des Jahres 1989.* Historische Forschungszentrum der Friedrich Ebert Stiftung 60. Bonn: FES, 2005.

Cohen, Jean, & Andrew Arato. *Civil Society and Political Theory.* Cambridge, MA: MIT Press, 1992.

Curran, Vivian Grosswald. "Formalism and Antiformalism in French and German Judicial Methodology." Draft manuscript, "Perceptions of Europe and Perspectives on a European Order in Legal Scholarship During the Era of Fascism and National Socialism," European University Institute Workshop, September 29–30, 2000.

Dahrendorf, Ralf. *Society and Democracy in Germany.* New York: Norton, 1967.

Davis, Belinda. "The Gender of War and Peace: Rhetoric in the West German Peace Movement of the Early 1980s," *Mitteilungsblatt des Instituts für soziale Bewegungen* (Special Issue "Peace Movements as Social Movements") 32 (December 2004), 84–114.

Deflem, Mathieu. "Habermas, Modernity and Law." *Philosophy and Social Criticism* (Special Issue) 20: 4 (1994).

Demirovic, Alex. *Der Nonkonformistische Intellektuelle: Die Entwicklung der Kristischen Theorie zur Frankfurter Schule.* Frankfurt am Main: Suhrkamp, 1991.

Denninger, Erhard. "Freiheitsordnung – Wertordnung, Pflichtenordnung." In *Verfassung, Verfassungsgerichtsbarkeit, Politik*, ed. Mehdi Tohidipur, 163–83. Frankfurt am Main: Suhrkamp, 1976.

"Bundesverfassungsgericht zwischen Recht und Politik." In *Das Recht der Republik*, ed. Hauke Brunkhorst & Peter Nielsen, 288–304. Frankfurt am Main: Suhrkamp, 1999.

"Judicial Review Revisited: The German Experience." *Tulane Law Review* 59 (1984–5), 1013–31.

Deppe, Frank. "Diskussion: Zum Stand der staatstheoretischen Debatte in der Bundesrepublik." In *Abendroth-Forum. Marburger Gespräche aus Anlass des 70. Geburtstags von W. Abendroth*, 295–327. Marburg: Verlag Arbeiterbewegung und Gesellschaftswissenschaft, 1977.

"Das Dilemma der verfassungspolitischen Diskussion der Linken in der Bundesrepublik." In *Probleme der Marxistische Rechtstheorie*, ed. Hubert Rottleuthner, 419–83. Frankfurt am Main: Suhrkamp, 1975.

Derrida, Jacques. "Declarations of Independence." *New Political Science* 15 (Summer 1986), 7–15.

Dews, Peter. *Autonomy and Solidarity. Interviews with Jurgen Habermas.* London: Verso, 1987.

Habermas: A Critical Reader. Oxford, England: Blackwell, 1999.

Dietrich, Barbara, & Joachim Perels, eds. *Wolfgang Abendroth: Ein Leben in der Arbeiterbewegung. Gespräche aufgezeichnet und herausgeben von Barbara Dietrich und Joachim Perels.* Frankfurt am Main: Suhrkamp, 1977.

Dietze, Hans-Helmut. *Naturrecht der Gegenwart.* Bonn: Rohrscheid, 1936.

Doehring, Karl von, ed. "Säkularisation und Utopie." In *Ebracher Studien. Festgabe für Ernst Forsthoff zum 65. Geburtstag.* München: C. H. Beck, 1967.

Drath, Martin. "Die Gewaltenteilung im heutigen deutschen Staatsrecht." In *Faktoren der Machtbildung*, 99–138. Berlin: Duncker & Humblot, 1952.

Dreier, Ralf, & Wolfgang Sellert, eds. *Recht und Justiz im "Dritten Reich."* Frankfurt am Main: Suhrkamp, 1989.

Dreier, Ralf. *Recht, Moral, Ideologie: Studien zur Rechtstheorie.* Frankfurt am Main: Suhrkamp, 1981.

Dubiel, Helmut. "Der entfesselte Reise? Die zivile Gesellschaft und die liberale Demokratie nach 1989." In *Wozu Politikwissenschaft? Über das Neue in der Politik*, ed. Claus Leggewie, 49–60. Darmstadt: Wissenschaftliche Buchgesellschaft, 1994.

Kritische Theorie der Gesellschaft. Eine einführende Rekonstruktion von den Anfängen bis Habermas. München: Weinheim, 1985.

Dubiel, Helmut, Ulrich Rödel, & Günter Frankenberg. *Die Demokratische Frage.* Frankfurt am Main. Suhrkamp, 1989.

Dürig, Gunther. "Verfassung und Verwaltung im Wohlfahrtsstaat." *Juristenzeitung* 8, 7/8, (April 15, 1953), 193–9.

"Der Grundrechtssatz von der Menschenwürde." *Archiv des öffentlichen Rechts* 81, 1 (1956), 2–54.

Duve, Freimut, ed. *Briefe zur Verteidigung der bürgerliche Freiheit. Nachträge 1978.* Reinbek bei Hamburg: Rowohlt, 1978.

Dyzenhaus, David L. "Legitimacy of Legality," *University of Toronto Law Journal* 46, 1 (Winter 1996), 129–80.

Legality and Legitimacy: Carl Schmitt, Hans Kelsen and Hermann Heller in Weimar. Oxford, England: Oxford University Press, 1997.

Law as Politics: Carl Schmit's Critique of Liberalism. Durham, NC: Duke University Press, 1998.

Edwards, G. E. *German Political Parties. A Documentary Guide.* Cardiff, Wales: University of Wales Press, 1998.

Ehmke, Horst. "Staat und Gesellschaft als verfassungstheoretisches Problem." In *Staatsverfassung und Kirchenordnung. Festgabe für Rudolf Smend zum 80. Geburtstag am 15 Januar 1962*, ed. Konrad Hesse, Siegfried Reicke, & Ulrich Scheuner, 23–49. Tübingen: J. C. B. Mohr, 1962.

Wirtschaft und Verfassung. Die Verfassungsrechtsprechung des Supreme Court zur Wirtschaftsregulierung. Berkeley-Kölner Rechtsstudien, Kölner Reihe, Vol. 2. Karlsruhe: C. F. Muller, 1961.

Eisfeld, Rainer, Michael Th. Greven, & Hans Karl Rupp, eds. *Political Science and Regime Change in 20th Century Germany.* New York: Nova Science Publishers, 1996.

Ellwein, Thomas. *Krisen und Reformen. Die Bundesrepublik seit den sechziger Jahren.* München: Deutscher Taschenbuch Verlag, 1993.

Eppler, Erhard. *Die tödliche Utopie der Sicherheit.* Reinbek bei Hamburg: Rowohlt, 1983.

Wege aus der Gefahr. Reinbek bei Hamburg: Rowohlt, 1981.

Erhard, Ludwig. *Prosperity through Competition*, trans. & ed. Edith Temple Roberts & John B. Wood. New York: Praeger, 1958.

Fechner, Erich. "Freiheit und Zwang im Sozialen Rechtsstaat." In *Recht und Staat in Geschichte und Gegenwart*, 73–95. Tübingen: J. C. B. Mohr, 1954.

Fehrenbach, Heide, & Ute Poiger, eds. *Transactions, Transgressions, Transformations: American Culture in Western Europe and Japan.* New York: Berghahn, 2000.

Fichter, Tilman, & Siegward Lonnendonker. *Kleine Geschichte des SDS: Der Sozialistische Deutsche Studentenbund von 1946 bis Auflösung.* Berlin: Rotbuch Verlag, 1977.

Finn, John E. *Constitutions in Crisis. Political Violence and the Rule of Law.* Oxford, England: Oxford University Press, 1991.

Fischer, Frank. "Einleitung: 'Die Entspannung unzerstörbar machen.' Internationale Beziehungen und deutsche Frage 1974–1982." In *Willy Brandt Ausgabe*, Vol. 9. Bonn: Dietz, 2003.

Flechtheim, Ossip Kurt, ed. *Grundlegung der politischen Wissenschaft*. Meisenheim am Glan: Hain, 1958.

Forsthoff, Ernst. *Die Verwaltung als Leistungsträger*. Stuttgart: Kohlhammer, 1938.

Forsthoff, Ernst, trans. and ed. *Vom Geist der Gesetze, Charles Louis de Secondat de Montesquieu*. Tübingen: Laupp, 1951.

"Verfassungsprobleme des Sozialstaats." In *Rechtsstaatlichkeit und Sozialstaatlichkeit: Aufsätze und Essays*, 145–64. Darmstadt: Wissenschaftliche Buchgesellschaft, 1968; originally published 1954.

"Begriff und Wesen des sozialen Rechtsstaates." In *Rechtsstaatlichkeit und Sozialstaatlichkeit: Aufsätze und Essays*, 165–201. Darmstadt: Wissenschaftliche Buchgesellschaft, 1968; originally published 1954.

Lehrbuchs des Verwaltungsrechts, 5th ed. München: C. H. Beck, 1955.

"Umbildung des Verfassungsgesetzes." In *Verfassung: Beiträge zur Verfassungstheorie*, ed. Manfred Friedrich, 117–52. Darmstadt: Wissenschafliche Buchgesellschaft, 1978; originally published 1959.

"Die Bundesrepublik Deutschland. Umrisse einer Analyse." *Merkur* 14, 9 (September 1960), 807–21.

Rechtsstaat im Wandel. Stuttgart: Kohlhammer, 1964.

ed. *Rechtsstaatlichkeit und Sozialstaatlichkeit: Aufsätze und Essays*. Darmstadt: Wissenschaftliche Buchgesellschaft, 1968.

Der Staat der Industriegesellschaft. Dargestellt am Beispiel der Bundesrepublik Deutschland. München: C. H. Beck, 1971.

Forsthoff, Ernst, Werner Weber, & Franz Wieacker, eds. *Festschrift für Ernst-Rudolf Huber. Zum 70. Geburtstag am 8. Juni 1973*. Göttingen: Verlag Otto Schwarz & Co., 1973.

Fraenkel, Ernst. *The Dual State*. New York: Oxford University Press, 1941.

Fraenkel, Ernst, & Heinrich von Gablentz, eds. *Staat und Politik*. Frankfurt am Main: Fischer Lexikon, 1959.

Frankenberg, Günter. "Why Care? The Trouble with Social Rights." In "Habermas on Law and Democracy: Critical Exchanges," ed. Michel Rosenfeld, Special Issue, *Cardozo Law Review* 17: 4–5 (March 1996), 1365–90.

Frei, Norbert. *Adenauer's Germany and the Nazi Past: The Politics of Amnesty and Integration*, trans. Joel Golb. New York and Chichester: Columbia University Press, 2002.

Friedmann, Wolfgang G. *Law and Social Change in Contemporary Britain*. London: Steven and Sons, 1951.

"Übergesetzliche Rechtsgrundsätze und die Lösung von Rechtsproblemen." In *Naturrecht oder Rechtspositivismus*, ed. Werner Maihofer, 405–28. Bad Homburg vor der Höhe: Hermann Gentner Verlag, 1962.

Friedrich, Manfred, ed. *Verfassung: Beiträge zur Verfassungstheorie*. Darmstadt: Wissenschafliche Buchgesellschaft, 1978.

Fucks, Wilhelm. *Formeln zur Macht Prognosen uber Volker, Wirtschaft, Potentiale*. Stuttgart: Deutsche Verlags-Anstalt, 1965.

Gehlen, Arnold. "Anthropologische Ansicht der Technik." In *Technik im technischen Zeitalter*, ed. Hans Freyer et al. Düsseldorf: Schilling, 1965.

Gerber, Hans. "Die Sozialstaatsklausel des Grundgesetzes." In *Verfassung: Beiträge zur Verfassungstheorie*, ed. Manfred Friedrich, 340–410. Darmstadt: Wissenschafliche Buchgesellschaft, 1978; originally published 1956.

Geyer, Michael. "Cold War Angst: The Case of West-German Opposition to Rearmament and Nuclear Weapons." In *The Miracle Years: A Cultural History of West Germany, 1949–1968*, ed. Hanna Schissler, 376–408. Princeton, NJ: Princeton University Press, 2000.

Girndt, Helmut, Jürgen Habermas, & Eberhard Simons. "Zum Legitimation politischen Handelns – Eine Auseinandersetzung mit Jürgen Habermas." In *Legitimationsprobleme politischer Systeme*, ed. Peter Graf Kielmannsegg, 35–78. Opladen: Westdeutscher Verlag, 1976.

Glotz, Peter, ed. *Ziviler Ungehorsam im Rechtsstaat*. Frankfurt: Suhrkamp, 1983.

Grass, Günter. *Widerstand Lernen. Politische Gegenreden 1980–83*. Darmstadt/Neuwied: Luchterhand, 1984.

Grebing, Helga. *Konservative gegen die Demokratie: konservative Kritik an der Demokratie in der Bundesrepublik nach 1945*. Frankfurt am Main: Europäische Verlagsanstalt, 1971.

Greiffenhagen, Martin. *Das Dilemma des Konservatismus in Deutschland*. München: Piper, 1971.

Grimm, Dieter. "Verfassungspatriotismus nach der Wiedervereinigung." In *Das Recht der Republik*, ed. Hauke Brunkhorst & Peter Niesen, 305–16. Frankfurt am Main: Suhrkamp, 1999.

Grote, Rainer. "Rule of Law, *Rechtsstaat*, and État de Droit." In *Constitutionalism, Universalism and Democracy – Comparative Analysis*, ed. Christian Starck. Baden-Baden: Nomos Verlagsgesellschaft, 1999.

Güggenberger, Bernd, & Tine Stein, eds. *Die Verfassungsdiskussion im Jahr der deutschen Einheit: Analysen – Hintergründe – Materialien.* München: Carl Hanser Verlag, 1991.

Günther, Frieder. *Denken vom Staat her: die bundesdeutsche Staatsrechtslehre zwischen Dezision und Integration, 1949–1970.* München: Oldenbourg, 2004.

Güsy, Christoph. "Die 'freiheitliche Demokratische Grundordnung' in der Rechtsprechung des Bundesverfassungsgerichts." *Archiv des Öffentlichen Rechts* 105, 2 (July 1980): 279–310.

Häberle, Peter. *Die Verfassung des Pluralismus.* Frankfurt am Main: Suhrkamp, 1980.

Habermas, Jürgen. "Mit Heidegger gegen Heidegger denken. Zur Veröffentlichung von Vorlesungen aus dem Jahre 1935." *Frankfurter Allgemeine Zeitung* (July 25, 1953). Reprinted in *Philosophisch-Politisch Profilen*, 3rd ed. (Frankfurt/Main: Suhrkamp, 1998), 65–71; originally published 1959.

"Unruhe, erste Bürgerpflicht: Römerbergrede gegen die Atombewaffnung des Bundeswehr." *Diskus* 8, 5 (June, 1958).

"Review of Koselleck and Kesting." Reprinted in *Philosophisch-politische Profilen*, 3rd ed., 435–44. Frankfurt: Suhrkamp, 1998; originally published 1959.

"Der Soziologen-Nachwuchs stellt sich vor. Zu einem Treffen in Hamburg unter der Leitung von Professor Schelsky." *Frankfurter Allgemeine Zeitung* (June 13, 1955).

"Comeback der deutschen Soziologie." A review of A. Gehlen & H. Schelsky, *Soziologie* (Düsseldorf, 1955) and W. Bernsdorf & H. Bülow eds., *Wörterbuch der Soziologie* (Stuttgart, 1955). *Frankfurter Allgemeine Zeitung* (July 23, 1955).

"Comeback der deutschen Soziologie." A review of A. Gehlen & H. Schelsky. "Zerfall der Institutionen." Reprinted in *Philosophische-Politische Profilen*. 3rd ed. 101–6. Frankfurt: Suhrkamp, 1998; originally published 1956.

"Comeback der deutschen Soziologie." A review of A. Gehlen & H. Schelsky. "Die Grenze in uns. Helmuth Plessner: 'Die verspätete Nation.' " *Frankfurter Hefte* 14 (1958), 826–31.

"Die Bundesrepublik – eine Wahlmonarchie?" Special Issue: "Woher-Wohin. Bilanz der Bundesrepublik." *Magnum* (Köln) (1961), 26–9.

"Reflexionen über den Begriff der Politischen Beteiligung." In *Student und Politik: eine soziologische Untersuchung zum politischen Bewusstein Frankfurter Studenten*, ed. Ludwig von Friedeburg, Christoph Oehler, & Friedrich Weltz, 11–55. Neuwied: Luchterhand, 1961

"Strukturwandel der Offentlichkeit. Untersuchungen zu einer Kategorie der bürgerlichen Gesellschaft. " In *Politica: Abhandlungen und Texte zur politischen Wissenschaft*, Bd. 4., ed. Wilhelm Hennis & Roman Schnur. Neuwied: Luchterhand, 1962.

Theorie und Praxis. Sozialphilosophische Studien. Neuwied: Luchterhand, 1963.

"Vom Ende der Politik." *Frankfurter Allgemeine Zeitung* (October 17, 1964).

"Diskussion über Revolution." In *Die Philosophie und die Frage nach dem Fortschritt*, ed. H. Kuhn & Fr. Wiedermann, 317–25. München: Pustet, 1964.

"Wissenschaft und Politik." *Offene Welt: Zeitschrift für Wirtschaft, Politik, und Gesellschaft* 86 (December 1964), 413–23.

Verwissenschaftliche Politik und öffentliche Meinung" [1963]. In *Humanität und Politische Verantwortung. Festschrift für Hans Barth*, ed. R. Reich. Zurich: Erlenbach, 1964.

"Wertfreiheit und Objektivität. Eine Diskussionbemerkung." In *Max Weber und die Soziologie heute*, ed. Otto Stammer, 74–81. Tübingen: J. C. B. Mohr, 1965.

"Technischer Fortschritt und soziale Lebenswelt." *Praxis* (Zagreb) 1–2 (1966), 217–28.

"Partisanenprofessor im Lande der Mitläufer. Der Marburger Ordinarius Wolfgang Abendroth wird am 2. Mai sechzig Jahre alt." *Die Zeit* (April 29, 1966), 24.

Zur Logik der Sozialwissenschaften. Tübingen: J. C. B. Mohr, 1967.

Antworten auf Herbert Marcuse. Eds. Herbert Marcuse and Alfred Schmidt. Frankfurt am Main: Suhrkamp, 1968.

"Technik und Wissenschaft als 'Ideologie.'" *Merkur* 243 (July 1968), 591–610; *Merkur* 244 (August 1968), 682–93.

Technik und Wissenschaft als 'Ideologie'. Frankfurt am Main: Suhrkamp, 1968.

ed. "Über einige Bedingungen der Revolutionierung spätkapitalischer Gesellschaft." Reprinted in *Kultur und Kritik: Verstreute*

Aufsätze, 70–86. Frankfurt am Main: Suhrkamp, 1973; originally published 1968.

Erkenntnis und Interesse. Frankfurt/Main: Suhrkamp, 1968.

Protestbewegung und Hochschulreform. Frankfurt am Main: Suhrkamp, 1969.

Towards a Rational Society: Essays on Student Protest, Science and Politics, trans. Jeremy Shapiro. Boston: Beacon Press, 1970.

Luhmann, Niklaus. Theorie der Gesellschaft oder Sozialtechnologie. Was leistet die Systemforschung? Frankfurt am Main: Suhrkamp, 1971.

"Die Deutsche Mandarine. *Minerva* (London)" 9: 3 (1971), 422–8.

Theorie und Praxis. Sozialphilosophische Studien. 4th ed. Neuwied: Luchterhand, 1971.

Knowledge and Human Interests, trans. Jeremy Shapiro. Boston: Beacon Press, 1971.

Theory and Practice, trans. John Viertel. Boston: Beacon Press, 1973.

Legitimationsprobleme im Spätkapitalismus. Frankfurt am Main: Suhrkamp, 1973.

Legitimation Crisis, trans. Thomas McCarthy. Boston: Beacon Press, 1975.

Zur Rekonstruktion des Historischen Materialismus. Frankfurt am Main: Suhrkamp, 1976.

Stichwörte zur geistige Situation der Zeit, Vol I: Nation und Republik; Vol. II: Politik und Kultur. Frankfurt am Main: Suhrkamp, 1979.

Communication and the Evolution of Society. Boston: Beacon Press, 1979.

"Modernity and Postmodernity." *New German Critique* 22 (Winter 1981), 3–14.

Philosophisch-politische Profilen, 3rd ed. Frankfurt am Main: Suhrkamp, 1981.

Theorie des kommunikativen Handelns, Vol. I: Handlungsrationalität und gesellschaftliche Rationalisierung, Vol. II: Zur Kritik der funktionalistischen Vernunft. Frankfurt am Main: Suhrkamp, 1981.

Kleine Politische Schriften (I-IV). Frankfurt am Main: Suhrkamp, 1981.

"Ziviler Ungehorsam – Testfall für den demokratischen Rechtsstaat. Wider den autoritären Legalismus in der Bundesrepublik." In *Ziviler Ungehorsam im Rechtsstaat*, ed. Peter Glotz, 29–53. Frankfurt am Main: Suhrkamp, 1983.

Theory of Communicative Action, Vol. I: Reason and the Rationalization of Society, trans. Thomas McCarthy. Boston: Beacon Press, 1984. Vol. II: *Lifeworld and System: A Critique of Functionalist Reason*. Boston: Beacon Press, 1987.

Vorstudien und Ergänzungen zur Theorie des kommunikativen Handelns. Frankfurt am Main: Suhrkamp, 1984.

ed. *Observations on 'The Spiritual Situation of the Age': Contemporary German Perspectives*, trans. Andrew Buchwalter. Cambridge, MA: MIT Press, 1985.

Der philosophische Diskurs der Moderne. Zwölf Vorlesungen. Frankfurt am Main: Suhrkamp, 1985.

Die Neue Unubersichtlichkeit: Kleine Politische Schriften V. Frankfurt am Main: Suhrkamp, 1985.

The Philosophical Discourse of Modernity: Twelve Lectures, trans. Frederick Lawrence. Cambridge, MA: MIT Press, 1987.

Eine Art Schadensabwicklung: Kleine Politische Schriften VI. Frankfurt am Main: Suhrkamp 1987.

"Wie ist Legitimität durch Legalität möglich?" *Kritische Justiz* 20:1 (1987), 1–18.

Nachmetaphysisches Denken. Philosophische Aufsätze. Frankfurt am Main: Suhrkamp, 1988.

Theorie und Praxis: Sozialphilosophische Studien, 5th ed. Frankfurt am Main: Suhrkamp, 1988.

"Law and Morality" (October 1–2, 1986). In *The Tanner Lectures on Human Values* Vol. 8., ed. S. M. McMurrin, 217–79, trans. Kenneth Baynes. Salt Lake City, UT: University of Utah Press, 1988.

On the Logic of the Social Sciences, trans. Shierry Weber Nicholsen & Jerry A. Stark. Cambridge, MA: MIT Press, 1988.

The Structural Transformation of the Public Sphere: An Inquiry into a Category of Bourgeois Society, trans. Thomas Burger with Frederick Lawrence. Cambridge, MA: MIT Press, 1989.

Die Nachholende Revolution: Kleine Politische Schriften VII. Frankfurt am Main: Suhrkamp, 1990.

Justification and Application. Cambridge, MA: MIT Press, 1990.

"Vorwort." In *Strukturwandel der Offentlichkeit. Untersuchungen zu einer Kategorie der bürgerlichen Gesellschaft*, 11–50. Frankfurt am Main: Suhrkamp Taschenbuch Verlag, 1990.

Erläuterungen zur Diskursethik. Frankfurt am Main: Suhrkamp, 1991.

Vergangenheit als Zukunft: Das alte Deutschland in neuen Europa. Zurich: Pendo, 1991.

"Recht und Moral." In *Faktizität und Geltung: Beiträge zur Diskurstheorie des Rechts und des demokratischen Rechtsstaats*, 541–99. Frankfurt am Main: Suhrkamp, 1992.

"Further Reflections on the Public Sphere." In *Habermas and the Public Sphere*, ed. Craig Calhoun, 431–61. Cambridge, MA: MIT Press, 1992.

Faktizität und Geltung: Beiträge zur Diskurstheorie des Rechts und des demokratischen Rechtsstaats. Frankfurt am Main: Suhrkamp, 1992.

"Further Reflections on the Public Sphere." In *Habermas and the Public Sphere*, ed. Craig Calhoun, 431–61. Cambridge, MA: MIT Press, 1992.

"Die zweite Lebenslüge der Bundesrepublik: Wir sind wieder 'normal' geworden," *Die Zeit* 51 (December 11, 1992). www.zeit.de/1992/51/Die-zweite-Lebenslüge-der-Br-Wir-sind.

"On the Pragmatic, the Ethical, and the Moral Employments of Practical Reason." In *Justification and Application: Remarks on Discourse Ethics*, trans. Ciaran Cronin. Cambridge, MA: MIT Press, 1993.

"Nachwort," In *Faktizität und Geltung: Beiträge zur Diskurstheorie des Rechts und des demokratischen Rechtsstaats*, 4th revised and enlarged edition, 661–80. Frankfurt am Main: Suhrkamp 1994.

Die Normalität einer Berliner Republik. Frankfurt am Main: Suhrkamp, 1995.

Die Einbeziehung des Anderen: Studien zur Politischen Theorie. Frankfurt am Main: Suhrkamp, 1996.

Between Facts and Norms: Contributions to a Discourse Theory of Democracy, trans. William Rehg. Cambridge, MA: MIT Press, 1996.

"Postscript." In *Between Facts and Norms: Contributions to a Discourse Theory of Democracy*, trans. William Rehg, 447–65. Cambridge, MA: MIT Press, 1996; originally published 1994.

"Popular Sovereignty as Procedure." In *Between Facts and Norms: Contributions to a Discourse Theory of Democracy*, trans. William Rehg. Cambridge, MA: MIT Press, 1996; originally published 1988.

"Reply to Symposium Participants, Benjamin Cardozo School of Law." In "Habermas on Law and Democracy: Critical Exchanges," ed. Michel Rosenfeld, Special Issue. *Cardozo Law Review* 17: 4–5 (March 1996), 1477–1558.

"On the Relation between the Nation, the Rule of Law, and Democracy." In *The Inclusion of the Other: Studies in Political*

Theory, ed. Ciaran Cronin & Pablo De Greiff, 129–54. Cambridge, MA: MIT Press, 1998; originally published 1996.

"Three Normative Models of Democracy." In *The Inclusion of the Other: Studies in Political Theory*, ed. Ciaran Cronin & Pablo De Greiff, 239–52. Cambridge, MA: MIT Press, 1998; originally published 1996.

"On the Internal Relation between the Rule of Law and Democracy." In *The Inclusion of the Other: Studies in Political Theory*, ed. Ciaran Cronin & Pablo De Greiff, 253–64, Cambridge, MA: MIT Press, 1998; originally published 1996.

"Carl Schmitt in the Political-Intellectual History of the Federal Republic." In *A Berlin Republic: Writings on Germany*, trans. Steven Rendall, Introduction, Peter Uwe Hohendahl. Lincoln, NE: University of Nebraska Press, 1997. Originally published in *Die Zeit* (December 3, 1993), 107–18.

"Bestiality and Humanity: A War on the Border between Legality and Morality," trans. Stephen Meyer & William E. Scheuerman. *Constellations* 6, 3 (1999), 264–72.

On the Pragmatics of Social Interaction: Preliminary Studies in the Theory of Communicative Action, trans. Barbara Fultner. Cambridge, MA: MIT Press, 2001.

Der Gespaltene Westen: Kleine Politische Schriften X. Frankfurt am Main: Suhrkamp, 2004.

Hansen, Klaus, ed. *Frankfurter Schule und Liberalismus. Beiträge zum Dialog zwischen kritischer Gesellschaftstheorie und politischen Liberalismus*. Baden Baden: Nomos Verlagsgesellschaft, 1981.

Hansen, Klaus, & Hans Lietzmann, eds. *Carl Schmitt und die Liberalismuskritik*. Opladen: Leske und Budrich, 1988.

Haller, Michael. *The Past as Future: "Vergangenheit als Zukunft." Jürgen Habermas Interviewed by Michael Haller*, trans. and ed. Max Pensky, Foreword Peter Hohendahl. Lincoln, NE: University of Nebraska Press, 1994.

Hartwich, Hans-Hermann. *Sozialstaatspostulat und gesellschaftlicher status quo*. Köln: Westdeutscher Verlag, 1970.

Hegel, G. W. F. *Grundlinien der Philosophie des Rechts*. Hamburg: F. Meiner, 1967.

Heigl, Richard. *Oppositionspolitik. Wolfgang Abendroth und die Entstehung der Neuen Linken, 1950–1968*. Hamburg: Argumentations-Verlag, 2008.

Held, David, & John B. Thompson, eds. *Habermas: Critical Debates.* Cambridge, MA: MIT Press, 1982.

Heller, Hermann. *Rechtsstaat oder Diktatur?* [1930], enlarged version of 1929. In *Gesammelte Schriften*, Bd. 2: *Recht, Staat, und Macht.* ed. Christoph Müller. Tübingen: J.C. B. Mohr, 1992.

Henne, Thomas, ed. *Das Lüth-Urteil aus (rechts-)historischer Sicht: die Konflikte um Veit Harlan und die Grundrechtsjudikatur des Bundesverfassungsgerichts.* Berlin: BWV, 2005.

Hennig, Eike, & Richard Saage, eds. *Konservatismus – eine Gefahr für die Freiheit? Festschrift für Iring Fetscher zum 60. Geburtstag.* Zürich: Piper, 1983.

Hennis, Wilhelm. *Öffentliche Meinung und Repräsentative Demokratie. Recht und Staat.* Tübingen: J. C. B. Mohr, 1956.

"Der Begriff der öffentlichen Meinung bei Rousseau." *Archiv für Rechts-und Sozialphilosophie* 43 (1957), 111–15.

"Zum Problem der deutschen Staatsanschauung." *Viertelsjahreshefte für Zeitgeschichte* 7 (1959), 1–23.

"On the Present Situation in Political Science." In *Politik und Praktische Philosophie: Eine Studie zur Rekonstruktion der politischen Wissenschaft.* Berlin: Luchterhand, 1963.

"Demokratisierung. Zur Problematik eines Begriffs." In *Demokratisches System und politische Praxis der Bundesrepublik. Festschrift für Theodor Eschenburg*, ed. Gerhard Lehmnruch, 68–96. München: Piper, 1971.

Die missverstandene Demokratie. Demokratie, Verfassung, Parlament: Studien zu deutsche Problemen. Freiburg im Breisgau: Herder, 1973.

"Legitimität. Zu einer Kategorie der bürgerliche Gesellschaft." In *Legitimationsprobleme politischer Systeme. Tagung der Deutschen Vereinigung für Politische Wissenschaft in Duisburg, Herbst 1975*, ed. Peter Graf Kielmannsegg. Opladen: Westdeutscher Verlag, 1976.

"Verfassung und Verfassungswirklichkeit. Ein Deutsches Problem." In *Verfassung: Beiträge zur Verfassungstheorie*, ed. Manfred Friedrich, 232–68. Darmstadt: Wissenschafliche Buchgesellschaft, 1978.

Herbert, Ulrich. "Liberalisierung als Lernprozess: Die Bundesrepublik in der deutschen Geschichte – eine Skizze." In *Wandlungsprozesse in Westdeutschland: Belastung, Integration Liberalisierung*, 7–49. Gottingen: Wallstein, 2002.

Herf, Jeffrey. *War by Other Means: Soviet Power, West German Resistance, and the Battle of the Euromissiles.* New York: Free Press, 1984.

Divided Memory: The Nazi Past in the Two Germanys. Cambridge, MA: Harvard University Press, 1997.

Hesse, Konrad. "Die Normative Kraft der Verfassung." *Recht und Staat* 222(Tübingen: J. C. B. Mohr, 1959), 3–24.

"Die verfassungsrechtliche Stellung der politischen Parteien im modernen Staat." *Veröffentlichungen der Vereinigung der Deutschen Staatsrechtslehrer*, 17. Berlin: de Gruyter, 1959.

Hippel, Ernst von. "The Role of Natural Law in the Legal Decisions of the Federal Republic." *Natural Law Forum* 4: 1 (1959), 107–10.

Hofmann, Hasso. *Legitimität gegen Legalität: Der Weg der politischen Philosophie Carl Schmitts*, 3rd ed. Berlin: Duncker & Humblot, 1995; originally published 1964.

Hollerbach, Alexander. "Auflösung der Rechtsstaatlichen Verfassung? Zu Ernst Forsthoffs Abhandlung 'Die Umbildung des Verfassungsgesetzes.'" In *Verfassung: Beiträge zur Verfassungstheorie*, ed. Manfred Friedrich, 11–38. Darmstadt: Wissenschafliche Buchgesellschaft, 1978; originally published 1960.

Holmes, Stephen. "Precommitment and the Paradox of Democracy." In *Constitutionalism and Democracy*, eds. John Elster & Rune Slugstad, 195–240. Cambridge, England: Cambridge University Press, 1988.

Holub, Robert C. *Jürgen Habermas: Critic in the Public Sphere*. New York: Routledge, 1991.

Höffe, Otfried. "Eine Konversion der kritischen Theorie. Zu Habermas's Rechts- und Staatstheorie." *Rechtshistorische Journal* 70: 12 (1993), 70–88.

Höffner, Josef. *Christliche Gesellschaftslehre*. Kevelaer, Rheinland: Butzon & Bercker, 1962.

Horkheimer, Max. *Eclipse of Reason*. New York: Continuum, 1974; originally published 1947.

"Survey of the Social Sciences in Germany." Washington: Library of Congress, Reference Department, European Affairs Division, 1952.

Eclipse of Reason. Oxford, England: Oxford University Press, 1947.

Horster, Detlev. *Jürgen Habermas*. Stuttgart: Metzler, 1991.

Howard, Dick. "Law and Political Culture." In "Habermas on Law and Democracy: Critical Exchanges," ed. Michel Rosenfeld, Special Issue. *Cardozo Law Review* 17: 4–5 (March 1996), 1391–1430.

Huber, E. R. *Wirtschaftsverwaltungsrecht*, 2 Aufl., Bd. I. Tubingen: Mohr, 1953.

Huyssen. Andreas. "Nation, Race, and Immigration: German Identities after Unification." In *Twilight Memories: Marking Time in a Culture of Amnesia*, 37–85. New York: Routledge, 1995.

Isensee, Josef. "Ein Grundrecht auf Ungehorsam gegen das demokratische Gesetz? Legitimation und Perversion des Widerstandsrechts." In *Frieden im Lande. Vom Recht auf Widerstand*, ed. Basilius Streithofen, 155–73. Bergisch-Gladbach: Bastei Lübbe, 1983.

Jackson, Thaddeus. *Civilizing the Enemy: German Reconstruction and the Invention of the West.* Ann Arbor, MI: University of Michigan Press, 2006.

Janowitz, Morris, et al., eds. *Political Behavior: A Reader in Theory and Research.* Glencoe, IL: Free Press, 1956.

Jay, Martin. "Reconciling the Irreconcilable? A Rejoinder to Kennedy." *Telos* 71 (Spring 1987), 67–81.

Fin de Siècle Socialism and other Essays. New York and London: Routledge, 1988.

Marxism and Totality. The Adventures of a Concept from Lukàcs to Habermas. Berkeley, CA: University of California Press, 1984.

Jarausch, Konrad H. *After Hitler: Recivilizing Germans, 1945–1995.* Oxford, England: Oxford University Press, 2006.

The Rush to German Unity. Oxford, England: Oxford University Press, 1984.

Aufbruch der Zivilgesellschaft. Zur Einordnung der friedlichen Revolution von 1989. FES Reihe "Gesprächskreis Geschichte," 55. Bonn: FES, 2004.

Jones, William David. *The Lost Debate: German Socialist Intellectuals and Totalitarianism.* Chicago, IL: The Univerity of Illinois Press, 1999.

Kalman, Laura A. *The Strange Career of Legal Liberalism.* New Haven, CT: Yale University Press, 1996.

Kaltenbrunner, Gerd Klaus, ed. *Die Herausforderung der Konservativen: Absage an Illusionen.* Freiburg (Breisgau): Herder, 1974.

Kaufmann, Arthur. "The Small-Coin Right of Resistance: An Admonition to Civil Courage." In *Prescriptive Formality and Normative Rationality in Modern Legal Systems: Festschrift for Robert S. Summers*, eds. Werner Krawietz & Neil MacCormick, 573–9. Berlin: Duncker & Humblot, 1994.

Kaufmann, Franz-Xaver. *Sozialpolitisches Denken: Die Deutsche Tradition.* Frankfurt am Main: Suhrkamp, 2003.

Kelsen, Hans. "Verteidigung der Demokratie." In *Demokratie und Sozialismus*, ed. Norbert Leser, 60–8. Wien: Europa Verlag, 1967.

Kennedy, Ellen. "Carl Schmitt and the Frankfurt School." *Telos* 71 (Spring, 1987), 37–66.

Kirchheimer, Otto. *Politics, Law and Social Change: Selected Essays of Otto Kirchheimer*, eds. F. Burin & Kurt Schell. New York: Columbia University Press, 1969.

"Review of Werner Weber." *American Political Science Review* 46:3 (September 1952), 885–7.

Kitzinger, Uwe W. *German Electoral Politics: A Study of the 1957 Campaign*. Oxford, England: Clarendon Press, 1960.

Koch, Claus, & Dieter Senghaas, eds. *Texte zur Technokratiediskussion*. Frankfurt am Main: Europäische Verlaganstalt, 1970.

Kogon, Eugen. *Die Restaurative Republik. Zur Geschichte der Bundesrepublik Deutschland*. Berlin: Quadriga, 1996.

Kohlberg, Lawrence. *Essays on Moral Development*. San Francisco: Harper & Row, 1981.

Kommers, Donald. *The Constitutional Jurisprudence of the Federal Republic of Germany*. Durham, NC: Duke University Press, 1989.

"German Constitutionalism: A Prolegomenon." *Emory Law Journal* 40 (1991), 837–73.

Kornhauser, William. *The Politics of Mass Society*. Glencoe, IL: Free Press, 1959.

Koselleck, Reinhart. *Critique and Crisis: Enlightenment and the Pathogenesis of Modern Society*. Cambridge, MA: MIT Press, 1988; originally published 1958.

Kraus, Rudolf. "Sozialstaatlichkeit und Soziale Marktwirtschaft. Verfassungsrechtliche Grundlinien und sozialphilosophische Postulate einer Gesellschaftsordnung in der Bundesrepublik Deutschland." PhD. dissertation, University of Basel, 1962.

Krausharr, Wolfgang, ed. *Frankfurter Schule und Studentenbewegung. Von der Flaschenpost zum Molotowcocktail, 1946–1995*. Hamburg: Hamburger Digital Edition, 2003; originally published 1998.

Krawietz, Werner, & Neil MacCormick, eds. *Prescriptive Formality and Normative Rationality in Modern Legal Systems: Festschrift for Robert S. Summers*. Berlin: Duncker & Humblot, 1994.

Krieger, Leonard. *The German Idea of Freedom: History of a Political Tradition*. Boston: Beacon Press, 1957.

Kriele, Martin. "Widerstandsrecht in der Demokratie? Über die Legitimität der Staatsgewalt." In *Frieden im Lande. Vom Recht auf Widerstand*, ed. Basilius Streithofen, 139–54. Bergisch-Gladbach: Bastei Lubbe, 1983.

Krockow, Christian von. "Die Versuchung des Absoluten." *Die Zeit* (September 2, 1983)

Kübler, Friedrich. *Verrechtlichung von Wirtschaft, Arbeit und sozialer Solidarität. Vergleichende Analysen.* Baden-Baden: Nomos Verlagsgesellschaft, 1984.

Kvistad, Gregg. *The Rise and Demise of German Statism: Loyalty and Poltical Membership.* Providence, RI: Berghahn Books, 1999.

Ladeur, Karl-Heinz. "Verfassungsgebung als Katharsis: Der Entwurf des 'Runden Tisches'." In *Die Verfassungsdiskussion im Jahr der deutschen Einheit: Analysen-Hintergründe-Materialien*, ed. Bernd Guggenberger & Tine Stein, 376–86. München: Carl Hanser Verlag, 1991.

Landeshut, Siegfried. "Zum Begriff und Gegenstand der Politischen Soziologie," *Kölner Zeitschrift für Soziologie und Sozialpsychologie* VIII (1956), 410–14

Larmore, Charles. *The Morals of Modernity.* New York: Cambridge University Press, 1999.

Lau, Heinrich. *Naturrecht und Restauration. Zur Kritik eines Legitimationsmuster in Justiz und Rechtstheorie der Nachkriegszeit.* Egelsbach: Hänsel-Hohenhausen, 1994.

LaVopa, Anthony J. "Conceiving a Public. Ideas and Society in Eighteenth Century Europe." *Journal of Modern History* 64, 1 (March, 1992), 79–108.

Lazarsfeld, Paul, et al., eds. *Voting: A Study of Opinion-Formation in a Political Campaign.* Chicago: The University of Chicago Press, 1954.

Leibholz, Gerhard. *Strukturprobleme der Moderne Demokratie.* Karlsruhe: C. F. Müller, 1958.

Lipset, Seymour Martin. *Political Man: The Social Bases of Politics.* New York: Doubleday, 1960.

Litowitz, Douglas. *Postmodernism, Philosophy and Law.* Lawrence, KS: University Press of Kansas, 1997.

Loewenstein, Karl. *Verfassungslehre.* Tübingen: J. C. B. Mohr, 1959.

"Militant Democracy and Fundamental Rights, II." *American Political Science Review* 31: 4 (August 1937), 638–58.

Lohmann, Ulrich. "Legitimation und Verfassung in der DDR." In *Modernisierung im Wiederaufbau: Die westdeutsche Gesellschaft der 50er Jahre*, ed. Axel Schildt & Arnold Sywotteck, 468–83. Bonn: Dietz, 1998.

Love, Nancy. "Disembodying Democracy: Gendered Discourse in Habermas's Legalistic Turn." In *Confronting Mass Democracy and Industrial Technology: German Political and Social Thought from Nietzsche to Habermas*, eds. William Scheuerman & John McCormick, 321–42. Durham, NC: Duke University Press, 2002.

Lübbe, Hermann. "Zur politischen Theorie der Technokratie"[1962]. In *Theorie und Entscheidung: Studien zum Primat der praktischen Vernunft*, 32–53. Freiburg: Rombach, 1971.

Luhmann, Niklas. *Politische Theorie im Wohlfahrtstaat*. München: Günter Olzog Verlag, 1981.

Lukàcs, Georg. *History and Class Consciousness: Studies in Marxist Dialectics*, trans. Rodney Livingstone. London: Merlin Press, 1971.

Maier, Charles S. *The Unmasterable Past: History, Holocaust, and German National Identity*. Cambridge, MA: Harvard University Press, 1988.

Dissolution: The Crisis of Communism and the End of East Germany. Princeton, NJ: Princeton University Press, 1997.

Maihofer, Werner, ed. *Naturrecht oder Rechtspositivismus*. Bad Homburg vor der Höhe: Hermann Gentner Verlag, 1962.

Mangoldt, Hermann von, Friedrich Klein, eds. *Das Bonner Grundgesetz*, 2nd ed., Vol. 1. Berlin: Franz Vahlen, 1957.

Manow, Phillip. "Ordoliberalismus als ökonomische Ordnungstheologie." *Leviathan* 29 (2001), 179–200.

Marcuse, Harold. *Dachau: The Uses and Abuses of a Concentration Camp, 1933–2003*. Cambridge, England: Cambridge University Press, 2001.

Matustik, Martin Beck. *Jürgen Habermas: A Philosophical-Political Profile*. London: Rowman and Littlefield, 2001.

Maus, Ingeborg. *Bürgerliche Rechtstheorie und Faschismus: Zur sozialen Funktion und aktuellen Wirkung der Theorie Carl Schmitts*. München: C. H. Beck, 1980.

"Gesetzesbindung der Justiz und die Struktur der nationalsozialistischen Rechtsnormen." In *Recht und Justiz im 'Dritten Reich'*, eds. Ralf Dreier & Wolfgang Sellert, 81–104. Frankfurt am Main: Suhrkamp, 1989.

"Justiz als Über-Ich. Zur Funktion von Rechtsprechung in der 'vaterlosen Gesellschaft.'" In *Sturz der Götter? Vaterbilder im 20 Jahrhundert*, eds. Werner Faulstich & Gunter E. Grimm, 121–49. Frankfurt am Main: Suhrkamp, 1989.

"Hermann Heller und die Staatsrechtslehre der Bundesrepublik." In *Der soziale Rechtsstaat. Gedächtnisschrift für Hermann Heller*

1891–1933, eds. Ilse Staff & Christoph Müller, 113–39. Baden-Baden: Nomos, 1984.

"Liberties and Popular Sovereignty: On Jürgen Habermas's Reconstruction of the System of Rights," Special Issue, "Habermas on Law and Democracy: Critical Exchanges." *Cardozo Law Review* 17, 4–5 (1996), 825–82.

McCarthy, Thomas. *The Critical Theory of Jürgen Habermas.* Cambridge, MA: MIT Press, 1979.

Ideals and Illusions: Reconstructions and Deconstruction in Contemporary Critical Theory. Cambridge, MA: MIT Press, 1993.

McCormick, John, ed. *Confronting Mass Democracy and Industrial Technology: German Political and Social Thought from Nietzsche to Habermas.* Durham, NC: Duke University Press, 2002.

McCormick, John. *Carl Schmitt's Critique of Liberalism: Against Politics as Technology.* Cambridge, England: Cambridge University Press, 1999.

McDermott, John. "Technology: The Opiate of the Intellectuals." *New York Review of Books* 23, 2 (July 31, 1969), 25–35.

Mehring, Reinhard. *Carl Schmitt zur Einführung.* Hamburg: Junius Verlag, 1992.

Menger, Christian-Friedrich. "Zur verfassungsrechtlichen Stellung der deutschen politischen Parteien." *Archiv des Öffentliches Rechts* 78: 2 (1952), 149–62.

"Der Begriff des sozialen Rechtsstaates im Bonner Grundgesetz." In *Rechtsstaatlichkeit und Sozialstaatlichkeit: Aufsätze und Essays*, ed. Ernst Forsthoff, 42–72. Darmstadt: Wissenschaftliche Buchgesellschaft, 1968.

Metzler, Gabriele. *Der deutsche Sozialstaat: vom bismarckschen Erfolgsmodell zum Pflegefall.* München: Deutsche Verlags-Anstalt, 2004.

Miller, Suzanne, & Heinrich Potthoff. *Kleine Geschichte der SPD. Darstellung und Dokumentation, 1848–1980.* Bonn: Verlag Neue Gesellschaft, 1983.

Miller, Russell, John LaMont, et. al. "40/68 – Germany's 1968 and the Law," *German Law Journal* 10, 3 (2009), 223–60. www.germanlawjournal.com, accessed December 1, 2009.

Mitchell, Maria. "Materialism and Secularism: CDU Politicians and National Socialism, 1945–49." *Journal of Modern History* 67 (June 1995), 278–308.

Moeller, Robert G., ed. *West Germany under Construction: Politics, Society and Culture in the Adenauer Era*. Ann Arbor, MI: University of Michigan Press, 1997.

War Stories: The Search for a Usable Past in the Federal Republic of Germany. Berkeley, CA: University of California Press, 2001.

Protecting Motherhood : Women and the Family in the Politics of Postwar West Germany. Berkeley, CA: University of California Press, 1993.

Möllers, Christoph. *Der Staat als Argument*. München: C. H. Beck, 2000.

Montesquieu, Baron von. *Vom Geist der Gesetze*, ed. and intro. Ernst Forsthoff. Tübingen: Laupp, 1951.

Moses, A. Dirk. *German Intellectuals and the Nazi Past*. Cambridge, England: Cambridge University Press, 2008.

Motzkin, Gabriel. "Habermas's Ideal Paradigm of Law." In "Habermas on Law and Democracy: Critical Exchanges," ed. Michel Rosenfeld, Special Issue. *Cardozo Law Review* 17: 4–5 (March 1996), 1431–40.

Mouffe, Chantal. *The Challenge of Carl Schmitt*. New York: Verso, 1999.

Muller, Jerry Z. *The Other God that Failed: Hans Freyer and the Deradicalization of German Conservatism*. Princeton, NJ: Princeton University Press, 1987.

"German Neoconservatism, ca. 1968–1985: Hermann Lübbe and Others." In *German Ideologies since 1945: Studies in the Political Thought and Culture of the Bonn Republic*, ed. Jan-Werner Müller. New York: Palgrave Macmillan, 2003.

Müller, Christoph, ed. *Hermann Heller: Gesammelte Schriften*. Tübingen: J. C. B. Mohr, 1992.

"Das Freund-Feind-Theorem Carl Schmitts: Fortwirkungen im Verfassungsdenken der Bundesrepublik Deutschland." In *Rückkehr zum starken Staat? Studien über Konservatismus, Faschismus und Demokratie*, ed. Richard Saage, 153–78. Frankfurt am Main: Suhrkamp, 1983.

Müller, Gerhard. *Naturrecht und Grundgesetz: Zur Rechtsprechung der Gerichte, besonders des Bundesverfassungsgerichts*. Würzburg: Echter-Verlag, 1967.

Müller, Ingo. *Furchtbare Juristen: Die unbewältigte Vergangenheit unserer Justiz*. Münich: Kindler Verlag, 1987.

Hitler's Justice. The Courts of the Third Reich. Cambridge, MA: Harvard University Press, 1991.

Müller, Ingo, & Eisfeld, Rainer. *Gegen Barbarei: Essays Robert M. W. Kempner zu Ehren*. Frankfurt am Main: Athenäum, 1989.

Müller, Jan-Werner, ed. *German Ideologies since 1945: Studies in the Political Thought and Culture of the Bonn Republic.* New York: Palgrave Macmillan, 2003.

Müller, Jan-Werner. *A Dangerous Mind: Carl Schmitt in Postwar European Thought.* New Haven, CT: Yale University Press, 2003.

Müller, Wolfgang, & Christel Neusüss. "Die Sozialstaatsillusion und der Widerspruch von Lohnarbeit und Kapital." *Sozialistische Politik* 2: 6–7 (June 1970), 4–68.

Narr, Wolf-Dieter, & Dietrich Thränhardt, eds. *Die Bundesrepublik Deutschland: Entstehung, Entwicklung, Struktur.* Königstein/TS: *Verlagsgruppe Athenäum, Hain/Scriptor/Hanstein*, 1979.

Naumann, Klaus, ed. *Nachkrieg in Deutschland.* Hamburg: Hamburger Edition, 2001.

Negt, Oskar, ed. *Die Linke antwortet Jürgen Habermas.* Frankfurt am Main: Europaische Verlagsanstalt, 1968.

"Autonomie und Eingriff," *Frankfurter Rundschau* (June 16, 1989)

Achtundsechzig. Politische Intellektuelle und die Macht. Göttingen: Steidl Verlag, 2008.

Negt, Oskar, D. Horster, J. Zimmerman, K. Christoph, H. Siebert, & G. Shafer. *Theorie und Praxis Heute: Ein Kolloqiuum zur Theorie und politischen Wirksamkeit von Jürgen Habermas.* Frankfurt/ Hannover: Materialis Verlag, 1990.

Nell-Breuning, Oswald von. *Streit um Mitbestimmung.* Frankfurt am Main: Europäische Verlagsanstalt, 1968.

Neumann, Franz, Karl Nipperdey, Ulrich Scheuner, & Otto Bachof, eds. *Die Grundrechte: Handbuch der Theorie und Praxis der Grundrechte.* Berlin: Dunckler & Humblot, 1955.

The Democratic and the Authoritarian State: Essays in Political and Legal Theory, ed. Herbert Marcuse. Glencoe, IL: Free Press, 1957.

Demokratischer und autoritärer Staat, ed. Herbert Marcuse. Wien: Europa Verlagsanstalt, 1967.

Behemoth: The Structure and Practice of National Socialism. New York: Oxford University Press, 1944.

Wirtschaft, Staat, Demokratie. Aufsätze 1930–54, ed. Alfons Söllner. Frankfurt am Main: Suhrkamp, 1978.

The Rule of Law: Political Theory and Legislative System in Modern Society. Providence, RI: Berg, 1986.

"Die Wissenschaft von der Politik in der Demokratie"(December 1952), *IWK* 25 (1989), 31–54.

Nicholls, Anthony. *Freedom and Responsibility: The Social Market Economy in Germany, 1918*–1963. Oxford, England: Oxford University Press, 1994.

The Bonn Republic: West German Democracy, 1945–90. New York: Longman, 1997.

Niclaus, Karlheinz. "Parlamentarischer Rat und Sozialstaatspostulat." *Politische Viertelsjahresschrift* (March 1974), 33–50.

Niethammer, Lutz, & Hans-Ulrich Wehler. "Sind die 68er politisch gescheitert?" *Frankfurter Allgemeine Lesesaal* (September 1, 2008) www.faz.net, accessed June 15, 2009

Offe, Claus. *Arbeitsgesellschaft – Strukturprobleme und Zukunftsperspektiven.* Frankfurt am Main: Campus, 1984.

Olsen, Kevin. "Rethinking the Welfare State: A Study in the Foundations of Social Democracy (Michel Foucault, Jürgen Habermas)." PhD. dissertation, Northwestern University, 1995.

Outhwaite, William. *Habermas: An Introduction.* Palo Alto, CA: Stanford University Press, 1995.

Papier, Hans-Jürgen, & Wolfgang Durner. "Streitbare Demokratie." *Archiv des Öffentlichen Rechts* 128 (2003), 340–71.

Paulson, Stanley. "Lon Fuller, Gustav Radbruch and the 'Positivist' Theses," *Law and Philosophy* 13, 3 (1994), 313–59.

"On the Background and Significance of Gustav Radbruch's Post-War Papers." *Oxford Journal of Legal Studies* 26, 1 (2006), 17–40.

Pensky, Max. "Jürgen Habermas and the Antinomies of the Intellectual." In *Habermas: A Critical Reader*, ed. Peter Dews, 211–40. Oxford, England: Blackwell, 1999.

"Universalism and the Situated Critic." In *The Cambridge Companion to Habermas*, ed. Steven K. White, 67–96. Cambridge, England: Cambridge University Press, 1995.

Perels, Joachim. "Die Restauration der Rechtslehre nach 1945." *Kritische Justiz* 17 (1984), 359–79.

Das juristische Erbe des 'Dritten Reiches.' Beschädigungen der demokratischen Rechtsordnung. Frankfurt am Main: Suhrkamp, 1999.

Entsorgung der NS-Herrschaft. Konfliktlinien im Ungang mit dem Hitler-Regime. Hannover: Offizin-Verlag, 2004.

Preuss, Ulrich K. *Legalität und Pluralismus: Beiträge zum Verfassungsrecht der Bundesrepublik Deutschland.* Frankfurt am Main: Suhrkamp, 1973.

"The Critique of German Liberalism: A Reply to Kennedy." *Telos* 71 (Spring 1987), 97–111.

"Perspektiven von Rechtsstaat und Demokratie." *Kritische Justiz* 22: 1 (1989), 1–18.

Revolution, Fortschritt, Verfassung. Frankfurt am Main: Fischer Taschenbuch Verlag, 1994.

"Communicative Power and the Concept of Law." In "Habermas on Law and Democracy: Critical Exchanges," ed. Michel Rosenfeld, Special Issue. *Cardozo Law Review* 17: 4–5 (March 1996), 1179–92.

Pühle, Hans Jürgen. "Konservatismus und Neokonservatismus: Deutsche Entwicklungslinien seit 1945." In *Konservatismus – eine Gefahr für die Freiheit?* Festschrift für Iring Fetscher zum 60. Geburtstag, ed. Eike Hennig & Richard Saage. München: Piper, 1983.

Radbruch, Gustav. "Gesetzliche Unrecht und Übergesetzliches Recht" [orig. *Süddeutsche Zeitung* 1 (1946), 105–8]; reprinted in *Rechtsphilosophie*, 6th ed. Stuttgart: Koehler, 1963; originally published 1932.

Rawls, John. *A Theory of Justice.* Cambridge, MA: Harvard University Press, 1971.

Redaktion Kritische Justiz, ed. *Der Unrechtsstaat.* Baden-Baden: Nomos Verlagsgesellschaft 1979.

Streitbare Juristen: Ein andere Tradition. Baden-Baden: Nomos Verlagsgesellschaft, 1988.

Rehg, William. *Insight and Solidarity: The Discourse Ethics of Jürgen Habermas.* Berkeley, CA: University of California Press, 1997; originally published 1994.

Deliberative Democracy: Essays on Reason and Politics. Cambridge, MA: MIT Press, 1997.

Rehg, William, & James Bohman, eds. *Pluralism and the Pragmatic Turn: Essays in Honor of Thomas McCarthy.* Cambridge, MA: MIT Press, 2001.

Remy, Steven P. *The Heidelberg Myth: The Nazification and Denazification of a German University.* Cambridge, MA: Harvard University Press, 2002.

Rheinstein, Max, ed. *Max Weber on Law in Economy and Society* (2nd ed. of *Wirtschaft und Gesellschaft*, 1925), trans. Edward Shils. Cambridge, MA: Harvard University Press, 1954.

Ridder, Helmut. "Enteignung und Sozialisierung." *VVDStRL* 10 (1952), 124–49.

Zur verfassungsrechtlichen Stellung der Gewerkschaften im Sozialstaat nachdem Grundgesetz fur die Bundesrepublik Deutschland. Stuttgart: Fischer, 1960.

Notstand der Demokratie, Referate, Diskussionsbeiträge und Materialien vom Kongress 1966 in Frankfurt, 2nd ed. Frankfurt: Europäische Verlagsanstalt., 1967.

Ringer, Fritz. *Toward a Social History of Knowledge: Collected Essays.* New York: Berghahn Books, 2000.

The Decline of the German Mandarins: The German Academic Community, 1890–1933. Hanover, NH: University Press of New England, 1990.

Rockmore, Tom. *Habermas's Reconstruction of Historical Materialism.* Indianapolis, IN: Indiana University Press, 1989.

Römer, Peter, ed. Der Kampf um das Grundgesetz: über die politische Bedeutung der Verfassungsinterpretation: Referate und Diskussionen eines Kolloquiums aus Anlass des 70. Geburtstages von Wolfgang Abendroth. Frankfurt am Main: Syndikat, 1977.

Rommen, Heinrich. *Die ewige Wiederkehr des Naturrechts*, 2nd rev. ed. München: Kösel, 1947; originally published 1936.

Rosenfeld, Michel, ed. "Habermas on Law and Democracy: Critical Exchanges." Special Issue. *Cardozo Law Review* 17: 4–5 (March 1996), 767–1685.

Rupp, Hans Karl. "Democratizing a Country and a Discipline: The (Re-)Establishment of Political Science as Political Education in West Germany after 1945." In *Political Science and Regime Change in 20th Century Germany*, ed. Rainer Esfeld, 55–108. New York: Nova Science Publishers, 1996.

Rüthers, Bernd. *Die unbegrenzte Auslegung. Zum Wandel der Privatsrechtsordnung im Nationalsozialismus.* Frankfurt am Main: Athenäum, 1973.

Entartetes Recht: Rechtslehren und Kronjuristen im Dritten Reich. München: Deutscher Taschenbuch Verlag, 1994.

Saage, Richard. "Rückkehr zum starken Staat? Zur Renaissance des Freund-Feind Denkens in Bundesrepublik Deutschland." In *Rückkehr zum starken Staat? Studien über Konservatismus, Faschismus und Demokratie*, 7–42. Frankfurt am Main: Suhrkamp, 1983.

Sachsse, Christoph, & H. Tristam Engelhardt, eds. *Sicherheit und Freiheit: Zur Ethik des Wohlfahrtstaates.* Frankfurt am Main: Suhrkamp, 1990.

Sarrazin, Thilo, Fritjof Spreer, & Manfred Tietzel. "Krise und Planung in marxistischer Sicht. Das Beispiel Habermas." In *Hamburger Jahrbuch für Wirtschafts- und Gesellschaftspolitik* 19, 293–318. Tübingen: J. C. B. Mohr, 1974.

Schelauske, Hans Dieter. *Naturrechtsdiskussion in Deutschland: ein Überblick über zwei Jahrzehnte; 1945–1965*. Köln: Bachem, 1968.

Schelsky, Helmut. "Über die Stabilität von Institutionen, besonders Verfassungen. Kulturanthropologische Gedanken zu einem rechtssoziologischen Thema." In *Auf der Suche nach Wirklichkeit: Gesammelte Aufsätze*, 35–55. Düsseldorf/Köln: Eugen Diederichs, 1965; originally published 1949.

Der Mensch in der wissenschaftlichen Zivilisation. Köln: Westdeutscher Verlag, 1961.

"Mehr Demokratie oder Mehr Freiheit." *Frankfurter Allgemeine Zeitung* (January 20, 1973).

Die Soziologen und das Recht: Abhandlungen und Vorträge zur Soziologie von Recht, Institution und Planung. Opladen: Westdeutscher Verlag, 1980.

Scheuerman, William E. "Neumann vs. Habermas: The Frankfurt School and the Rule of Law." *Praxis International* 13 (1993), 50–67.

"Between Radicalism and Resignation: Democratic Theory in Habermas's Between Facts and Norms." In *Habermas: A Critical Reader*, ed. Peter Dews, 153–77. Oxford, England: Blackwell, 1999.

Between the Norm and the Exception: The Frankfurt School and the Rule of Law. Cambridge, MA: MIT Press, 1994.

ed. *The Rule of Law under Siege: Selected Essays of Neumann and Kirchheimer*. Berkeley, CA: University of California Press, 1996.

Carl Schmitt: *The Fate of Law*. Oxford, England: Rowman & Littlefield, 1999.

"Unsolved Paradoxes: Conservative Political Thought in Adenauer's Germany." *Confronting Mass Democracy and Industrial Democracy: German Political and Social Thought from Nietzsche to Habermas*, ed. John McCormick, 221–41. Durham, NC: Duke University Press, 2002.

Scheuner, Ulrich. "Die staatliche Intervention im Bereich der Wirtschaft: Rechtsformen und Rechtsschutz." *Veröffentlichungen der Vereinigung der Deutschen Staatsrechtslehrer*, 11. Berlin: de Gruyter, 1954.

Schildt, Axel. *Zwischen Abendland und Amerika. Studien zur Westdeutschen Ideenlandschaft der 50er Jahre*. München: Oldenbourg, 1999.

Schildt, Axel, & Arnold Sywotteck. *Modernisierung im Wiederaufbau: Die westdeutsche Gesellschaft der 50er Jahre.* Bonn: Dietz, 1998.

Schlink, Bernhard. "Why Carl Schmitt?" *Constellations* 2–3 (1996), 425–44.

"Abenddämmerung oder Morgendämmerung? Zu Jürgen Habermas' Diskurstheorie des demokratischen Rechtsstaats." *Rechtshistorische Journal* 70, 12 (1993), 57–69.

"The Dynamics of Constitutional Adjudication." In "Habermas on Law and Democracy: Critical Exchanges," ed. Michel Rosenfeld, Special Issue. *Cardozo Law Review* 17: 4–5 (March 1996), 1231–8.

"Die Enthronung der Staatsrechtswissenschaft durch die Verfassungsgerichtsbarkeit." *Der Staat* 28 (1989), 161–72.

Schlink, Bernhard, & Arthur Jacobson, eds. *Weimar: A Jurisprudence of Crisis*, trans. Belinda Cooper. Berkeley, CA: University of California Press, 2000.

Schluchter, Wolfgang. *Entscheidung für den sozialen Rechtsstaat: Hermann Heller und die staatstheoretischen Diskussion in der Weimarer Republik.* Köln: Kiepenheuer & Witsch, 1968.

Schmid-Noerr, Günzelin ed. *Max Horkheimer: Gesammelte Schriften*, Bd. 18: *Briefwechsel 1949–73.* Frankfurt am Main: Suhrkamp, 1996.

Schmidt, Ute. "Die Christlich Demokratische Unions Deutschlands." In *Parteien-Handbuch: die Parteien der Bundesrepublik Deutschland: 1945–1980*, Vol. 1, ed. Richard Stöss. Opladen: Westdeutscher Verlag, 1983.

Schmitt, Carl. *The Crisis of Parliamentary Democracy*, ed. Ellen Kennedy. Cambridge, MA: MIT Press, 1984; originally published 1923.

Verfassungslehre, 5th ed. Berlin: Duncker & Humblot, 1970; originally published 1927.

Legalität und Legitimität, 5th ed. Berlin: Duncker & Humblot, 1993; originally published 1932.

Legality and Legitimacy, trans. and ed. Jeffrey Seitzer, with an Introduction by John P. McCormick. Durham, NC: Duke University Press, 2004.

Der Begriff des Politischen (1927, 1932), 5th ed. Berlin: Duncker & Humblot, 2002.

The Concept of the Political [1932], trans. George Schwab, with a Foreword by Tracy Strong. Chicago: The University of Chicago Press, 1996.

"Der Weg des deutschen Juristen," *Deutsche Juristen-Zeitung* 39, 11 (1934), 692–5.

"Über die Drei Arten des rechtswissenschaftlichen Denkens" (1934), 2nd ed. Berlin: Duncker & Humblot, 1993.

"Das Problem der Legalität." In *Verfassungsrechtliche Aufsätze aus den Jahren 1924–1954: Materialien zu einer Verfassungslehre.* Berlin: Duncker & Humblot, 1958; originally published 1950.

"Nehmen, Teilen, Weiden: ein Versuch der Grundfrage jeder Sozial- und Wirtschaftsordnung vom Nomos her richtig zu stellen." In *Rechtsstaatlichkeit und Sozialstaatlichkeit: Aufsätze und Essays*, ed. and intro. Ernst Forsthoff, 95–113. Darmstadt: Wissenschaftliche Buchgesellschaft, 1968; originally published 1953.

Schneider, Hans. "Über Einzelfallgesetze." In *Festschrift für Carl Schmitt zum 70. Geburtstag*, ed. Hans Barion, Ernst Forsthoff, & Werner Weber, 159–78. Berlin: Duncker & Humblot, 1959.

Schorn, Hubert. *Der Richter im Dritten Reich.* Frankfurt am Main: Klostermann, 1959.

Schnur, Roman. "Die normative Kraft der Verfassung." In *Verfassung: Beiträge zur Verfassungstheorie*, ed. Manfred Friedrich, 100–17. Darmstadt: Wissenschafliche Buchgesellschaft, 1978.

Schumacher, Björn. "*Rezeption und Kritik der Radbruschen Formel.*" Ph.D. dissertation, University of Göttingen, 1985.

Seifert, Jürgen. *Kampf um Verfassungspositionen. Materialen über Grenzen und Möglichkeiten von Rechtspolitik.* Köln: Europäische Verlagsanstalt, 1974.

"Haus oder Forum. Wertsystem oder offene Verfassung?" In *Stichwörte zur Geistigen Situation der Zeit*, Vol. 1: *Nation und Republik*, ed. Jürgen Habermas, 321–39. Frankfurt am Main: Suhrkamp, 1979.

"Der 'neue Dezisionismus' die Orientierungslosigkeit der 'Linken' und gesamtdeutsche Verfassungsberatungen." *Vorgänge: Zeitschrift für Bürgerrechte und Gesellschaftspolitik* 107, Jg. 29, H. 5 (October 1990), 1–6.

"Fragmentierte Politik: Ein Entwurf." *Vorgänge: Zeitschrift für Bürgerrechte und Gesellschaftspolitik* 108, Jg. 29, H. 6 (December 1990), 51–60.

"Vom '58er' zum '68er.' Ein biographischer Rückblick," *Vorgänge: Zeitschrift fur Bürgerrechte und Gesellschaftspolitik* 124, Jg. 32, H. 6 (Dec. 1993), 1–6.

Seitzer, Jeffrey. *Comparative History and Legal Theory: Carl Schmitt in the First German Democracy.* London: Greenwood Press, 2001.

Senghaas, Dieter. *Abschreckung und Frieden. Studien zur Kritik organisierter Friedlosigkeit* [1969], rev. ed. Frankfurt: Europäische Verlagsanstalt, 1981.

Simitis, Spiro. *Die Faktischen Vertragsverhältnisse*. Ph.D. dissertation, University of Marburg, 1956.

Der Sozialstaatsgrundsatz in seinen Auswirkungen auf das Recht von Familie und Unternehmen. Habilitationsschrift, J. W. Goethe University (Frankfurt), 1963.

Simon, Dieter, ed. *Rechtswissenschaft in der Bonner Republik*. Frankfurt am Main: Suhrkamp, 1994.

Skuhr, Werner. "Die Stellung zur Demokratie in der Deutschen Nachkriegsdiskussion über den 'Demokratischen und Sozialen Rechtsstaat' dargestellt unter besonderer Berücksichtigung der Beiträge Ernst Forsthoffs." PhD. dissertation, University of Berlin, 1961.

Sladeczek, Heinz. "Zum konstitutionellen Problem des Widerstands." *Archiv für Rechts-und Sozialphilosophie* 43 (1957), 367–98.

Smend, Rudolf. "Verfassung und Verfassungsrecht." In *Staatsrechtliche Abhandlungen und andere Aufsätze*. Berlin: Duncker & Humblot, 1955; originally published 1928.

"Zum Problem des Öffentlichen und der Öffentlichkeit." In *Forschung und Berichte aus dem Öffentlichen Recht. Gedächtnisschrift für Walter Jellinek, 12. Juli 1885 – 9. Juni 1955*, ed. Otto Bachof, 11–20. München: Isar Verlag, 1955.

"Integrationslehre." In *Handwörterbuch der Sozialwissenschaften*, Vol. 5: *Handelsrecht-Kirchliche Finanzen*, ed. Erwin von Beckerath, 299–302. Stuttgart: Fischer Verlag, 1956.

"Staat." In *Evangelisches Kirchenlexikon: Kirchlich-Theologisches Handwörterbuch*, Vol. 3, ed. Heinz Brunotte. Göttingen: Vandenhoeck & Ruprecht, 1959.

Smith, Gordon. *Democracy in Western Germany: Parties and Politics in the Federal Republic.* New York: Holmes and Meier, 1986.

Söllner, Alfons. "Jürgen Habermas und die Kritische Theorie des gegenwärtigen Rechtsstaates – Versuch einer wissenschaftlichen Einordnung." *Leviathan: Zeitschrift für Sozialwissenschaft* [1982], 97–131. Opladen: Westdeutscher Verlag, 1983.

"Normative Westernization? The Impact of the Remigres on the Foundation of Political Thought in Post-War Germany." In *German Ideologies since 1945: Studies in the Political Thought and Culture of the Bonn Republic*, ed. Jan-Werner Müller, 40–60. New York: Palgrave Macmillan, 2003.

"Beyond Carl Schmitt: Political Theory in the Frankfurt School." *Telos* 71 (Spring 1987), 81–97.

Söllner, Alfons, Rainer Elsfeld, Michael Th. Greven, & Hans Karl Rupp, eds. *Political Science and Regime Change in 20th Century Germany*. New York: Nova Science Publishers, 1996.

Sontheimer, Kurt. "Review of J. Habermas, *Strukturwandel der Öffentlichkeit*." *Frankfurter Allgemeine Zeitung* (September 28, 1962), 17.

"Zum Begriff der Macht als Grundkategorie der politischen Wissenschaft." In *Wissenschaftliche Politik. Eine Einführung in Grundfragen ihrer Tradition und Theorie*, ed. Dieter Oberndörfer. Freiburg: Verlag Rombach, 1962.

Das Elend unserer Intellektuellen: Linke Theorie in der Bundesrepublik Deutschland. Hamburg: Hoffmann & Campe, 1976.

Sternberger, Dolf. *The Social Sciences in Western Germany: A Postwar Survey*. Washington: Library of Congress European Affairs Division, 1950.

"Bemerkungen über den Gegenstand der Politik." *Kölner Zeitschrift* 8, 3 (1956), 396–409.

Verfassungspatriotismus. Frankfurt am Main: Insel-Verlag, 1990.

Staff, Ilse. "Der soziale Rechtsstaat. Zur Aktualität der Staatstheorie Hermann Hellers." In *Der soziale Rechtsstaat. Gedächtnissschrift für Hermann Heller 1891–1933*, eds. Ilse Staff & Christoph Müller, 25–41. Baden-Baden: Nomos, 1984.

"Das Lüth-Urteil. Zur demokratietheoretischen Problematik materialer Grundrechtstheorie." In Das Lüth-Urteil aus (rechts-) historischer Sicht: die Konflikte um Veit Harlan und die Grundrechtsjudikatur des Bundesverfassungsgerichts, ed. Thomas Henne, 315–26. Berlin: BWV, 2005.

Stammer, Otto, ed. *Max Weber and Sociology* [1965]. Oxford, England: Blackwell, 1971.

Stolleis, Michael. *Geschichte des öffentlichen Rechts in Deutschland, Vol. 2: Staatsrechtslehre und Verwaltungswissenschaft, 1800–1914*. München: Verlag C. H. Beck, 1992.

Geschichte des öffentlichen Rechts in Deutschland, Vol. 3: Staats-und-Verwaltungsrechtswissenschaft in Republik und Diktatur, 1914–1945. München: C. H. Beck, 1999.

Recht im Unrecht. Studien zur Rechtsgeschichte des Nationalsozialismus. Frankfurt am Main: Suhrkamp, 1994.

ed. *Juristen: ein biographisches Lexikon; von der Antike bis zum 20. Jahrhundert*. München: C. H. Beck, 1995.

The Law under the Swastika: Studies on Legal History in Nazi Germany, trans. Thomas Dunlap. Oxford, England: Oxford University Press, 1998.

"Der Methodenstreit der Weimarer Staatsrechtslehrer – ein abgeschlossene Kapitel der Wissenschaftsgeschichte?" In *Sitzungsberichte der Wissenschaftlichen Gesellschaft an der Johann-Wolfgang-Goethe Universität, Frankfurt am Main*, Bd. 39, No. 1. Stuttgart: Steiner 2001.

"Die Staatsrechtslehre der fünfziger Jahre." In *Das Lüth-Urteil aus (rechts)historischer Sicht: die Konflikte um Veit Harlan und die Grundrechtsjudikatur des Bundesverfassungsgerichts*, ed. Thomas Henne, 295–300. Berlin: BWV, 2005.

Streithofen, Basilius, ed. *Frieden im Lande. Vom Recht auf Widerstand.* Bergisch-Gladbach: Bastei Lübbe, 1983.

Tamanaha, Brian Z. *On the Rule of Law: History, Politics, Theory.* Cambridge, England: Cambridge University Press, 2004.

Thomas, Nick. *Dissent and Democracy: Protest Movements in West Germany*. London: Berg, 2003.

Thompson, John B., & David Held, eds. *Habermas: Critical Debates.* Cambridge, MA: MIT Press, 1982.

Thornhill, Christopher. "Jürgen Habermas." In *Political Theory in Modern Germany: An Introduction*, 130–73. London: Polity Press, 2000.

Tohidipur, Mehdi, ed. *Der Bürgerliche Rechtsstaat.* Frankfurt am Main: Suhrkamp, 1978.

Torpey, John. "Introduction: Habermas and the Historians." *New German Critique* 44 (Spring–Summer 1988), 5–24.

Tully, James. *Meaning and Context: Quentin Skinner and his Critics.* Princeton, NJ: Princeton University Press, 1988.

Van Laak, Dirk. *Gespräche in der Sicherheit des Schweigens – Carl Schmitt in der Geistesgeschichte der frühen Bundesrepublik.* Berlin: Akademie, 1993.

"From the Conservative Revolution to Technocratic Conservatism." In *German Ideologies since 1945: Studies in the Political Thought and Culture of the Bonn Republic*, ed. Jan-Werner Müller. New York: Palgrave Macmillan, 2003.

Varon, Jeremy. *Bringing the War Home: The Weather Underground, the Red Army Faction, and Revolutionary Violence in the Sixties and Seventies*. Berkeley, CA: University of California Press, 2004

Voigt, Rüdiger, & Wolfgang Luthardt, eds. "Von Dissidenten zu Klassikern. Eine Situationsanalyse der Veröffentlichungen der Vereinigung der Deutschen Staatsrechtler." In *Historisische Soziologie der Rechtswissenschaft*, ed. Eric Volkmayer Heyen, 135–55. Frankfurt am Main: Klostermann, 1986.

ed. *Verrechtlichung: Analysen zu Funktion und Wirkung von Parlamentarisierung, Bürokratisierung und Justizialisierung sozialer, politischer und ökonomischer Prozesse*. Königstein: Athenäum, 1980.

Vollrath, Ernst. "Allgemeine Staatslehre." In *Culture in the Federal Republic of Germany, 1945–1995*, ed. Reiner Pommerin. Oxford, England: Berg, 1996.

Von Hippel, Ernst. "The Role of Natural Law in the Legal Decisions of the Federal Republic." *Natural Law Forum* 4, 1 (1959), 106–18.

Walther, Manfred. "Die Positivismus-These als Selbstanklage? Hat der juristische Positivismus die deutschen Juristen wehrlos gemacht?" *Kritische Justiz* 21 (1988), 263–80.

Ward, Ian. *Kantianism, Postmodernism and Critical Legal Thought*. Dordrecht, The Netherlands: Kluwer Academic Publishers, 1997.

Weber, Max. "Politik als Beruf." In *Gesammelte Politische Schriften*, 2nd ed., ed. Johannes Winckelmann. Tübingen: J. C. B. Mohr, 1958.

Economy and Society: An Outline of Interpretive Sociology [1920], ed. Günther Roth & Claus Wittich, trans. Ephraim Fischoff et al. Berkeley, CA: University of California Press, 1978.

Weber, Werner. *Spannungen und Kräfte im westdeutschen Verfassungs system*, 2nd ed. Stuttgart: Vorwerk, 1958.

"Die Teilung der Gewalten als Gegenwartsproblem." In *Festschrift für Carl Schmitt zum 70. Geburtstag*, ed. Hans Barion, Ernst Forsthoff, & Werner Weber, 253–72. Berlin: Duncker & Humblot, 1959.

Weinkauff, Hermann. "Der Naturrechtsgedanke in der Rechtsprechung des Bundesgerichtshofes." In *Naturrecht oder Rechtspositivismus*, ed. Werner Maihofer, 554–76. Bad Homburg vor der Höhe: Hermann Gentner Verlag, 1962.

Die Deutsche Justiz und der Nationalsozialismus. Stuttgart: Deutsche Verlags-Anstalt, 1968.

Welte, Bernard. *Über das Wesen und den rechten Gebrauch der Macht: eine philosophische Untersuchung und eine theologische These dazu*. Freiburg: Rombach, 1960.

Werner-Müller, Jan. *A Dangerous Mind: Carl Schmitt in Postwar Europe*. New Haven, CT: Yale University Press, 2003.

ed. *German Ideologies since 1945: Studies in the Political Thought and Culture of the Bonn Republic*. New York: Palgrave Macmillan, 2003.

Wesel, Uwe. *Aufklärungen über Recht. Zehn Beiträge zur Entmythologisierung*. Frankfurt am Main: Suhrkamp, 1981.

White, Steven, ed. *The Cambridge Companion to Habermas*. Cambridge, England: Cambridge University Press, 1995.

Wiggershaus, Rolf. *The Frankfurt School: Its History, Theories and Significance*, trans. Michael Robertson. Cambridge, MA: MIT Press, 1994.

Jürgen Habermas. Reibeck bei Hamburg: Rowohlt, 2004.

Winckelmann, Johannes. *Legitimität und Legalität in Max Webers Herrschaftssoziologie*. Tübingen: J. C. B. Mohr, 1952.

Wingert, Lutz. "Jürgen Habermas: *Faktizität und Geltung* – Der Prozess des Rechts in den Satzungen der Macht." In *Klassische Werke der Philosophie. Von Aristoteles bis Habermas*, ed. Reinhardt Brandt & Thomas Sturm, 345–78. Leipzig: Reclam, 2002.

Winkler, Heinrich A. *Der Lange Weg nach Westen*. München: C. H. Beck, 2000. Trans. *Germany: The Long Road to the West*. Oxford, England: Oxford University Press, 2006.

Winterling, Peter. "Das Gewissen der Demokratie. Der Philosoph Jürgen Habermas wird 80" (June 18, 2009).

Zacher, Hans. "Das Sozialstaatsziel." In *Handbuch des Staatsrechts der Bundesrepublik Deutschland*, Bd. I, ed. Josef Isensee & Paul Kirchhof, 1085–1111. Heidelberg: C.F. Müller, 1987.

Index

4211028R00154

Printed in Great Britain
by Amazon.co.uk, Ltd.,
Marston Gate.